NEWHAVEN-ON-FORTH

Port of Grace

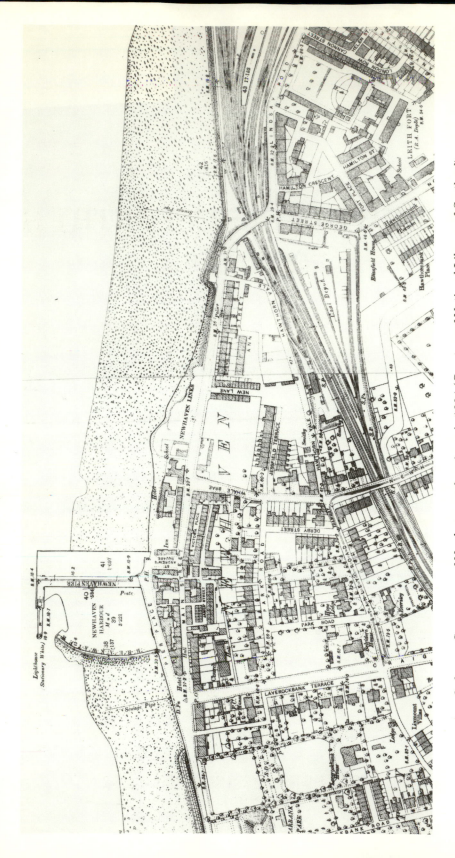

Ordnance Survey map of Newhaven and environs in 1894 (Courtesy of National Library of Scotland).

NEWHAVEN-ON-FORTH
Port of Grace

TOM McGOWRAN

With Drawings by Ronald Penn

Foreword by
W. LOGAN WILSON
Boxmaster, The Society of Free Fishermen of Newhaven

JOHN DONALD PUBLISHERS LTD
EDINBURGH

TO MY WIFE

ISBN 0 85976 130 4

Printed in Great Britain by Bell & Bain Ltd., Glasgow

FOREWORD

This excellent and evocative work by Tom McGowran on the village of Newhaven and the fishing areas of the River Forth brings to life so vividly scenes and characters from bygone days. His painstaking research has been well rewarded by this fascinating blend of historical fact, amusing anecdotes and exciting episodes on the contraband trade and the days of the Press Gangs.

It is amazing that this topic has been bypassed for so long by writers of local history. Probably the author's own family connection with Newhaven fired his enthusiasm in this venture to trace the life of the fisherfolk through its pends and closes.

I am sure you will enjoy this book as much as I have and hope it may bring alive again the many facets of this active community which was the fishing village of Newhaven

W. Logan Wilson, Boxmaster,
Society of Free Fishermen of Newhaven

Preface

This is the story of a village which lived and died within the space of four hundred and fifty years and particularly it is a tribute to the folk who lived there. In part it is also Scotland's story of those years.

Compiling it has been an enthralling experience, not least for the pleasure of making so many new acquaintances and of meeting so much kindness and helpfulness in the quest, and for the constant thrill of finding another piece of the jigsaw.

A book such as this must be indebted to a great number of sources and many of these are gratefully acknowledged in the bibliography. But in particular, my gratitude is expressed to all the Newhaven men and women who shared their memories of the village as it was, and whose encouragement and advice were invaluable. I mention especially Sandy Noble whose encyclopaedic memory and wit were an inspiration, Sarah Dyer who kindly placed at my disposal the tapes of her oral history project, Drew Sime for his companionship, George Liston for his help with historical detail and illustration, W. Logan Wilson, Boxmaster of the Free Fishermen for his patient attention to the manuscript, Peter Carnie of the Peacock Hotel, the Rev. Alex. R. Aitken, and the ever-helpful staffs of the Edinburgh Room of the Central Library and Leith Library, who seemed to enjoy the search as much as I did.

Tom McGowran

Contents

CHAPTER 1

Jewel of the Sea

The trouble with James the Fourth - and it proved fatal in the end - was that he could never resist a chance to unfurl the flag. So having built the biggest ship in the world he now set out to try to sink her.

Laughter and high spirits animated the kirkmen, courtiers, craftsmen and fisherfolk crowded for the spectacle on Newhaven pier and the boats in the harbour. Many of them had worked for four years on the splendid ship dressed overall with flags and streamers, which lay at anchor on the sunlit water a few cable-lengths out in the roads. The King was about to fire a cannon at her. The great gun had been manhandled on to the pier. Hans, the German gunner, had mixed and rammed home the saltpetre, charcoal and sulphur, supervised the loading of the stone shot then trained the iron giant on the great ship.

Behind him, at a distance showing respect of his artistry and some doubt about the outcome, the court had gathered. The King, glowing match in hand, acknowledged the gunner's nod and strode forward. With a roar and a belch of flame, the cannon reared and recoiled. From the distant vessel was heard a faint cheer. The King had blooded his new ship.

'It has done her little skaith' he said later, peering from his galley into the gash above the waterline where the cannonball lay embedded. 'Have our wrights heal this scratch.' Then the King 'taking pleasure to pass into her and to dine and sup in her with his Lords, did let them see the order of his Ship.'

When James came to the throne in 1488 he brought a boyhood ambition to build a powerful navy. He saw the navy as the readiest and most powerful argument his impoverished country could use in the concourse of Europe.

The basis had already been laid by a new race of merchant skippers whose freebooting voyages had recently spread terror of the Saltire from the Baltic to the Canaries. These skeely skippers, Wood, Barton, Merrimonth, Brownhill, Paterson, Lamb, all of Leith, had, several of them, approval from the crown to carry on a kind of state-licensed piracy; in return they gave their ships to the King's service when needed, bringing an efficiency, power and ruthlessness that daunted other seafaring nations. In no other port of Europe at this time could there have been found so many bold and skilful captains.

Chief among them was Sir Andrew Wood. It was said of him that there were no ten ships in Scotland would give combat to his two ships the *Flower* and the *Yellow Carvel*. The *Yellow Carvel*, a three-masted carrack of 300 tons, belonged to the King and was hired at so much a voyage while the *Flower* was Wood's own vessel. His route to high places was unusual in that he had started as a simple apprentice, bypassing the burgess ticket. He had stood high with James III and after that King was overthrown Wood's two ships were hovering

1

A facsimile of the map of the siege of Edinburgh Castle in 1573, shows the village of Newhaven at the head of a lagoon whose entrance has been narrowed by earth works.

in the Forth to take aboard wounded Royalists. It was thought the King might be among them and Wood was brought before James IV who demanded : 'Sir, have you my father?' 'Sir, I have not your father, but would to God he were on my ships, I would keep him skaithless.'

Reconciled with the new king in 1489 he was the hero of several brilliant exploits. Five English privateers were spreading destruction up and down the coast and none dared go against them but Wood, who sailed with his two ships, grappled and boarded the enemy off Dunbar and after a long fight brought all five back to Leith. The English court was furious. Sir Stephen Bull an English privateer seeking favour with his king, sailed with three ships into the Forth in the summer of 1490 and lay off the May Island in the hope of trapping Wood on his way back from Flanders. He had captured some local fishermen and made them climb to the fighting tops to tell him of Wood's approach. Under threat they identified two approaching sail as the *Yellow Carvel* and the *Flower*.

Aboard Wood's ships the English had been sighted and he ordered out the wine and every man drank to the other. 'Set yourselves in order, each man in his own place. Let the gunners charge their artillery and the cross-bows be made ready, and the lime pots at the mast heads, and the two-handed swords, let them too be ready.'

By now the sun was high and the English opened fire with their heavier guns. Wood, seeing he would be outgunned, got to windward and closed with them. All through the long summer day the farmers and fisherfolk on the coast of Fife watched the ships locked in bloody embrace as the hand to hand fighting swayed to and fro with such blind fury that neither captains nor sailors noticed that the ships were drifting on to the sandbanks at the mouth of the Tay. The English ships, of greater draught, ran aground and being helpless, at last surrendered. James in a chivalrous gesture sent them and their crews back to England with a warning: Next time they would not loup home so dryshod. Andrew Wood was knighted and given lands at Largo.

Another famous family were the Bartons. John the father had skippered the *Yellow Carvel* before Wood, and his three sons Andrew, Robert and John were all celebrated mariners. For nearly a hundred years they carried on a family war with the Portuguese, the quarrel having begun in 1476 when John, homeward bound from Flanders had his ship captured and was set adrift in a small boat. He later made his way to Lisbon to seek redress but in vain so he obtained a warrant from the Scots King to seize Portuguese vessels until the debt of £6000 - an enormous sum - was paid. In his zeal he tended to classify all foreign flags as Portuguese. Among his captures were two Moorish lasses who were taken into the Court by James, one being made Queen at a jousting tourney. Dunbar wrote of her:

> When she is claid in rich apparel
> She blinks as bright as ane tar barrel
> My ladye with the mekle lyppis.

About this time a small fleet of Scottish ships was attacked by Dutch pirates and the crews were thrown overboard. Andrew Barton was despatched by James to avenge this act and to prove that he had cleansed the coast of Dutch pirates he sent the king a barrel full of their heads. The King apparently liked his style - the Bartons were favoured at court and Robert was knighted and given the lands of Barnton.

The King's Navy

With the help of these tough sailors James planned his navy at a meeting in Robert Barton's house at Leith. No longer would they rely on the yards of Holland and France - Scottish ships would now be built at Dumbarton and Leith. But the trouble with James was that his soaring ambitions were a kite tied to the hand of a barefoot kingdom. In this poor marsh-strewn realm, timber was so scarce that it was said 'had Christ been betrayed in this country... Judas had sooner found the grace of repentance than a tree to hang himself on.' Timber was used for everything and centuries of reckless cutting and the ravages of war had led Parliament to grieve that 'the wode of Scotland is utterlie destroyit.'

So James wrote to his good friend Louis XII of France telling him: 'We have been busy with the building of a fleet for the protection of our shores... and we labour at it with great zeal. Since there is a greater abundance of building material in your realm we have sent our men thither to fetch beams and oak-wood from a friendly nation and to bring shipwrights to us.'

When the first French wright, John Lorans, arrived in 1502 work began on the *Margaret*, a 21-gun carrack of 600 tons, twice the size of Sir Andrew Wood's *Yellow Carvel*. She took a thousand oak trees and two and a half years to build and cost £6000 and there was a great sounding of trumpets at her launch and further rejoicing when the masts were erected with coins placed under the heel of each for luck. But when they came to haul her out into the Forth her great hull stuck like a stranded whale across the sandbank at the mouth of the Water of Leith. She had to be dismasted, stripped and buoyed with a hundred casks and floated off at the highest tide. Leith had proved too limited for James's ambitions.

But a mile to the west was the perfect bay, a natural haven with deeper water lapping the strand on which clustered the huts of a small fishing community. The sandy links, though they supported several orchards and a windmill, were mostly covered in coarse grass and whins and the Abbot of Holyrood who owned them readily agreed to exchange 143 acres stretching from the Chapel of St Nicholas in North Leith to Wardie Brae on the west, for richer lands around the palace of Linlithgow. And so the fisherfolk acquired a royal landlord.

A kind of prefabricated wooden pavilion was brought down from Edinburgh Castle in 1504 and erected on the links to house the local labourers and incoming craftsmen from France, Flanders, Denmark and Spain. Teams of oxen dragged 163 great trees from the neighbouring estate of Inverleith (the original name for the land around the mouth of the Water of Leith) to build a village of one broad street. A yard was laid out with warehouses for chandlery and workshops for sawyers and carpenters, a ropewalk set up, a dock excavated and the soil and rubble used to build a breakwater and support a pier and every detail was supervised by the King down to the provision of drink silver to encourage 'the marinaris that setis up the bulwarks of the New Haven.'

Devoted to the Church like his mother, he built in 1505 a stone chapel at the centre of the village dedicated to the Virgin and St James, presenting a silver chalice and communion cup. From this chapel the village became known popularly in its early years as Our Lady's Port of Grace or Maryport. In charters it is named as Novus Portus de Leith, or Newhaven. Some say that this is to distinguish it from the Old Haven which they have assumed to be Blackness, hitherto a port of significance servile to Linlithgow but it is more likely that the name meant precisely what it said, the New Haven of Leith. (It is confusing to find references in old documents to Newhaven which appear to place it on the other side of Edinburgh. The reason is that in 1526 James V granted a charter to some Preston Grange monks, nine miles east, to construct a port in their

The Yellow Carvel, 300 tons, a fighting merchantman of the late 14th century, brilliantly sailed by Sir Andrew Wood of Largo, part trader, part pirate, pare naval skipper.

own lands from which they might export coal. They too called their port Newhaven, but this rival did not keep its name for long, reverting to its original name of Acheson's Haven, latterly known as Morrison's Haven. It was the site of extensive salt pans and glassworks and a haunt after the Reformation of 'Jesuitis, sainmarie and mespreistis').

In this fine new naval dockyard the King's ambition took flight - he would build the biggest ship in the world and all Scotland would be recruited to the grand design. This plan grew out of his sense of guilt at his father's murder for ever since that day he had worn next to his skin an iron belt and had promised himself a pilgrimage to the Holy Land. The idea got built upon with the years until it grew into a plan for a grand all-Europe crusade against the Ottoman. He would lead it himself in a great flagship and he even got as far as ordering his goldsmiths to make the gold chain and whistle of a High Admiral.

Scotland's Greatest Artefact

So in 1507 the keel was laid of the ship that was to be 'to admiration the biggest that any man had seen sail on the ocean'. Sir Andrew Wood was in overall authority, the principal shipwright was Jaques Terrell of Normandy and Sir Andrew Melville was in charge of what now became the single largest project and employer of labour in the kingdom.

James sent his agents with Scottish hides, wool, salted fish and pearls to almost every maritime country of Europe. They brought back timber from the Baltic, ropes, cables and guns from Flanders, sails and rigging from Rouen and Dieppe, tar, pitch, brass tackle blocks and more timber from Denmark, mast poles from Norway, copper sheathing for the hull from Cornwall (got via Antwerp because England took a dim view of all this enterprise), anchors from Cadiz and the latest in lanterns, hourglasses to record the watch, and compasses from Middelburg fetched at the King's command by George Paterson member of an old Leith seafaring family.

This frenzy of foreign buying was matched by the demands now made on Scotland herself. The Treasurer's Accounts for these years read like a rollcall of Lowlands and Highlands. Rosshire gave forest timber, the woods of Darnaway where Janet Kennedy mourned the loss of her Royal lover, supplied great trees, all the oak woods of Fife except around the hunting lodge at Royal Falkland were razed and fed into the great maw; there was more wood from Cambuskenneth, Cawder, Kincardine and Loch Ness, from Logan and Tulliallan. At Edinburgh Castle and at Cambuskenneth forges glowed in the night casting armaments. At Newmills of Louden John Campbell made lanterns and John Hunter produced nails and staples. The single street of the new-built village echoed to the rumble of heavy drays and the squeal of sledges; around the cocooned giant the wrights clambered in the scaffolding while the four-men saws gave a metronome beat to the clamour of a hundred hammers, the rasping cough of adze and axe. Booths were set up near the yard to sew flags and banners to deck out the great ship. Dunbar describes the scene:

> Carpenters,
> Builders of barks and ballingars.
> Masons plying upon the land
> And shipwrights hewing upon the strand

How big was she? James had declared his ambition to produce the greatest ship in Christendom but the true dimensions will probably never be known. The fleet with which Columbus fifteen years before had crossed the Atlantic would it seems have fitted comfortably in her hull. Sir David Lindsay of Pitscottie, whose world was all superlatives, writing some 20 years after the event, may have mixed poetic licence and historical fact in the only extant account of her:

> 'In this same year (1511) the King of Scotland bigged the great ship called the Great Michael which was the greatest ship and of most strength that ever sailed....for she was so strong and of so great length and breadth, all the wrights of Scotland, yea, and many other strangers were at her device, by the King's Commandment...jests of oak in her wall and boards on every side, so stark and so thick that no cannon could go through her. This great ship cumbered all Scotland to get her to the sea...and if any man believe that this description of the ship be not of verity, as we have written, let him pass to the gate of Tillibardin, and there, after the same, ye will see the Length and Breadth of her planted with hawthorn by the wright that helped to make her. As for other properties of her, Sir Andrew Wood is my author who was quartermaster of her; and Robert Barton who was Master-Skipper'.

Newhaven by Mary Cameron, 1887

The building of the *Great Michael* by Alex Jamieson, 1929
(Courtesy of the artist's daughter)

Newhaven Pier by Alex R Smith
(Courtesy of Edinburgh City Libraries)

Caller Herrin' by Alexander Roche, RSA

Newhaven Minstrels by Keely Halswell, 1869

Newhaven at the Chain Pier from Wardie
(Courtesy of Edinburgh City Libraries)

The Great Michael, the largest ship of her day, built by James IV principally for prestige purposes. The envy of England and France, she boasted an armament of more than 300 guns.

Pitscottie's account has been proved in some respects. The hawthorns of Tullibardine are mentioned in the Athole Papers and more than three hundred years later are referred to in the Second Statistical Account of Scotland which reports only three trees as having escaped the ravages of time and the plough. In 1883 T. Hunter in *'Woods, Forests and Estates of Perthshire'* says the area was filled with water to make an ornamental pond; despite this, 'the shape of the vessel is still distinctly visible and it will take a long time before it is thoroughly obliterated'. But although attempts have been made at aerial photogrphy from the nearby small aerodrome, signs are now hard to find since the stream has been diverted from its original course.

The numbers Pitscottie gives for the crew are confirmed in an existing nominal roll. But 'a year and a day' to build was obviously a poetic way of saying 'a long time'. The size he gives to the ship (240 ft. long by 56 ft. wide, the sides being ten feet thick) is however, the most fascinating puzzle. Carracks, or floating forts, tended to be tubby vesels with a length of approximately two and a half times the breadth. But the shape and construction of a ship depended almost entirely on the personal judgment, knowledge and experience of the shipwright. The eye and hand played more part than the head and there were no drawings, tests or models. Writers have tended to assume that Pitscottie overstated the length and that 180 ft might be nearer the truth. But Pitscottie's dimensions become more plausible when it is realised that nearly a century earlier Henry V had had a ship building at Bayonne which was almost as large - she was 186 ft from stem to sternpost with a beam of only 46 ft. This ship was never finished but the *Grace Dieu* built at Southampton in 1419 was even larger. Examination of her remains in the Hamble River in 1933 show that her keel was 13 ft longer than that of Henry V's ship.

These giants, like dinosaurs, left only the occasional skeleton to point to an evolutionary dead-end - by the middle of the 16th century a reaction had set in and the biggest ship of Elizabeth's reign was the *Triumph*, only 100 ft long in the keel. There were other features about the *Michael* which were novel. Carracks had large aftercastles and triangular overhanging forecastles, fighting platforms from which, with the fighting tops at the mastheads, the men-at-arms, archers and spearmen would fight as from battlements until the vessels closed for boarding and hand-to-hand fighting. War at sea between floating forts was at this time very much an extension of warfare on land. The artillery to be effective had to be carried high in the ship and so was rarely heavy enough to do great damage to the opposing hull.

Not so with the *Great Michael*. She carried heavy guns, fitted down in the hull between decks and fired through gunports close to the waterline. These gunports are believed to have been first used in Brittany about six years earlier. It was the fitting of these to the *Mary Rose*, some twenty-five years later which probably led to her disastrous flooding and capsize. In the following century the Swedish warship *Vasa* suffered a similar fate. Gunports had to be closed when the ship heeled under sail. Making them totally watertight was difficult when ships were clinker-built of overlapping planking, giving an uneven skin to the hull, and it is a reasonable assumption that the *Michael* had smooth edge-to-edge, planking, the carvel build, which was beginning to appear in Northern countries at the start of the 16th century. This was another Breton innovation though it had been common building practice in the Mediterranean for centuries.

The *Michael* had four masts with eight very large and heavy sails richly painted with coats of arms. The two forward masts were square-rigged and the two after masts triangular or lateen-rigged, another southern feature, designed to give her good down-wind speed yet the ability to point closer into the wind. All these features are shown in the models of the ship in Edinburgh Castle and the Royal Scottish Museum. The model maker, Richard Paterson of Lasswade, used the *Henri Grace a Dieu* of 1514 partly as his basis.

Robert Borthwick, master gunsmith, had for months plied the furnaces at Edinburgh Castle, forging some of the 32 large cannon with which she would be armed, six on either side between decks and three great Bassils, guns of 160lb shot, two pointed aft and one forward. The largest number of guns however, came from Flanders including many of the three hundred shot of small artillery with names a poet must have dreamed up: 'that is to say, Myand and Battert-falcon ... Pestillent Serpents and Double-dogs, Hagtor and Culvering, crossbows and hand-bows'. (Pitscottie). James boasted to the English ambassador that she had more guns than ever the French king had brought to a siege, though the latter took this with a pinch of salt, describing it in letters home as a 'crack'.

A Pleasure in his Ship

This mediaeval *Queen Mary* had, from the start, excited the nation's pride and was a burning obsession with James who was seldom away from Newhaven during her building. If he was at Holyrood or Linlithgow he would saddle up his favourite steed Gray Gretano and be in Newhaven at first light, taking disjonit (dejeuner) at the house of his French shipwright whose wife had a reputation as a cook, before going up to the Castle to supervise the casting of brass cannon for the ship. Or if he was at Dunfermline he would have himself rowed over by way of Inchcolm.

His enthusiasm never relaxed, infecting and urging on the whole workforce. Candles and lanterns were lit for those that wrought by night for even darkness brought no respite. Yet he was a great favourite. His kindly consideration, attractive manner and deep interest earned love and respect from all. More than a dozen payments of a groat to buy strawberries are recorded to a little lass at Newhaven he used to take by the hand round the dockyard, and the Treasurer's Accounts show him buying honey pears at the pierend. One of his foreign shipwrights died and was buried in the chapel at Newhaven. The King paid all the expenses and sent the widow back to Rouen. The poor charwoman that kept the court that led to the works was not forgotten when she fell sick nor the 'puir wyff whose husband brek his leg at the kinggis wark and had naething to amend it with.' Sometimes he would try his hand at the adze or spend a morning rowing over the oyster beds with the 'dreggers', accompanying their interminable work-songs on his lute or sit on a barrel on the pier listening to a tale-teller to whom he paid 9s. It has been written that these Newhaven years were the most care-free any Scottish monarch ever spent.

There is no mention of the formal launching though she is said to have 'danged a' the men o' Scotland to get her to the sea.' But there is mention of a payment to trumpeters and a drummer at the 'outputting of the kinggis gret schippe' and it must have been a gala occasion on that October day in 1511, Michaelmas by the old calendar, with the Queen and all the glittering court gathered with the artisans and fisherfolk to see the climax the greatest and most splendid artefact to come out of Scotland.

That night boatmen brought out to the anchored hulk 'candill and necessaries to the maister cuik for the Kinggis supper on the gret schipe.' It was an impromptu picnic for the hull was bare of cabins or comforts but there was food and wine and music and on the lamp-lit decks the elation and mutual congratulations at an enterprise accomplished, the King toasting the foreign wrights who had made it possible.

From January to March the King was at Newhaven, every day taking pleasure in his ship. He delighted to entertain aboard and would swagger around the decks with the foreign ambassadors after a sumptuous meal, to the music of troubadours or Highland harpers.

Then in March, like ants swarming around a helpless beetle, the boats of the Newhaven fishers towed the great ship upstream to dock at the Pool of Airth. Throughout 1512 a force of 200 workmen lived aboard as fitting out then commissioning was completed. James was again a frequent visitor and when at Linlithgow sometimes brought his Queen and court to dine aboard. He ensured that the workforce was well looked after and there is a record of a Dunfermline baker supplying 600 loaves of bread while on the same day in July 400 fish and 140 gallons of ale were taken on board. The wage rates of these skilled men was 3s to 4s a week, top rates for the times, and they were bedded and boarded on the ship with cooks to make their meals. But relations between the Scots and the foreign wrights were not always harmonious and it is recorded that the son of Jaques Terrell was killed in a brawl.

Though much remained to be done, *the Michael* was now ready for sailing trials. To modern eyes the massive rudder portrayed in the models of the ship seems so narrow as to be useless. But it was used only for fine adjustments of the course; it was the sails that played the most important part in determining the direction of the ship and each time a change of course was needed the setting of the sails was changed. The sails of a carrack were huge and heavy and those of the *Great Michael* were the hugest and heaviest. She was cumbersome and wayward to navigate; she was also of deeper draught than any other ship and during one of her trips she ran aground under full sail off Burntisland and there was great trouble getting her afloat again. As a result three French pilots were put aboard to navigate her and to mark out the shoals which were not well charted in those days. Shortly afterwards the water level inside the hull began to rise so that bailing became necessary but throughout all this the fitting out continued. The 'tween-deck guns could not protrude beyond the enormously thick walls so the gunports were lined with leather, 190 hides being used, to prevent the wood from burning. On the towering poop and foc'sle artists and woodcarvers on improvised platforms worked to bring to flower this great artefact of the King's ambition. Andrew Chalmers, the principal painter is said to have earned the small fortune of £140 between 1511 and 1513.

In February 1513 Jaques Terrell, his work ended, sailed with the French Ambassador, de la Motte, in the Ambassador's little barque, the *Gabriel* escorted by William Brownhill with three ships. Though they carried a cargo of wool fleeces and salted hides and pretended they were en route for Flanders, their real purpose was to recruit French gunners for the *Michael*. Off the Northumberland coast they fell in with an English ship with a cargo of wine which they captured and sent back to Leith under a prize crew.

In March the *Michael* returned to her birthplace to be drydocked. This was accomplished by sailing her up into the dock, building behind her a wall of clay and heather at low tide then bailing out the trapped seawater. Under her hull were lit fires of heather for 'blazing', then she was scraped clean of marine growth, her seams caulked with hemp and tallow and the whole tarred with mops. The mainmast having proved too tall, new masts were fitted and the main deck and 'cowbrigging', the fighting platform in the poop, below which were the captain's quarters, were finished. Twenty-three large horn lanterns were fitted around the decks.

The *Great Michael* now took up station behind Inchkeith, a thing of splendour and renown, her gunwales supporting walls of shields bearing the Royal arms and the arms of the nobles and knights serving with her, a multitude of great flags, standards amd pennants streaming in the breeze, her towering stern a glorious burst of art and colour.

Down to the Sea

The Scottish navy in the middle of 1513 consisted of three large ships undermanned and undergunned and a fourth ship with apparently no crew at all. These, in addition to the *Michael*, were the *James*, under the command of Lord Ross of Hackett, the *Margaret* under Lord Fleming of Cumbernauld and the *Ship of Lynn* which had been captured by Brownhill. There were also ten smaller ships or sloops without fo'csles and some crayers or barques including the *Mytone*, the *Barque d'Abbeville* bought from France for £300, Chalmers's barque, the *May and the Crown*, which private merchants had been persuaded to lend, and the 60-oar *Rose Galley* which had been built as a tender for the *Michael*. Messengers were now sent out to every part of the kingdom to enlist sailors, guns were brought down from Edinburgh Castle, 50 carts in convoy rumbling through the night down Easter Road then the principal road to Leith. From the King's Wark on the Shore at Leith 32 workmen toiled day and night carrying artillery and provisions to the boats which plied between shore and fleet. Into the *Michael* were poured stores to equip her for a 40-day voyage, including 289 barrels of ale, 7250 gallons of wine, 200 stones of cheese, 42 stones of butter, 5300 stock fish, 13,000 loaves, five barrels of biscuits, also eggs, salmon, salted porpoise, honey, pepper, spices, and 'to the gret schip the day sche salit, xx fresche mutone and iij fresche martis (beef)'. Only one quarter of this task had been completed when July came and the mobilisation of sailors had to be postponed for a week. When fully crewed, the *Michael* had a complement of 300 mariners impressed partly from the fishing communities of the Forth and in addition to captains, skippers and quartermaster, 120 French and Flemish gunners, a thousand men-at-arms, three priests, three barber-surgeons and a musician. Half the Scottish navy, it seemed, had been crammed into this one ship. Only the *Mytone* with 130 crew approached anywhere near her, the others averaging 50 apiece.

By contrast the English navy comprised 24 ships carrying 6480 sailors and mariners with a portage of 8460 tons. James was sensible of the imbalance. He was never averse to twisting the English lion's tail when its back was turned but he was reluctant to commit himself irrevocably to war in spite of the blandishments of the French king with his promise of help for the grand crusade and of the French Queen with her loveletter and turquoise ring asking him to be her true knight and advance three feet into England for her sake. Against such flattery was the insistent pressure of his own Queen who had never cut her English ties and of the more cautious of his counsellors. There was too the threat of papal excommunication should he break his treaty with Henry VIII. In May he tried to temporise with England but was rebuffed by Henry who, saying it was a ruse to get the Scots fleet to France unmolested, provokingly asked him to hand over the *Great Michael*. With no knightly alternative left, James on 25th July 1513 ordered the Scottish navy to sea.

James Hamilton, Earl of Arran was in command. Although Sir Andrew Wood had previously been appointed Commander of the *Michael* and Robert Barton its master, it seems that these positions were honorary or were outranked by others. There is no record that Wood or Barton sailed with her. The fleet that now set forth with James himself on board the flagship until the Isle of May was reached, consisted of at least nine and possibly 11 vessels.'The King's glittering toys' were off to war.

But not quite yet, for even while he sent word to France that the fleet had sailed James prevaricated. The general view is that Arran in sailing northabout through the Pentland Firth and in bombarding the coast of Northern Ireland was disobeying orders and that James, furious at this *lese majeste*, tried subsequently to replace him with Wood.

This is unlikely. Arran was an experienced commander, having seen naval service in the Baltic at the siege of Lubeck. He had also been responsible for subduing the Northern Isles with Wood as his lieutenant. Nothing in his record suggests that he would take on himself to initiate high policy.

The safest route to France was via the west coast of Scotland and much trade went out of Ayr and Dumbarton to avoid sailing too near the English coast. In 1512 the English Channel had been swept clear of French shipping by Sir Edward Howard in his flagship the *Mary Rose* of 600 tons, leading an English fleet of 24 ships, some much larger but none so nimble. The Scottish fleet if it had taken the direct route would have had to fight its way to the Seine against a much superior force.

Then again, James had gained an uncertain ally in Hugh O'Donnell of Tyrconnel who arrived in the early summer at the Scottish Court accompanied by his harper. Although O'Donnell's probable objective was to recruit Scottish help in his long-standing feud with the O'Neills of Antrim, James no doubt hoped that with a little encouragement he might attack Carrickfergus, an English stronghold - another tweak of the lion's tail. In any case a treaty was signed in June when James took O'Donnell under his protection and promised to send ships whenever he asked for them. He gave him guns too, which O'Donnell discarded on his way back to Ayr.

Having rounded Cape Wrath and shown the flag in the Hebrides the fleet sailed down to Belfast Bay and bombarded and plundered Carrickfergus in an orgy of rape and loot then returned to Ayr to unload the spoils, re-provision and at last sail for France. This small irrelevance may had served to introduce the untried crews to the canon's roar.

Meanwhile Louis, who had expected the Scottish fleet to arrive at Brittany about the middle of August, another indication of their roudabout route, had instructed the Grand Master of Brittany to have seven ships to sail northward with it as soon as it arrived and join the squadron of Norman ships lying at the mouth of the Seine. All through the last fortnight in August the *Petit Louis* lay off Villerville waiting to pilot the Scots into Honfleur where the *Lion*, Robert Barton's new French-built ship, lay at its moorings. The fleet, having been knocked about by equinoctial gales and delayed further by the grounding once again of the *Michael*, did not appear off the French coast until late September. By then James and the cream of Scottish chivalry were dead at Flodden and Henry was making peace with France. For all the effect it had had on the outcome the Scottish fleet might have stayed in the Forth.

Early in November Arran and Fleming brought home the storm-battered fleet but three of the finest ships had disappeared into the limbo of lost things. *The Great Michael* and two others had been left in the service of the French king to replace the *Cordeliere* destroyed at sea. On 2nd April 1514 it is recorded among the Acts of the Lords of Council that 'the Lords ratify the selling of the King's grat ship called the *Michael* with tackle and apparel for 40,000 francs to the French king. Done for the public weal and profit of the Realm.' The Duke of Albany had negotiated the sale which is said to have raised only a fraction of her original cost.

What became of her is unknown. Someone reported her damaged in a fight at sea; someone else saw her rotting in the harbour at Brest; a third reported her burned to the waterline two years later. Yet again it was claimed that she served for another decade in the French Navy, being broken up at last and her timbers used to build houses. In many ways the story of this jewel of the sea parallels that of the golden King out of whose mind she sprang. She was too large and splendid for her time, held in pride and high regard by all, wayward and heedless of restraint, squandering the riches of her homeland in ostentation and at last going down to a meaningless and doubtfilled extinction. Judged by the nation's balance sheet she was a failure, and no attempt was made to rebuild a large Scottish navy. But what magnificence, what style!

CHAPTER 2

The Yellow Butterflies

Newhaveners who talk about the building of the *Great Michael* as though it happened yesterday, have a tradition that, when the shipyard declined with the death of James IV, many foreign wrights stayed on to marry with the fisherfolk and imparted a strange style of dress, custom and architecture.

But some think the Flemish connection is even older and more deeply rooted. Mrs George Cupples who wrote a book about it a hundred years ago, claimed that the village had first been colonised in the 15th century from a Flemish fishing settlement on the Isle of May with maybe a dash of Spanish blood for flavour. Other writers have taken the same line and traces of this settlement on May, including Flemish pottery shards, were discovered last century. This early incursion, she believed, was later supplemented by refugees from the tyranny of Spanish domination in the Netherlands.

She first fell under the spell of Newhaven while on holiday visits to her uncle, who like many fashionable folk took a house there for a summer month to enjoy the sea breezes. Later she came to live in the village with her husband the novelist George Cupples. She says that to any one familiar with their village ways, customs, idioms, family names and costumes, it is indisputable how much they resemble Flemish and Dutch fisherfolk in skill and industry, thrift and shrewdness and well-conditioned habits. 'We may observe these resemblances in various ways, such as their women's manifold petticoats, lace caps, trim stockings conspicuously shown, all these and a special household care for elaborate collections of crockery and for furniture made to last.'

She goes on: 'In complexion and general physique they often exemplify the old Flemish descent, some being blond as any Netherlander and some being dark as any typical Spaniard, comparatively few intermediate. And among their children you may see any day broad-beamed little Dutchmen toddle across the street costumed as if fresh from Flanders itself. Dear flaxen-haired wee lassies whose doll-like cheeks and eyes carry out the picture, both being grouped at ends of narrow high-sided alleys that are crossed overhead by clothes lines of parti-coloured garments.'

Charles Reade draws the same picture in his Newhaven novel *'Christie Johnstone'*. Describing his heroines he says the character and cleanliness of their female costume pointed to their Flemish ancestry. 'They wore on their heads caps of Dutch or Flemish origin with a broad lace border, stiffened and arched over the forehead about three inches high, leaving brow and cheeks unencumbered.'

It is true that from the early Middle Ages there was a good deal of to-ing and fro-ing with the Dutch and Flemish coasts. An early Dutch chart shows the Firth of Forth as Mare Frisicum, the Friesian Sea, and many records tell of the

Jeannie Wilson, Newhaven fishergirl, photographed by David Octavius Hill and Robert Adamson in 1843 (Courtesy of the Scottish National Portrait Gallery).

presence every year at this 'Dutch gold mine' around the Isle of May of enormous fishing fleets - up to 2000 Flemish, Dutch and German broad bottomed herring busses, boats with two masts, of 20 Ton burden, each carrying three or four small skiffs which would be lowered when the fishing grounds were reached.

Part of this great fleet on one occasion brought fear and alarm to Newhaven, Leith and Edinburgh. Two hundred and fifty Flemish busses fishing off the coast attended by nine lighters were surprised by fourteen great Biscayen Spanish ships which set upon them and sank three of the lighters. The whole of

Another fine calotype by Hill and Adamson, pioneers in photography. This one is of Mrs Elizabeth Hall of Newhaven (Courtesy of the Scottish National Portrait Gallery).

the busses took flight and about sixty of them fled up the Forth where when this great fleet in half-moon formation was first seen as if in readiness for battle, everyone thought it was an army of Spaniards. The Privy Council ordered all men under pain of death to arm themselves on the seashore on the first touk of the drum. Canon were brought down from the Castle and the towns ordered under arms, 'every man resolved better than another to abide the worst till death or they put the enemy to destruction. About ten at night word came by two boats that were sent out from Leith that they were our friends and were only a number of busses fled from tyranny and then the canon were trailed back again to the castle and the people commanded to rest.'

Many of the Forth fishing towns, it is claimed, were populated by people cast ashore on this wave of commercial enterprise, or who were refugees from Spanish occupation of the Netherlands, or who had come from Friesland in the early Middle Ages, forced to leave because of incursions of the Angles and Saxons and again in the 12th century when a disastrous series of storms broke the ancient Dutch dykes (just as in 1933 when 1200 people were drowned in Holland). Much of the land was submerged throughout the Middle Ages driving people over to Scotland to find a firmer foothold and place-names of the East Neuk of Fife indicate a very ancient settlement of Frisians.

Shipwrecks too added to the immigrant population. In the 16th century a Flemish vessel was wrecked on the Fife coast and the sailors forced to take up their habitation in what is now Buckhaven. As they spoke Flemish and could scarcely understand the locals they were for long the laughing stocks of the surrounding countryside.

But not everyone accepts the Flemish origin of Newhaven and some writers have pointed out that the names which are commonest in Newhaven are from the common stock of Scottish surnames. It was usual for a sea community to receive recruits from other coasts through constant contact and shipwreck and it was these accidental additions which gave rise to the traditions. (The Spanish colouring which Mrs Cupples and others remarked among a minority of Newhaveners may have come from the large numbers of survivors of the Armada ships wrecked on the wild western coasts, who made their way to Leith and Newhaven where they settled until they could get a passage back home). Added to which, the fishers by economic necessity lived apart and had their own customs and the easiest way for their peasant neighbours to explain this difference was to attribute it to foreign origin.

In any case there are records of fishing folk being on the site of Newhaven from the earliest times. Prehistoric remains on the coast include kitchen middens, dugout canoes and burial urns. Much later, the Welsh-speaking barbarian tribes of the area are recorded as supplying the Roman port at Cramond with fish. The Forth formed a natural funnel for thousands of years of seaborne invasion and these Celtic tribes were driven out around the seventh century by the Angles who were hard-driven in later centuries by the Danes.

By Norman times there is evidence of a more settled state with rude fishing villages along the shores. Reference is made to this in a charter of 1143 granted by David I to Holyrood Abbey of among other things fishing tithes, which refers to North Leith as the home of fisherfolk, serfs of the Church of St Cuthbert, and another charter a couple of centuries later in which Bruce granted the oyster beds to Edinburgh.

These earliest fishing communities tended to be the disadvantaged, ousted from the meagre fields onto the bare fringe of a hard living, cast up on the economic tides like spume around the sea's brim. Their turf huts turned their backs upon the land, crowding the shore as though to be closer to the sea and

Mrs Hall (centre) and two unknown fishergirls. This Hill and Adamson study was used for Hill's painting of 'Edinburgh from the Castle', 1847 (Courtesy of the Scottish National Portrait Gallery).

their boats. For centuries they lived apart, worked apart and married wives of their own sort, drawing away from the landward community even in physical aspect, for the work of the oar moulded their form - their ambition to be left to live by the sea to the noise of the sea.

One of these communities, a mile west of the Water of Leith, scarcely more than a dozen hovels in the embrace of a sandy bay, for centuries dredged oysters from the rich beds of the Forth and sold them to the poor of Edinburgh. It was here that James IV chose to plant his naval dockyard.

A Race Apart

Those of us who are romantics at heart will toss cool logic over the housetops and staunchly stride to the support of Mrs Cupples' feminine intuition. But whatever their origin they marched to a different drum - long isolation, not only physical but of the spirit, and the demands of their employment, made of them strangers in their own land.

My young cousin, Sarah Dyer, who has made a fascinating oral record of reminiscences from among the generation which still recalls Newhaven as a living community says: 'Marriage outside the community was generally frowned upon and worse than anything was marriage to a 'Leither'.' She quotes

Mrs Barbara Flucker, fisherwife of Newhaven, selling from the creel. The fish were gutted on the spot after having been chosen by the customer (Hill and Adamson, Courtesy of the Scottish National Portrait Gallery).

Esther Liston, one of Newhaven's last fishwives: 'It's an awfy job the Leith and Newhaven - you hadnae to cross the bridge (at Anchorfield) to get married - oh, they thought that was something terrible.' And Sarah's grandmother, Alexandrina Barnes said: 'It was because the Newhaven folk earned more money from the sea that kept them apart, they were better off. The morning my mother Margaret Noble was born (1868) her father's catch was £50. That was his catch for one morning!' Mrs Margaret Colley, for many years secretary of the Fishermen's Society in Newhaven said: If a girl married a tradesman outside the village, they would worry - 'Do you get your meat?'. And if their son married a stranger they would say 'What use is a girl like that? Can she bait a hook?'

Newhaven fisherwives between trains at Edinburgh Waverley Station around 1900. They travelled far and wide daily, filling the waiting time by knitting. (Courtesy of the Pennycook Glazing Company Ltd).

The prolific intermarriage accentuated the physical distinction. The 2nd Statistical Account of Scotland referred to the fisherfolk as having a distinctive cast of countenance and physical constitution, above average height, robust and well-shaped, the men being muscular healthy and active and the women pretty and remarkable for their florid health and regular features as also for the neatness and cleanliness of their personal appearance. George IV who had some pretensions to authority on the subject, said the Newhaven fishwives were the handsomest women he had ever beheld. Moray McLaren also used the superlative to describe the younger Newhaven fish lassies: 'There is an appealing sweetness which comes partly from a complexion (for softness and freshness unrivalled in Europe) and partly from the expression of the eyes and mouth, sometimes shyly humorous, sometimes shyly serious which is quite enchanting.'

Poets and painters and the early photographers loved these colourful creatures. W.H.Ogilvie the border poet wrote:

> And the wind was on our faces and the salt was on our lips
> And our hearts were set adancing with the heave of little ships
> For these kind and comely women brightly kilted to the knee
> Brought home the sway of tangle and the clean scent of the sea

The Newhaven Fisherlasses Choir on-stage at the Assembly Hall during a performance of 'Hail Caledonia' at the 1954 Edinburgh Festival (Courtesy of Sandy Noble).

Charles Reade on the same subject: 'It is indeed a race of beauty that the Northern sun peachifies instead of rosewooding... She was fair, with a massive but shapely throat as white as milk; glossy brown hair, the loose threads of which glittered like gold, and a blue eye, which being contrasted with dark eyebrows and lashes, took the luminous effect peculiar to such rare beauty.

'Their short petticoats revealed a neat ankle and a leg with a noble swell; for Nature, when she is in earnest, builds beauty on the ideas of ancient sculptors and poets, not the modern poetasters, who with their airy-like sylphs and their smoke-filled verses, fight for want of flesh in women and want of fact in poetry as parallel beauties.'

'These women had a grand corporeal tract; they had never known a corset! so they were straight as javelins: they could lift their hands above their head! Actually! Their supple persons moved as Nature intended; every gesture was ease, grace, and freedom. What with their own radiance, and the snowy cleanliness and brightness of their costumes, they came like meteors into the apartment.'

Each port had its distinctive dress but the Newhaven women were the 'yellow butterflies' among the Forth fishwives. It was the colourful costumes they wore to the London Fisheries Exhibition in the Crystal Palace in 1883 which caught Queen Victoria's eye and got a party of 18 invited to Windsor Castle. Colston in *'The Town and Port of Leith'* says that at the exhibition they proved a great attraction.

The other choir, the Newhaven Fisherwomen's Choir, with their conductor Mrs Ritchie, M.B.E., and her two daughters who later continued her work with the choir. (Courtesy of Sandy Noble).

Princess Beatrice of the Royal party was greatly astonished to be addressed by one of them, Margaret Flucker: 'Hoo's yer mither, ma lamb?' She replied that the Queen was very well.

The Prince of Wales, realising the situation, said: 'You will not know who I am?' 'Toots, mon, wha doesnae ken you! You're the Queen's auldest son.'

'And do you know that fellow over there?' 'Yes, that's your next brither, the Duke o' Edinburgh. Ye ken he gets his title frae oor pairts.'

The story got back to Newhaven before the fishwives did and earned Mrs Flucker the byname, 'The Honourable Margaret'. Her grand-daughter Mrs Margaret Barker said: 'After that, when she was ill, her customers used to come down in their carriages to call on her and my uncle would run up the stair and tell her the carriages were coming. She used to tell her visitors, 'The bairn'll no go away until he gets a bit sixpence.'

As a result of their London visit, for a short while, their dress became a fashion copied in silks and satins by enthusiastic young ladies all over the country. Reade describes the costume: 'They had cotton jackets, bright red and yellow, mixed in patterns, confined at the waist by the apron strings, but bobtailed below the waist; short woollen petticoats with broad vertical stripes, red and white, most vivid in colour; white worsted stockings, and neat, though high-quartered shoes. Under their jackets they wore a thick spotted cotton handkerchief about one inch of which was visible round the lower part of the throat.

'Of their petticoats the outer one was kilted or gathered up to the front and the second, of the same colour, hung down in the usual way.'

But they had too, a more practical outfit for workaday purposes which the Queen saw when she drove through Newhaven in 1872 noting 'Many very enthusiastic but not in their smartest dress.' Sarah Dyer quotes her grandmother Rena Barnes looking at a picture of the Fisherwomen's Choir: 'That's not what they wore when they went to sell the fish. They wore navy blue petticoats, the outer kilted around the hips to pad the creel and a navy blue and white striped apron and the pocket was coloured and the blouse was coloured but always with the white cuffs and the sleeves turned up above the elbow. There was a navy blue cape they used to put on, black shoes and stockings, but they didn't wear hats when I was wee. Grannie Henny (Henrietta Paterson) always wore a lace hat like that, and even going to the meeting on a Sunday night in the Fishermen's Hall they wore these caps. When they went to church on Sunday they wore lovely bonnets and there was a woman in Tolbooth Wynd made them. They went to the Meeting with their fishwives' dark blue petticoat, two tucks in it, and a nice shawl, maybe a wee tartan one or something like that round their shoulders, but they didn't dress up like they did for Church.'

Though to most folk all fishwives seemed to dress alike, the Newhaven dress was distinguished from even its near neighbour, Fisherrow. The Fisherrow fishwives had a longer skirt and their creelbands were always of leather, while that of the Newhaven women was usually canvas which was well scrubbed each week to match their usual trig appearance. Though the young girls went bareheaded the married women often wore a frilled cap, though they too might simply go bareheaded, their ample hair brushed smooth and close with a centre-parting.

Working Wives

Apart from the Kirk there were few occasions for dressing up for the Newhaven fisherwomen. Here's Scott's Jenny Rintherout on the fishwife's lot: 'A wheen poor drudges ye are. As sune as the keel o' the cobble touches the sand deil a bit mair will the lazy fisher loons work, but the wives mon kilt their coats and wade into the surf to tak the fish ashore. And then the man casts aff the wat and puts on the dry, and sits down wi' his pipe and his gill stoup ahint the ingle, like ony auld houdie and ne'er a turn will he do till the coble's afloat again! And the wife she maun get the scull on her back and awa wi the fish to the next burrows town and scauld and ban (curse) wi' ilka wife that will scauld and ban wi' her till it's sauld - and that's the gait fisherwives live, puir slaving bodies.'

But Mrs Mucklebackit was having none of that: 'Slaves? - Gae wa' lass!- Ca' the head o' the house slaves? Little ye ken aboot it, lass. Show me a word my man daur speak, or a turn he daur do about the house without it be just to tak his meat, and his drink, and his diversion, like ony o' the weans. He has mair sense than to ca' onything about the bigging his ain, frae the roof tree down to the crackit trencher on the bink (beach). He kens weel eneugh wha feeds him

The young idea - fishergirls in their finery. The costumes are faithful replicas of those worn by their mothers (Courtesy of George Liston).

and cleeds him and keeps a' tight, thack and rape (thatch and rope) when his coble is jowing awa' in the Firth, puir fallow. Na' na' lass! - Them that sells the goods guide the purse - them that guide the purse rule the house.'

There's no doubt Maggie Mucklebackit had the rights of it. For the fishing was a partnership of equals, with the women more equal than the men, a practical matriarchy induced by the long absences of the men at sea.

The 1st Statistical Account (1793) says of Lothian fishwives: 'as a great share in the maintenance of the family depends on the industry of the wife she has no small sway in it. Indeed she considers herself the head of the house as may be inferred from a remark about a young woman about to marry: 'Hout, her keep a man? She can hardly keep hersel'.' As they do the work of men their manners are masculine and their strength and activity equal to what they have to perform. Dextrous at bargaining they have a species of eloquence and facility at expressing their ideas by words and gestures. They are well acquainted with the world and not abashed. There seems to be no employment more conducive to good health and spirits than the one they follow. Some of them have been brought to bed with child and gone to Edinburgh with their creels on their backs within a week. Two days of the week are devoted to gathering bait and putting it on hooks and four to carrying fish in creels to Edinburgh.' They hauled the boats and helped launch them and sometimes carried the men on their backs out to the boats to keep them dry.

Describing the bait-gathering Janet Cadell writing in 1884 said: 'A painter might go far before he found a more tempting subject than a troup of these bait girls, their plentiful hair covered by gaily coloured kerchiefs, clean print gowns drawn up over ample layers of dark blue petticoats sufficiently short to allow a sight of shapely ankles and feet. The bait-gathering is carried on according to the state of the tide and as early as two o'clock our slumbers were often broken by the patter of many shoeless feet and by the merry laughter and the singing of secular ditties or more frequently of those hymns which have of late become popular, as they set forth for the distant sands.'

'The weight carried by these women' according to the Statistical Account, 'varies from 150 lbs upwards. When their husbands' boats arrive late so as to leave them with bare time to reach Edinburgh before dinner, it is not unusual for three of them to carry one basket by turns shifting it from one to the other every hundred yards'. Russell in *'The Story of Leith'* tells of the Edinburgh poet James Ballantine helping a fishwife to hoist her creel on to her back. He was astonished at the weight but her cheery reply as she adjusted her strap against her forehead 'showed a happiness and contentment with her lot as unexpected as was the beauty and poetry of the words in which it was expressed: 'Oo, aye, but ilka blade o' gress keps its ain drap o' dew.' Yet it was a load they bore with joy for a well-filled purse gave them superiority over other working women. And they took delight in the banter with customers. Maggie Mucklebackit speaks here for the sisterhood: 'And div ye think' (arms akimbo) 'that my man and my sons are to gae to the sea in weather like yestreen and the day - sic a sea as it's yet outby - and get naething for their fish, and be misca'd into the bargain? It's no fish ye're buying -it's men's lives.' Oh, they loved to turn the tap of sentiment:

> Ah, little ken ye gentle folk wha grudge the price o' fish
> O' the risin' o' the bree
> An' little think ye, leddies gay, that hae your every wish
> O' the dangers o' the sea
> Oh, listen to the mother's cries, oh hear the wail o' wives
> An' mind that to provide your fare men sacrificed their lives
> Oh, the wailin o' the bree
> Oh, the soughin' o' the sea
> Oh, hearken to the widow's cry
> Send my laddies back to me.

What comfortable Victorian housewife with a social conscience could resist that? Or this heart-wrenching speil quoted by Alastair Mackenzie: 'Twa shillings ower muckle mem, and the cod far ower dear? Ay, weel, I wat they're dear mem, they were gey dear to me. Ken ye what that boat o' fish cost me mem? It cost me the life o' a guid husband and the father o' fower bairns mem, stretched on my ain table wi' the salt sea drippin' from his hair mem. They are mebbe dear to you that buys mem, but they are dearer, ay, far ower dear to us that sells.'

As her creel emptied the fisherwife usually knitted whenever her hands were free keeping herself and family well-supplied with stockings and ganzies or jerseys. There was also a modest export trade in woollens to Holland. 'Such was the force of habit,' said Sir Walter Scott, 'that on the homeward journey the women would often ballast their baskets with stones and even take them scrubbed and weighted to kirk on Sunday.'

And as though that were not enough they kept the man, kept the house, kept the family and kept the siller too. Sandy Noble, whose knowledge of old Newhaven is encyclopaedic told me how these women ordered their week. 'In those days in the kitchen there was usually two shelves and they were full of china. And at the top shelf there was a table-set and at the bottom was two possibly three sets of the most beautiful china that was going of the day. Now just putting a question to you. My dear friend, you talk about keeping the Sunday. That was the wife's day off. Now when you got married, it was invariably that the best maid gave the bride a set of china. And about the first thing that they ever sought to buy was a dinner set. Somebody would say: Why have two sets of china that is always up on the shelf? But you see, unless they had that they couldnae keep the Sunday. Because they washed the dishes on Monday. You'll have heard the saying: You may not cut hair or horn on a Sunday. The point was that if these things were to be done it wasn't to occupy their Sunday. It was not that they were holy, holy. It was that Monday was washing, cleaning and ironing, Tuesday out on the town selling fish, Wednesday fish, Thursday fish, Friday fish, and Saturday maybe cleaning and it might be fish in the morning. What time had you for anything? Her Sunday was precious to her, not only that, it was essential. Their life was doing, doing, doing. A fishwife going along and seeing four young women standing talking: 'Could you not put a sock in your hand?' But the point is, not wasting time.'

Was it any wonder that marriages were seldom made outside the village? No landward maid could have borne the load.

Unlike the fishing villages of the North East where a fisher lass, once she reached the age of 14, was expected to join her sisters and cousins in following the fleets around the coast as herring gutters, Newhaven girls rarely left the village, there being full employment for them in retailing the local catches or in the kippering yard or the net factory at Granton. Girls from other ports, particulaly Peterhead did, however come to Newhaven during the season, and the occasional marriage resulted.

They had a proper notion of themselves, the womenfolk - they were among the earliest in the Suffragette Movement. When in 1796 their men were praised by the county gentry of Mid Lothian for rushing to man the fleet in a moment of national peril, and were presented with a silver medal and chain by the Duke of Buccleuch for their courage, the womenfolk protested they should get recognition too. It was them that had persuaded their men to go and they would have been the sufferers if their menfolk had been killed. The gentry conceded and presented a valuable brooch which is still worn by the wife of the Boxmaster of the Free Fishermen's Society on formal occasions. Inside the brooch is inscribed 'Our love shall be the pledge of courage' and on the outside 'They'll fight for us, their children and their King.'

But they held their men in respect too. When George IV visited Edinburgh in 1822 a trades procession was held in which the Newhaven fishermen had their place. When they appeared on the scene 'like marine puff-balls' in their jerseys and long leather seaboots some with top hats raked aft like tug-boat funnels, others in felt hats exploded upwards like a primitive form of sombrero, several fisherwomen who were collected at the Tron Kirk called out 'Ah, there's a wale (choice) o' men!'

CHAPTER 3

The Free Fishers

The men caught less of the public eye. Their attire was less colourful than their womenfolk, the most distinctive feature (apart from a varied collection of headgear from sou'wester to woollen cap to a primitive sombrero to tophat), consisting of leather sea boots reaching above the knees and folded down when ashore. These boots were all hand-sewn and had to be kept soft since the salt water tended to harden and crack them. Every week they were treated by the women with cod liver oil or a mixture of lard, melted over the fire and worked well into the seams with some black boot polish or maybe a wee drop of tar added. These boots, so much a part of their way of life, were also one of their biggest hazards for if a man fell overboard while wearing them he would go to the bottom. More than one drowned man has been found floating upright, weighted by his boots, his hair barely showing on the surface. Beneath the boots they wore flap-over trousers - for buttons were a hazard with the nets - of pilot-cloth and two or three pairs of long knitted stockings and above that innumerable dark indigo blue wool jerseys which buttoned at the neck the whole giving the impression of what is now pictured as the pirate. To protect the jersey a loose-fitting brown linen jumper known as a slop was sometimes worn at sea. Oilskin jackets, sou'wester and oilskin trousers reaching just below the knee in bright yellow were universal wear along the East Coast during heavy weather. Ashore they might wear white canvas trousers and Guernsey shirts and a sleeved waistcoat.

Their work they performed out of public sight - at sea - and the sea was exclusively the male domain. No woman was permitted to intrude on this male preserve. (It was Charles Reade's description of Christie Johnstone's boat trip to the herring which damned his novel out of hand for Newhaveners).

Here is John Buchan on these men: 'They had the decorum of men for whom the world was both merry and melancholy. They faced death daily so even in their cups they could not be children. Mighty eaters and drinkers, good fare only loosened their tongues. Here was the chief fisher, a mountainous man with a beard like moses and far sighted blue eyes beneath pent-house brows. There were gaps in the company, one had lost his boat and his life off the Bass in the great January storm, and another had shipwrecked at Ushant and was now in a French gaol. But here were old friends one who had sailed his smack far into the unpermitted Baltic, an old man who had been a pirate in western waters. There were men who had been pressed for the Navy and had seen Trafalgar, whalers who sailed regularly for the Faroes and Iceland, men who had manned privateers and fought obscure fights in forgotten seas and skippers who leavened their lawful merchantry with commodities not approved by law.'

31

The Newhaven men were described in the middle of last century as pre-eminent for their industrious and frugal habits, being muscular healthy and active. There were at that time (1845) upwards of 300 fishermen and pilots in the village (with an average of five children to each household - giving a total population of 2103). The men were employed on oyster fishing through the winter and in summer in line fishing in the firth or herring fishing off the north coasts. The distances to which they often went in their small boats in search of cod and ling and even in stormy weather was hardly credible. The fishing banks were in general 30 to 40 miles from the shore. Daniel Defoe in *'Tour through the Whole Islands'* says that the Forth oyster fishers in 23-ft open cob-bles would sometimes land their catches as far south as Newcastle -often hav-ing to row a good part of the way. Until around1850 boats were undecked and crews were exposed to the winds rain and sea and when bad weather overtook them during the night which often happened they were obliged to make for land which in some instances they never reached. In one night the loss of two boats left 10 widows and 53 children destitute. Yet it was amazing what seas they could survive unscathed for they had a hereditary instinct which exercise had sharpened until aided by skill and nerve they could weather storms where great vessels might founder. They themselves felt safer in their small boats than they would have in large ships.

Writing in 1849 James Thomson in *'The Scottish Fisheries'* says: 'Perhaps in the world generally it is not thought of how constant and unremitting the toil of the Scottish fishermen is, particularly during the eight weeks of the herring season. In every seven nights they are only two nights in bed on the Saturday and Sunday, this is from the time the nets are sent into the fields to dry till when they have again to be collected and carried to the boat. During the other five they may have a little slumber for an hour or two in the middle of the day. Unquiet and restless closing of the eye induced by fatigue in a moment of rest at the fishing ground, partakes of little of the good of nature's sweet restorative - a bare board of the boat, the couch, the canopy of heaven for covering.'

The Press Gangs

The ultimate element in their lives was the North Sea in all its moods. They might go out there and earn their living, they might go out there and lose their lives: the sea was indifferent. Its rages and its calms were not concerned with them.

Far more to be dreaded were the Press Gangs. Impressment was something of a feudal hangover and throughout the latter part of the 17th and 18th cen-tury a kind of legalised anarchy broke sporadically upon the ports as bands armed with sword and pistol roistered in search of their prey. The Free Fisher-men's Society records contain several references to demands upon the village to fulfill its quota of men for the King's Navy where they might serve for seven years or more in badly-equipped vessels, undermanned, underfed, underpaid

Three early 19th century picture cards representing a romantic view of the fishermen of Newhaven (Courtesy of Edinburgh City Libraries).

and treated brutally. In 1652 with the English at war with Holland the impressment of 500 Scots seamen was especially unpopular because Scotland's relations with the Dutch were commercially beneficial. Newhaven and Leith were to contribute twenty men, Musselburgh and Fisherrow four, Prestonpans three and Cockenzie two. The Privy Council commanded that all must be respectable seamen and fishermen and not robbers and sickly as had on previous occasions affronted the country. Many fled abroad to avoid the duty so skippers of merchant ships were forbidden to sail until the quota had been met. (The same quotas were demanded again in 1664 and 1672 for the second and third Dutch Wars). It was the difficulties the Government met in extracting the required men by quota that led to the setting up of gangs of armed bullies licensed to rampage in search of likely seamen. Disguised as a collier their gun brig might steal into harbour then led by spies burst upon the sleeping village at midnight, rum-enraged and cutlass in hand. Perhaps forewarned, the fisherman might escape through a trapdoor under the bed or hide in a kist till danger passed. Nor at sea was he safe. No smuggler was ever more cautious to avoid discovery than the fisher, going about his own business, to evade the cruising war brig. Yet many an empty fishing boat was found floating in the Forth, none knowing whether its crew had drowned or been taken for Naval service.

An issue of *'The Scotsman'* in 1875 carried the obituary of a Fife seaman, David Wilson, (83), whose story can be found repeated in essence in other records of the time. A farm boy, he ran away at the age of 12 aboard a little Kirkcaldy smack, later joining a Greenland whaler out of Dundee. One September day when on return from the Arctic they looked hopefully for the hills of home, they saw the dreaded war brig *Pinkie* cruising like a wolf in their tracks. As the only hope of escape the old ship was instantly trimmed under all sail before the freshening breeze. As quickly up flew the top gallant and studding sail on the brig which followed in the chase like a hound at the heels of a wild boar. The rising gale swelled the broad mainsail of the old hulk till tack and sheet snapped again and her huge bows were fairly buried in the foam and spray, and yet after all her fleet pursuer broadly ranged alongside. Then the brig like a maddened bull charged across the bows of the whaler and David Wilson who was at the wheel, put the cruiser's helm down hard in the nick of time. To save them from the serious consequences of denying a King's ship, the Captain and officers were herded into a cabin and locked in. 'Round off or I'll shoot ' thundered from the brig's quarter deck, but even the ship's boy, fired by the moment's wild enthusiasm waved defiance from the yard arm. The guns were ranged round - whiz, whiz flew the deadly shower and the spokes were struck twice from David's hands but now sail and rigging fell about the deck and the disabled hulk lay at the mercy of the cruiser.

David was clapped in irons as a mutineer, a heavy 6-ft iron bar across his legs and his hands rivetted to ring bolts. Befriended by a crew member, a disgraced London lawyer, he successfully pleaded his case before the London magistrates but though he escaped hanging for mutiny he was condemned into the King's service. On board the war brig, David distinguished himself as a brave and expert sailor and was set fair for promotion when he and his boat's company deserted ship in Jersey. There he joined a packet trading to the Mediterranean but in Biscay Bay the ship was captured by French privateers. The prisoners were put ashore and driven like cattle into an ancient church where on a scanty truss of straw they lay for the night. But someone fired the straw and the old sanctuary was quickly wrapped in flames. David lived to tell the scene when, as William Tennant says:

> Pinnacle cam doon and tow'r
> And Virgin Maries in a shower
> Fell flat and smashed their faces

After many hardships they were set free by Wellington's victorious march on Paris. Returning to Fife David found himself a hero for his stand at the helm of the old whaler.

A similar fate befell another Fife whaler, Robert Pratt of Cellardykes who

Willie Liston 'redding' (cleaning) the line, a Hill and Adamson study in customary shoregoing attire (Courtesy of the Scottish National Portrait Gallery).

was seized off Inchkeith but sprang from the forechains of the brig on to the rigging of a passing ferry smack and was back in Fife in a twinkling. He obtained a berth in a trader to London but was seized again in the Thames. Slipping overboard off Greenwich he served for several years in a variety of ships before being captured by a French privateer. By means of a marlin spike and a rope of blankets he escaped from an old castle in a snow storm and with the help of friendly villagers got a passage to Falmouth. Thereafter he returned to whaling and made 37 voyages to the Arctic before settling down to sailmaking in Cellardykes.

During the twenty-two years of war with Revolutionary France the gangs were particularly active. Reasoning that it was better to be volunteers than

James Liston and his yawl, probably best-known of the Hill and Adamson photographs (Courtesy of the Scottish National Portrait Gallery).

pressed men, the Newhaven Society in 1796 wrote to the Admiralty offering to form themselves into a marine force, aboard any gunboat or vessel of war the Government might appoint, from the Red Head of Angus to St Abbs Head and to go further if necessary. This patriotic if practical offer caught the public imagination. The Admiralty ordained that they should be formed into a corps of Sea Fencibles and they were given authority to draw cannon and ammunition as they might judge necessary. The Lord Provost and Magistrates presented the Society with a handsome stand of colours. The Duke of Buccleuch on behalf of the gentry of the Lothians went to Newhaven with several gentlemen

The tophat, often worn at a rakish angle and varnished against the weather, popular headgear ashore (Hill and Adamson, Courtesy of the Scottish National Portrait Gallery).

and presented the Boxmaster of the Society with a handsome silver medal and chain. On the medal is inscribed: 'In testimony of the brave and patriotic offer of the Fishermen of Newhaven to defend the coasts against the enemy this honorary mark of appreciation was voted by the County of Midlothian, *Agmine remerum celeri* (By their swift band of oars). The medal is still worn on ceremonial occasions though a Boxmaster wryly lamented that he could remember when the chain was longer.

A more qualified offer was made by the Society in 1803: 'We whose names are hereto subscribed, sensible of the blessings we enjoy under His Present Majesty's Government and our happy constitution and willing at all times to do what in our power lies in support of both, beg leave to offer our services as volunteers for the protection of the Firth of Forth without fee or reward unless our services are so required as to prevent us from providing for our families in our usual way.'

These offers were finally taken up in 1806 when the Admiralty called on the Society to furnish a crew for the 64-gun two-decker, *HMS Texel*, under Captain Donald Campbell, R.N., which was to proceed to sea from Leith Roads and give chase to some French frigates which had been preying upon shipping in the Greenland seas. Two hundred men of the Sea Fencibles volunteered and Mrs Cupples records that *'the Texel* captured the French frigate *'La Naydenne'* and brought her as a prize to Yarmouth Roads after which they came home to Newhaven with great eclat. For years it was the pride of those old salts who are now sleeping near the ruined walls of Our Lady's and St James' Chapel to recall the days when 'I was aboard the *Texel*'.'

For this exploit they received a decorative letter from George III (since lost) and the gratitude of the City of Edinburgh expressed by way of a sum of £250 and an elegant silver cup from Captain Brodie, one of His Majesty's officers presented to James Noble, Boxmaster. Engraved on the cup is a tribute to the volunteers who manned the *Texel* and: 'This cup is dedicated to their posterity to show what they did when their services were required to meet the enemies of their country - James Vashon, Rear Admiral.' The cup is still in the Society's possession.

It was an accepted custom to buy substitutes to meet a quota and men were willing to sell themselves into the Navy. Mention is made of this custom shortly before the *Texel* adventure when the village again fell under a quota. The Rev Dr Johnston of North Leith Church petitioned the Lords of the Admiralty 'in favour of the fishermen concerning the demand for men from the town of Newhaven when they had paid a man out of every five only a few years before and the town was all volunteers and always willing to tender their services on demand.' Their Lordships granted the petition.

A later petition met with less success. In 1812 Newhaven had already met part of its quota when a letter was received on behalf of the Admiral in Command at Leith demanding 'that the fishermen at Newhaven immediately furnish the remainder of their proportion of quota men for His Majesty's Naval service. As no further time can be allowed, and on their failure of doing so there will be immediate necessary direction given for impress.' The Society's reaction was to send out a petition to appeal for financial support for the provision of substitutes to 'The Gentlemen Shipowners and others in Leith, Edinburgh and the vicinity, the Petition of the Fishermen and Pilots of Newhaven humbly sheweth that in consequence of the late great and disastrous losses at sea it has pleased the Honourable His Majesty's Commissioners of the Admiralty to order a quota of men to be raised from among the fishers at Newhaven, hitherto protected as sea fencibles, and that either by personal service or by substitutes. Should the former of these ultimately happen it will be attended with the ruin of their families (they being in general married men) who must become a burden on the public, and as they are unable to be at the expense or substitutes without the assistance of the gentlemen, merchants and others in Leith and Edinburgh, this application is made for their assistance. May it therefore please the gentlemen, merchants, shipowners and others in about Leith and Edinburgh to take your petitioners' case into consideration and to grant them such assistance as to them shall seem proper, and they, as in duty bound will ever pray. (Signed) William Linton, for himself and other fishermen at Newhaven.'

The appeal did not provoke an overwhelming response. Seven individuals, including Henry Bell, builder of the steamship *Comet*, contributed five guineas each and one individual two guineas. The fishermen appear to have had a whip

Titled 'A Newhaven Pilot', this calotype was exhibited by Hill and Adamson at the Royal Scottish Academy in 1845 (Courtesy of the Scottish National Portrait Gallery).

round among themselves for a total of £70 was handed over which was sufficient to provide three substitutes. They still had to provide from among their own ranks as it is recorded that 'the fishermen of Newhaven were drilled in Leith Fort'. It was rumoured at the time that a letter had been received sometime after the *Texel* adventure that since the Newhaven fishermen had been the first volunteers they would be protected in all times coming from impress. Mr James Wilson in recording the incident wrote: 'The letter was sealed with the King's Seal. This letter was never seen after the first time by the fishermen and at the change of office-bearers the committee asked for the letter but there was no letter produced and the Boxmaster never gave any satisfaction about it. I have heard many of the old men speak often about it.'

A later record of Naval service is contained in the Society's papers. In 1854 during the Crimean War over a hundred fishermen volunteered. They trained for a month on a warship stationed at Queensferry and thereafter served in the Navy for five years after which many of them elected to serve a further term.

In the First World War eighty Newhaven men gave their lives, most serving in the Navy or in minesweepers. A marble war memorial was erected to them by a Leith businessman, John Pottinger, on the front of a tenement building on Main Street. Some fishing continued to be carried on inside the May Island under the protection of a Q-ship, a trawler equipped with a 6" gun which retracted into the galley, the purpose being to surprise the U-boat when it surfaced to attack the fleet of a dozen trawlers. This was successful if the trawlers stayed together. Mrs Johan Wilson recalls how her grandfather, Seaton Hall, was fishing a few miles from the rest of the fleet when a German submarine surfaced. The captain was very polite: 'We are going to put you in a small boat. There is the rest of your ships over there and here is food and a course. All we require to come aboard is the skipper.' One of the trawler's crew, a bit of a card said 'Here, take me instead, I am just a useless old b......' 'Precisely. That is why we take him,' said the German. They put a couple of rounds in the trawler and submerged. Seaton Hall spent the rest of the war as a prisoner in Germany. After his release he represented the Scottish fishermen at the unveiling of the War Memorial at Edinburgh Castle.

In the Second World War Newhaven men were equally active in the Navy and minesweeping, their basic skills making them particularly suitable for the latter work. 'Nearly all the fishermen of service age were in minesweepers or corvettes and auxiliary craft, very few on the big stuff,' said Tom Hall. As skipper of a minesweeper he swept ahead of the D-Day invasion fleets and he says that the storm which almost postponed the invasion was a blessing in disguise. 'The Germans had invented a new kind of mine we hadn't heard about - it reacted to the water pressure above it. There were tens of thousands of them from Calais right down to Normandy. But the stormy weather caused these mines to rise to the surface and explode because of the wave action. It was an act of God.'

Though they resisted forced service in the Navy there was never any shortage of volunteers from Newhaven to crew the merchant ships out of Leith. Privateering was popular since the rewards of this legalised piracy were great and it was an acceptable form of commercial enterprise. Leith had established an early lead. In 1476 John Barton, sailing out of Leith had his barque captured by a fleet of Portuguese pirates and declared a one-man war against entire Portugal. He secured letters of marque from the King to recover his loss, but seems to have had difficulty in distinguishing between foreign flags. As a way of getting rich, if you felt strong enough, it certainly beat the slow acquisition by honest industry. His three sons continued the plunder, using

Newhaven as their base and to the great annoyance of the burgesses of Edinburgh disposing of their plunder to the unfreemen of Leith. The Bartons were only the most notorious of a large number of pirates out of Leith and things reached such a pitch eventually between Scotland and Portugal that the Privy Council intervened in the commercial interests of both countries and an attempt to suppress piracy resulted in the letters being withdrawn. Anyone found guilty of piracy was to be hanged in irons between the tidemarks on Leith sands.

But piracy continued to flourish and was especialy rife in the Mediterranean. In 1615 four mariners of Leith were captured by Barbary pirates and sold as slaves at Algiers. The Privy Council asked all churches to make a collection to buy their release. A few years later the *Lion of Leith* with a crew of ten suffered a similar fate from Turkish pirates and collections were taken throughout Fife and the Lothians for their ransom. There were many other recorded instances. The last execution for piracy took place on the sands of Leith in 1822 when two Frenchmen were hanged on a gibbet at the foot of Constitution Street.

Arctic whaling, which for centuries had drawn recruits from Scottish fishing villages, took its quota of oarsmen from Newhaven. They had learned their skills closer to home for whales had been stranding themselves around the Fife and Lothian shores from prehistoric times and there is a tradition that the Whale Brae got its name from a school of 17 whales which grounded itself there. In the 12th century Malcolm IV granted the abbot and monks of Dunfermline the heads of whales that might be stranded off their shore, though he reserved the tongue as a delicacy for the royal household.

The active hunting of whales by small boat and harpoon followed, the last recorded capture, noted by Chalmers in *Historical and Statistical Account of Dunfermline* being off Queensferry in 1843 when the ferrymen put out and succeeded in striking several harpoons in the whale's back. A great battle ensued, 'the whale at one time darting from his assailants, at another throwing volumes of water into the air while he lashed the water with his tail.' The contest lasted for about an hour after which the whale, weakened by loss of blood, was despatched by the oarsmen and towed ashore. It was 51 feet in length.

Similar captures took place around the other fishing villages, but it was with the whaling fleets to Spitzbergen, Greenland and the Davis Straits that the serious whaling was done. From 1616 until the beginning of this century, when the Greenland right whale became almost extinct, whaling ships left Leith and Newhaven annually. The heyday was between 1750 and 1840 when the annual sailing in April of these splendid ships of 400 tons burden was a gala occasion, thousands thronging the pierhead to see them stand out to sea. Their return in the Autumn was often, however, an occasion for mourning for the death-toll was high. Sometimes the ships became ice-locked and this was a virtual death sentence for most, though a Cockenzie crew survived the entire harsh winter in Baffin Bay on a diet of blubber and prayer and strictest discipline.

The cargoes of blubber brought back were boiled in vats at the Fishermen's

Park area of Newhaven and the Shore at Leith. Leading up from the Shore was
Boiling House Close which gave on to the building where the processing took
place, the resulting smell being known as Wood's Scent from the name of the
brothers who owned the yard. The oil from the blubber was used in soapmak-
ing and for lamps and the whalebone for a variety of uses.

The Pilotage

Newhaven fishermen had the reputation of knowing the bed of the Forth better than they knew their own, of being able, almost to see under water. (During
the 1926 miners' strike they knew exactly where to dredge for large quantities
of coal). And their closeness to Scotland's major port made them the natural
pilots for the Forth - in one year alone (1788) all but three of the 29 candidates
certified as competent pilots by Trinity House were Newhaven fishermen.
They achieved a wide reputation, one of them, Edward Brown, serving as pilot
to Admiral Duncan on his flagship *H.M.S. Venerable* at the battle of Camperdown. He was later harbourmaster at Leith. Brown is shown in the painting of
Admiral de Winter's surrender aboard the Venerable. His portrait hangs in
Trinity House today. Another, David Dryburgh, as pilot to the Czar of Russia,
received the gift of a magnificent chiming watch which among other things told
the tides, and which is still in the possession of his descendants. And so the
record runs, up to the present day when several Forth Pilots have
Newhaven roots.

The pilot was at the apex of a stratified though barely acknowledged social
structure, the base of which was comprised by the boatless fisherman who was
either a member of someone's crew or 'walked the pier'. Above that was the
man who owned only a cobble, then there was the yawl-owner, who probably
also had a cobble for oyster dredging. Pilots would employ boatmen to act as
lookouts for approaching sail and to put them aboard the ship off the May or
Dunbar and conduct her up through the hazards of the Forth, a journey that
might take days if the winds were adverse. In November 1888 Thomas Wilson,
a Newhaven pilot got driven out into the North Sea and spent the next ten days
with the ship lying on her broadsides under bare poles until the gales
subsided.

But the pilots did not confine themselves to taking ships up and down the
Forth - they served too as a rescue and salvage service. If a vessel put up a distress signal, Newhaven pilots would put out into the storm to succour her. During a heavy storm in December 1816 the brig *South Esk* of Montrose ran up on
the Glasshouse rock off Leith Harbour. Twelve Newhaven pilots sailed out as
day dawned in two boats to her rescue. For seven days in the face of appalling
weather they struggled to save her, finally winning into Leith. But with the
master it was a case of

> The Devil was ill, the Devil a saint would be
> The Devil was well, the devil a saint was he

A Newhaven pilot and his family in 1845. The pilots were the elite of the little community and required to have served seven years before the mast. (Courtesy of the Scottish National Portrait Gallery).

The £50 bargain he had struck in the teeth of the gale now in calm waters appeared to him extortion. He refused to pay. The pilots appealed to Trinity House who adjudged them worthy of their hire.

The same year the Swedish brig *Venus*, lying in the roads off Leith, was driven in a violent storm despite her two anchors to within two cable-lengths (approximately 400 yards) of the rocks of Inchkeith. Eight Newhaven pilots including William Linton, Robert Carnie and George Robertson, saw her distress signal flying in the tearing wind and put out into the violent seas and with great risk managed to get three of their number over the brig's stern. They found the master preparing to cut away the mast and having persuaded him that the ship could be saved, they cut away the port anchor and ran up a topmast sail. This caused the vessel to veer towards the Leith shore and having established her headway they cut away the other anchor and slipped her through a narrow channel between two rocks. The danger cleared, they brought her safely into Elie. Again Trinity House had to be invoked to secure the agreed payment of one hundred guineas. Sometimes the House had to intervene for the shipmasters. In 1801 James Carney and John Seaton of Newhaven appeared before the committee following a complaint of the master of the ship *May* of Newcastle of extravagant charges. They had demanded twenty-five guineas for piloting her into Burntisland after she had fouled the

Herriot Rock. When the master refused they had left her in her plight. They were found guilty and as a result Trinity House laid down a scale of charges which would thereafter have to be adhered to, the standard rate being three guineas from the May Island to Leith Roads.

Trinity House, ancient and wealthy, had been instituted at Leith in 1380 as a charitable institution to stand by the seafarers in their 'hourly hazards and the fear of extreme poverty and beggary'. To do this it levied 12d Scots on every ton of goods passing through the port. This tribute, known as Prime Gilt, helped too in the upkeep of harbours and the building of South Leith Church. Later the House took to itself other duties, guarding the safety of ships at sea and the supervision of lights. A coal fire had been kept burning on top of a tower on the Isle of May from 1636. The architect who built the tower drowned on his way back to Pittenweem and so rampant were witch-hunts in Fife at the time that several old women were burned alive at Pittenweem, St Monance and Anstruther for raising the storm. This coal fire continued to serve until it was replaced in 1815 by one of the Stevenson oil-fired lighthouses which in 1886 was replaced by electric light.

As time went on Trinity House tended to tighten up on the regulations for pilots. In future, they commanded at the beginning of last century, pilots would have to be able to read and write. How else would they read the regulations and warning notices and write out reports? They should have served three years before the mast on a square-rigger and to have been at sea for at least seven years. They also proposed that a pilot ought to be sober before he took out a ship. Yet despite these considerable hurdles Newhaven continued to supply the bulk of the pilotage.

The Great Storm

Danger was the unseen crewman in every boat and scarcely a year passed without two or three drownings. Writing in 1828 the Newhaven Boxmaster noted: 'This has been a remarkable year in our Society indeed. There is about 220 members belonging to our Society and who have been prosecuting their lawful calling and now at this time we are all well, not a single accident happened to none of us in the course of this year. Thank God for it.'

But that was the exception. Esther Liston recalls: 'There was Beenie Carnie's man, he was drooned when his wheelhouse was blown off. You remember the *Margaret Paton* went down and nobody ever heard tell what happened. None of them were ever found. And there were two brothers, the skipper and his brother and another two brothers aboard that boat. Even no many years back now Joey my eldest son, they picked up a mine and he thought it was full o' barnacles and they didn't know what it was and he told the crew not to touch it and they hung it up but you see there were two of them very inquisitive to know what it was for the sake of getting the copper of it and it exploded. It was a mine. And there was not a bit of the two of them left, nothing but dungarees lying on the deck. And there was Jean Noble's brother on the pilot boat - he was blown over, he was drowned. His brother jumped in to get him but he was dead. And that week oor Willie died George Meikle was drowned at Ayr. They got his body at Irvine. I doubt it has been stepping aboard the boat at night and of course they would never notice. Like a' these wee fishing villages there has been a few tragedies.'

Storms in the Forth were a part of their lives but separated sometimes by a decade, sometimes two, would come the great storms which could wipe out an entire fleet. One of these occurred in January 1868. In the early morning when the sea was calm 50 fishing boats, mostly open boats of 23 ft length, left Newhaven for the oyster dredging. As the morning wore on the sea became boisterous and at midday the storm suddenly burst out around them with great force. The boats at that time were about a mile off-shore spread out between Leith and Granton. With the exception of a dozen boats they succeeded in reaching home with great difficulty. The less fortunate, unable to make headway with oars, cast anchor. By this time the storm had increased in violence and vast clouds of spray hid the boats from the anxious eyes on shore. Three steam tugs put out from Leith at great risk and gradually with difficulty the crews were rescued by throwing ropes to the men who tied them around their waists and jumped into the sea to be pulled aboard the tugs. But one boat with James Flucker, Hugh Stevenson and young James Dryburgh aboard lost its anchor and was swept off down the Forth. Dryburgh said: 'The sea caught us on the off-side and broke over the boat carrying me and three oars with me overboard. As the boat rocked to the side on which I was I seized hold of her side but she rose so high and the sea was so strong that I could not hold on with one hand and I again dropped into the water. When the boat again rocked to my side Stevenson got hold of me and hauled me aboard. We continued to be driven northwards though during this time we didn't know where we were and could see nothing at all. The boat was always filling with water and it required James Flucker and Stevenson to do all they could to bail it out. After some time we came near Kinghorn Ness when another sea broke on the quarter with great violence and carried away the tiller and knocked me up against the mast. Flucker and Stevenson then came aft and got hold of me and placed me again at the stern of the boat where for want of a tiller I required to turn the rudder with both hands while the other two bailed out the water which was like to fill the boat. When we came nearer the shore Flucker himself came to steer. We saw Kirkcaldy harbour and tried to make for it but we were driven past and just by chance we were thrown upon the sands about 30 yards to the East. For a good distance from the shore the bottom was level and though the water was not deep a long distance lay between our boat and the shore. We were so benumbed by cold and so worn out with our labours that we could not of ourselves get out of the boat but about a dozen men who were standing on the shore waded into the water where our boat was beached and carried us to land. We were taken to Mr Paterson's house where the people used us very kindly. Our boat is completely destroyed.'

No lives were lost in this storm, but during the terrible winter which succeeded, 13 were lost. Altogether one hundred Newhaven men were lost at sea
between 1820 and 1890, 17 in one disaster alone -the Great Storm of 1881 -
when in the Forth 31 boats and 189 lives were lost to the North Sea, 129 of the
men from Eyemouth. Of the 17 Newhaven men, eleven left widows and 44
fatherless children.

The summer had been cold and wet giving way to a turbulent autumn which
kept the boats harbour-bound. After a week of gales the men were impatient to
be away and when there was an easing of the wind on Thursday evening, 13th
October the womenfolk busied themselves at baiting the lines and the nets
were got aboard. The Newhaven fleet sailed at midnight, the bigger boats for
the deep-sea line fishing, the others for the waters around the Isle of May.

The morning of Friday 14th October dawned gloriously in a burst of sun and
gulls wheeled in the bright blue sky with no more than a breath of wind to rip-
ple the sparkling waters of the Forth. It was a morning to set the spirits dancing
after a week of stormy weather. There were uneasy looks though among those
who had not sailed as they gathered at the pier to inspect the glass for the pressure had fallen as low as any had ever seen, having dropped an inch in the
night. But on so enchanted a morning all misgivings fell away.

Then around 10 o'clock a telegram was received at Newhaven which read:
'Deep depression crossing Scotland. Hoist North cone for North-West to
North gale.' The warning was not needed, for already the women, tuned to
such things, had sensed a change. They gathered at their doors feeling that
something awful was coming. Sea and sky and land all seemed to be turning a
blue-grey and a dreadful silence fell over everything. As though of one mind
they began to run to the pier then someone cried 'Look at the sea'. A great wind
had sprung up lifting the sea into a writhing torment, at war with itself, towering mountains of water surging by, the air full of foam and spray so dense and
dark that sight was almost blotted out. From the women a wail of panic and
fear was snatched away in the hellish roar of the storm.

The fleet too, now on the fishing grounds and joined by boats from other
coastal villages, received little warning. They too recalled a dead calm, a great
stillness on the waters. The blue sky almost at once was washed out by swirling
black clouds and a fierce wind sprang snarling out of the North, snapping
masts like twigs, tearing away sails while they were being furled, tossing boats
clean out of the water and lashing the sea into a furious sympathy. Stunned by
the suddenness and the overwhelming noise, the men clung helpless before
the onslaught. Boat after boat turned turtle or broke under the raging ele-
ments as the darkness thickened. Some Berwickshire boats struggled about
and fought their way inshore and as the crews tried to fetch into storm-lashed
harbours, heart-breakingly were drowned before the eyes of their families. At
Fisherrow the *Alice* was seen from the pier to be running under shredded sails
for the harbour when she was struck by a heavy sea. She staggered and
recovered then was struck by a second and went straight to the bottom. Those
on the shore were powerless to help owing to the impossibility of
launching the lifeboat.

Most of the boats that survived were said to have beaten against the storm with reefed sails. About a score of deep-sea boats beat into Burntisland harbour, among them several from Newhaven.

Others threw out sea anchors or, trailing a sail, scudded with bare poles before the holocaust to find easier conditions further out to sea. One man recalled: 'I never saw my boat go so fast with sail as she did that afternoon without any.'

One surviving skipper was quoted as saying 'a boat which was alongside us was struck by a giant sea and overturned. We saw her twice afterwards but none of the men rose to the surface. The sea was getting heavier, we put the head of the boat to the sea and bore away out having tied the laddie to the mast. We came upon a second boat bottom up. On the air clearing of smoke (spume) we discovered we were about five miles to leeward of the harbour and as it was impossible to beat up we lifted the ballast to the front of the boat, so as to put her in a better position to meet the waves and decided to have the sea for our friend for the night rather than venture near the land.' Throughout the 25 hours of the gale the skipper sat alone at the helm singing hymns to his crew. Of another skipper it was said that so twisted and wedged were his legs beneath the bench at the helm that when they finally made port 44 hours later he had to be carried ashore.

'The noise was like thunder and the air was like smoke,' recalled another. 'Waves were mountains high and breaking all round us. Three times we were thrown on our beam ends and it looked as though we should all be gone. We kept about 30 to 40 miles out from land and the gale blew with great violence until nearly daylight on Saturday then it eased. On Saturday afternoon it began to blow again as hard as ever. We had some provisions, half of a quarter loaf each and we managed to keep our fire. But the bread was soaked with salt water and we had little heart to eat anything.'

The toll of merchant shipping was equally severe. A schooner sighted at midday off Dunbar was found to have had her entire crew washed away. She later became dismasted and rolled ashore. Another about dusk was driven ashore but the crew were more fortunate, being able to climb the yard arm and slither down a rope to the beach unscathed. It was said that for weeks afterwards the wreckage of unknown and unreported vessels was being cast up as well as the bodies of their crews.

Several Newhaven pilots helped man a lifeboat from Leith and went to the aid of a German schooner which, running up the Forth for safe anchorage, had had her sails torn to shreds and was in danger of being driven on the rocks to the east of Leith harbour entrance. She let go her anchor and was brought up within yards of the Black Rocks. The lifeboat was towed clear of the harbour by the tug *Blue Bonnet* then cast off in the great seas, often disappearing from sight. She fell back on the schooner and with great difficulty got four men aboard but, though she was labouring mightily, the German refused to take a tow from the tug and all three vessels bobbed and twisted for three hours until the gale abated, when a tow was put aboard and the German safely brought to port.

During a lull around five o'clock the four-oared Newhaven pilot-boat *Concord* manned by three brothers Johnston set out in search of the Newhaven boats. Finding conditions impossible they tried to make for Dunbar but were sunk by a heavy sea dashing over them and all drowned. A day later the body of John Johnston, the skipper, was washed ashore at Dunbar.

The incredible violence of the storm which had snuffed out the fleets at sea blasted the land from Orkney to the English Channel, blowing down houses, rooting up great forests, flooding rivers, covering hills in snow and wiping out telegraphic communication. All work stopped, schools and shops closed. In Newhaven where lamp-post tops and slates had been sent birling and shop windows had been shattered a little knot of women and children clung together on the pier soaked by the spray and rain or cowered down for fear of being blown away, seagulls coorying beside them. Through the murk hour after hour while the seas raged around the new breakwater, the women strained fearful eyes to the east. Towards evening their vigil was rewarded as the first of the broken fleet struggled under low canvas in through the harbour-mouth to the unreal calm within the walls.

In her novel *Fisherfolk* Janet Cadell describes the aftermath: 'Straining eyes watched their coming, striving to recognise by some well-known mark such as a patch on the sail the particular boats which were bringing relief to the anxious hearts. Half an hour later the boats reached the harbour. The faces of the crew showed a look of deep sadness as they silently busied themselves with preparations for landing. 'Do ye ken anything about the *Morning Star?*' was the question put by many lips but not answered as the men bent over their gear. 'There's something far wrong wi' the *Morning Star*' said an old man beside me. 'They canna bring themselves to speak aboot it. Willie,' he said to the man who had that moment sprung upon the pier, 'can ye no' set oor minds at rest. What's become o' Jimmy Erskine's boat?' 'She's lying in 20 fathoms off the Ness. She capsised afore oor e'en when the squall came on and we had nae po'er to help.' A wail of sorrow rose from the crowd of women and girls.

'The following morning the boats left harbour not to fish but to recover the bodies of the sunken crew. Late afternoon of the second day they were seen rowing slowly up over the calm grey sea for it was a sultry day with silvery haze filling the sky. 'They maun hae gotten something or they wouldnae have left the ground so early. It's the *Morning Star*, bottom up, wi' corpses tangled in the rigging.' We heard the steady fall of the oars and the drip of the water from the blades but we heard no sound of speech from the men who plied their heavy task with strong but wearied arms for they had rowed many a tedious mile. On each face was a sad repression of feeling that told of its depths. As the first boat passed the pier head a strong sobbing wail pased through the mass of people gathered there.'

By Saturday morning all the Newhaven boats had been accounted for except four - the *Perseverence*, the *Stormy Petrel*, the *Robina* and the pilot boat *Concord*. News came in soon from a pilot named Wilson who was out on Saturday along the beach in the direction of Dunbar and arrived home to report that the boat *Concord*'s mast, oars and rudder had been washed ashore. He also identified an oar from the boat *Robina*.

A steamer arrived at Burntisland and reported having seen a fleet of fishing boats off the Isle of May and hope flared again. Arrangements were quickly made to despatch a steam tug in search and a party of returned fishers got a horse-van and started down the coast to comb the beaches. A Mr Merrilees reported from Dunbar having fallen in with the mast, tiller and rigging of the pilot boat *Stormy Petrel* but no trace of the large deep-sea fishing vessel *Perseverence* had yet been found. On the beach at Dunbar body after body was being washed in, men wading up to the waist to draw the corpses ashore using grapnels.

Many of the bodies were naked, stripped by the sea. But not all came ashore and it was believed that the bodies which had not been recovered would come to the surface on the ninth day. The bodies were reverently taken back to the village where they were laid out on the table and prepared by the females of the house for 'kistin' the placing of the body in the coffin so that it might be viewed by friends and relatives. There was no questioning of fate, only a sad serenity. So interconnected by blood and marriage were they that death brought most of them something to mourn and this showed itself in different ways: with the younger women and the girls there was unrestrained weeping, the older women congregated in each others' houses and the men went silently to work.

Any hope that the *Robina* might have survived were dashed when the lighthouse keepers on the May Island reported having seen her about half a mile to the south making great exertions to gain the island. The boat suddenly disappeared and was seen no more.

But surely the *Perseverence* must have survived? She was one of the largest of the 204 boats that were then registered at Newhaven. But as day succeeded day and no news came all hope died. It was surmised that she had been loath to leave the fishing, and at last run before the storm and been swamped.

As though in a final gesture of grim irony the sea threw out a fifth Newhaven boat, the *Hope* which had been lost six months previously, rolling it up the shore like a barrel.

The four Newhaven boats lost were:

> *PERSEVERENCE*, 7 men (near the May Island): John Carnie (32), left a widow and 5 children, the oldest 7 years; William Inglis (30), married with two children; Peter Inglis (18), his brother; Johnston Wilson (21); Boreas Hall (31), married with three children; Wlliam Liston (Rutherford) (37); and David Lyle (25).
> *STORMY PETREL*, yawl, 3 men: David Stevenson (58), left a widow and 7 children; and his two sons Hugh (32), married with one child; and Philip (30), married with 4 children.
> *ROBINA*, yawl, 4 men: Walter Rutherford, who left a widow and 5 children; Alexander Noble (42), widower, who left 9 of a family, the youngest only two months; Matthew Hume and William Liston (20) both unmarried.
> *CONCORD*, pilot boat, 3 crew, swamped off Dunbar: John Johnston (37); his brother James Johnston (30); his brother William Johnston (23).

Great crystal-sided hearses, each drawn by two blue-black horses with silver-studded harnesses and nodding plumes of ostrich feathers, white for the young men - stood before the stricken homes while neighbours in sympathy drew their blinds and shops put up their shutters and long processions followed on foot up Bonnington to Rosebank Cemetery. In so close-knit a community there were few who had not lost a relative.

The Scotsman published a long poem expressing the anguish of the fishing villages the first verse of which ran:

> Half o' us drooned i' the Forth
> Hearses at each other door.
> No' a dry e'e on the shore!
> No' a hoose but has its corpse,
> Father or cousin or brother;
> Nane o' us stands by himsel!
> We are a' sib to each other.

Yet to the outside world they preserved a stoic calm. The Rev Dr. William Graham who was for 37 years parish minister in Newhaven noted the marvellous calmness of the stricken ones in 'homes clean and comfortable and betokening a practise of domestic virtue. There is not now as formerly the wild shreiking and wailing in the homes of the bereaved, but calm resignation and Christian hope.'

They knew the cost of the sea's companionship and were not unprepared.

Had the fates tried to deprive Newhaven of the best men in the village, said Councillor Cook of Leith Town Council, in calling for a national disaster fund, it could not have been more effectually done than in the case of this calamity. In support, the Lord Advocate said a more courageous hardy and prudent people than the East Coast fisherfolk could not be found. The fund was widely subscribed, the Queen herself making a handsome donation.

For weeks after, the correspondence columns of the newspapers were busy with letters analysing, discussing, suggesting, theorising on one sailing rig over another, steam over sail, decked over open boat, inshore over off-shore fishing. Within a week or two public attention drifted elsewhere and the fishermen had resumed their calling, a calling which, unique in the expanse of human endeavour, required a routine meeting with hardship and peril and the risking of their whole possessions to gain a livelihood.

CHAPTER 4

The Way They Lived Then

A century ago the focus of village life was the harbour and its sandy beach. Here the drying nets looped on the seawalls were backcloth to the rich drama of shoreside life. On a stage that would have graced an opera set, fishing cobbles dreamed inactive in the blue water within the embrace of the pier, or, stranded on the sands, loomed strangely large over the pageant of colourful pirates and theatrical peasantry busy about their endless attendance upon the sea and its harvest.

Here the fisher mends his gear or stands knee-deep among the slippery wealth of his labours. There a knot of gaffers, pipes at the ready, surmise on the ownership of a passing sail far out on the Forth and close by a mariner, newly ashore, sleeps against his boat, straw hat tilted forward and knees drawn up to chin like any Mexican peon. Women in their kilted skirts bend to the creel and pause often to exchange the social currency of the place, the kindly gossip, or press around the fruit stalls, set up in sculls atop herring barrels. Bare-legged children scamper on the boats at their favourite game of scranning - searching the bilges for the undiscovered fish that they may hawk around the doors of Trinity. And over all the sense of a community busy about a common purpose, the babble of their own Doric and the wonderful strong smells of sea and fish and tarry rope. Beyond, the sparkling Forth is alive with the noiseless passage of every size of craft and the purple hills of Fife prepare to disappear in the summer haze.

They lived in harmony with one another and every door was open, perhaps because they were all inter-related or perhaps because a tradition of mutual help and concern had been fostered by a Church reluctant to assume responsibility for the sick and poor of so hazardous a life. At any rate they had long been noted for their peaceful and law-abiding ways. When the warren of tenements and wynds of the Canongate and the Kirkgate were havens for vagabonds and sturdy beggars, Newhaven knew none of this. Unlike fisherfolk in other parts of Scotland, they were thirled to no laird, they owned their houses and their boats and their freedom. Their pleasures were visiting each other's houses, their recreation the church.

Yet the idyll was flawed. Though they kept themselves apart they could not escape the consequences of the country's backwardness. Perhaps in no other nation was sanitation so neglected as in this last corridor of Europe, the gutters serving as open sewers. Newhaven was no different from Edinburgh and Leith in this respect. The consequence was that death was a frequent visitor.

Plague

The insanitary conditions were the forcing beds but the seeds came from elsewhere. The earlier visitations were of bubonic plague brought in on trading ships from Europe and the Near East. Leith, Scotland's largest port, was prone to frequent outbreaks and during the 16th century there were no fewer than seven major occurrences most of which erupted in a foul tide onto her neighbours, killing thousands. In 1585 Edinburgh had its worst outbreak since the Black Death of 1349. The year before, the *William*, trading out of Bruges, arrived at Leith with three of the crew infected. Though she was ordered at once to Inchcolm which had been cleared as a hospital camp, her deadly message sped ashore, raging along both coasts of the Forth, killing 1400 in Edinburgh, a considerable portion of the total inhabitants, and causing the University to take flight to Linlithgow. So difficult did the Council find it to confine those suspected of being afflicted that they ordered all such as were found outdoors to be executed. The grey-robed plaguemasters with white St Andrew Cross stitched to their gowns and bearing the white staffs of their office, carried fire and death to parents who hid their sick children. Children under 15 found roaming the streets were taken to the stocks and scourged. But by the New Year the danger seemed past and the crew of the *William* was set-tled in Newhaven which was to remain clean while all suspected ships would be channeled into Leith which would remain isolated.

The measures the authorities took to stamp upon the outbreaks were sim-ple, effective and terrible. Robert Louis Stevenson described them: 'In times of pestilence the discipline had been sharp and sudden and what we now call stamping out contagion was carried out with deadly effect, adding the terror of man's justice to the fear of God's visitation. The living who had concealed the sickness were drowned if they were women in the quarry holes and if they were men were hanged and gibbeted at their own doors and wherever the evil had passed furniture was destroyed and houses closed. And the most bogeyish part of the story is about such houses; two generations back they still stood stark and empty. People avoided them as they passed by, the boldest schoolboy only shouted through the keyhole and made off, for within it was supposed the plague lay ambused like a basilisc, ready to fly forth and spread blain and pustule throughout the city. What a desirable next-door neighbour for superstitious citizens.'

Social disorder resulting fom the plague was dealt with harshly. In Leith a man who forged papers to acquire a tenement of land belonging to a plague victim, was brought to the Tron and bound fast with a paper on his head declaring his fault. Then the common hangman drew out his tongue with a pair of blacksmith's forceps and ran it through with a red-hot poker.

There were fewer outbreaks during the first half of the 17th century, though an Order of the Privy Council of 1635 prohibited ships from the Low Coun-tries landing persons at Newhaven until the authorities were satisfied that the ships were free of the plague. Logan of Sheriffbrae was charged to see that the

A Newhaven couple, Mr and Mrs George Main, in their braws for the photographer. The photograph, taken in the late 19th century, shows Mrs Main wearing the lace cap which some trace back to a Flemish origin (Courtesy of Mrs M Colley).

ordinance was carried out. Cramond was plague-struck the same year and six cleaners from Newhaven were sent to clear and burn the infected houses and bury the dead.

The last major outbreak was in 1645 and for Leith and Newhaven it was the worst of all. The pestilence , which this time was possibly typhus, a disease spread by lice, was carried to all parts of the country by the marching armies of the Covenant. The rattle of the tumbrills and the clang of the warning bells became the night sounds in Leith where the outbreak was so bad that it became impossible to separate the clean from the unclean and in a town of 4000 people fewer than 1600 survived.

Besides bubonic and typhus there were other scourges. Leprosy, from which Robert the Bruce suffered, was said by some to come from eating raw or stale fish. An outbreak occurred just after some stale fish had been given to the poor at the Castle gate. But no one was sure and the only fact beyond dispute was that isolation prevented its spread. So they made an isolation colony on Inchkeith. That island was also used when the virulent French Pox or Grand Gore which Columbus was said to have brought back from America and which the free and easy morality of the times encouraged, swept through the land at the beginning of the 16th century. The sick were lined up at the Shore at Leith and ferried across to the island. Anyone ignoring the summons was branded on the cheek and banished from the town.

Malaria debilitated many low-lying areas along the Forth, Cramond in particular, and farmers would take on six men to do the work of four on the expectation that two would collapse with the ague. But seafaring people appeared to be immune and Newhaven was unaffected. The disease disappeared by the end of the 18th century as land drainage improved.

But cholera and typhoid from polluted drinking water were a hazard in a village which had no freshwater streams - the nearest being the Anchorfield Burn - and relied on several public wells. There was an outbreak of typhus in 1838 when many families in the village were isolated in their homes and many more were sent to the Royal Infirmary. They found that institution a great relief in their distress. The Free Fishermen's Society sent the Infirmary a donation of £20 in gratitude.

Throughout the 17th century plague eased its grip and the population increased. Then a new scourge appeared. Seven cold winters and wet summers ended in 1699 with a great famine which so burned itself into the popular mind that a century later many of the reports in the 1st Statistical Account told of its terrible coming. From the rough plenty that travellers had found among the Lothian peasantry they were plunged into the depths of destitution. People were found dying by the roadside with grass in their mouths, trying to drag themselves towards the churchyards and a Christian burial. It was one of the great killing times and villages were wiped out never to recover. Yet again Newhaven was fortunate in having its own plentiful food supply to hand though the herring shoals had temporarily departed the Forth at this time.

Solace in the tribulation of these recurring catastrophes they found in their religion, and safeguard they found in beliefs more ancient.

Touch Cauld Ir'n

Like fishing communities the world over the Newhaven folk recognised a hidden world whose malignant spirit must constantly be propitiated. Older than their religion, this superstitious dread existed for the same purpose, to save their lives in a dangerous world and to attempt to explain the inexplicable.

They recognised no incongruity in this twin allegience, though they had probably been more at ease with the old Catholicism which preceded the Refor-

A typical Newhaven close in the 1840s photographed by Hill and Adamson. Life and work tended to spill over into the streets (Courtesy of the Scottish National Portrait Gallery).

mation, where the fundamental doctrines had become blurred by association with pagan survivals. As, for example, the 13th century parish priest of Inverkeithing who had all the maidens of the village dance naked beneath the full moon to celebrate the feast of Priapus, though whether he himself played the part of the horny old diety is not recorded.

Calvinism did not eradicate their superstition but it made them furtive in its exercise. Unlike the priest, the Presbyterian minister was kept apart for he could not approve or condone these irrational practices. 'My father brought a minister to the hoose and afterwards my brother burned a handfu' o' saut on the fire,' one Newhaven housewife told me.

Sandy Noble recalled being told: 'If you were going to the fishing and met a minister, you'd turn back. The minister says: 'Nice to see you, Willie.' And he'd reply: 'Minister, you're the last person on this earth I had hoped to meet. If I go down to the harbour and tell them I spoke to you the whole of the fishermen would go home.'

'They never liked to mention them on board. They would call them 'sky pilots'. There was the time they took the minister aboard the pilot boat and it broke down. The minister said: 'There must be a Jonah aboard.' 'Aye, minister, it's you.' Then there's the story of the young minister over in Fife who thought he would have a service of dedication prior to the beginning of the herring fishing and he not having any idea, he takes as his text the story of the prodigal son. Now any mention of pig is taboo to the fisherfolk. And when he got to the bit which says 'He would fain have filled his belly with the husks that the swine did eat,' there was a shuffling in the church as the congregation reached surreptitiously to touch their heels or sought under the pews for iron fittings and a murmur of 'touch cauld irn'. And again it happened and this time the murmur was louder and the searching less surreptitious. But the third repetition of the text was too much for them. They stood up as one, and shouting 'touch cauld irn', scailed out.'

The younger generation tended to be less affected. The Rev. Daniel McIver in his book on Eyemouth tells how a youngster got hold of a little pig and placed it on the seat at the stern with a sou'-wester over its head. 'In due course one of the three brothers who owned the cobble came down with his scull and line and having laid it in the cobble he leisurely took out pipe and tobacco in preparation for a smoke. When in the act of cutting the 'baccy his eye fell on the pig. 'Eh, man! ye're there afore us!' Having thus saluted the pig the fisherman lifted his scull and made for home. When passing the wynd foot he was met by a brother who also carried his scull. 'Whaur'e gaun? What's wrang?' 'He's yonder afore oo,' was all the reply. The second brother proceeded aboard as did the first, and when he caught sight of the pig, all that he could say was 'Eh, ye're there are ye!' Taking up his line he returned home also. Meeting with the third brother the second was asked: 'Anything wrang?' 'Aye, he's yonder afore oo!'. Not knowing to what his brother referred the third man went down to the cobble to discover the object which was responsible for all this mysterious conduct. 'Richt enough,' said he, as he looked at the queer picture of the wee piggie with the sou'-wester on his head, and sitting defiantly at the rudder, 'ye're there afore us!' and saying this, he also took up his tackle and returned home. Not one of the brothers mentioned the word 'pig' and they did not sail that day!'

It was the journey down to the harbour, the preparation for the act of fishing, that was most fraught with taboos. In Newhaven if a black cat, a red-haired woman or someone with a physical deformity crossed the path of a fisherman on his way to the pier he would turn back. Esther Liston recalls: 'If a man was going doon to the market or the pier and he met a man coming up and the man said 'Good morning' before he said 'Good morning' he would go away back because he would think it wasnae worth gaun oot because he wouldnae get ony fish.'

Once aboard, if someone was sweeping the deck and happened to touch a net, that was bad - he would be sweeping the luck overboard. Lighting your pipe, one of the first rituals aboard, had its own rights. It was unlucky to give another man a light from your pipe, and if you gave him a match, you would break a little piece off so that you weren't giving your luck away. Leaving harbour you must always turn your boat with the sun, from East to West. Then at sea you mustn't mention certain things by name, rabbits or hares or foxes or beetles or cockroaches or salmon all had their other names, the beetle was the

No need for pedestrian precincts in the early 19th century. A cart trundles by while women work in Main Street at baiting the lines.

'bum-clock', the salmon was 'the red felly' or 'the queer felly'. Peter Carnie, proprietor of the Peacock Inn, recalls that when his dad was working on the trawlers his mother put a tin of salmon in his piece box. 'The crew called him for everything.' To turn the bailer upside down was a sign of disaster, of a boat returning bottom-up. And you must wait until the nets had been shot before you cut bread or all the haddock would be eaten by the dogfish.

There were unlucky days. Things could not be borrowed or lent on a Monday or they did away with your good luck for the week. Most villages did not fish on the Sabbath but at Prestonpans it was regarded as lucky to start fishing on the Sunday, a case of 'The better the day the better the deed.' No one went to sea on a Friday, it was an unlucky day except for weddings and laying down the keel of a new boat. Then there were lucky and unlucky boats and some shipwrights claimed they could tell with the first blow of the adze on the keel how a boat would turn out.

Superstition had not ten commandments but a thousand. The taboos were legion and most were held in common but some were particular to a village. In Newhaven for instances any talk of a man called 'Brounger' was sure to cause consternation. 'Brounger', who might better have been called 'scrounger' made his living as he grew too old to fish, by asking oysters and fish from the fishermen on their return. If he didn't get what he wanted he would curse them and wish that on their next trip ill-luck would go with them and sometimes so it fell out. So the shout 'John Brounger's in your headsheets' was enough to make a boat go round three times in a circle to break the spell.

And some superstitions were peculiar to one fisherman. Tom Hall, whose father sailed his own trawler out of Newhaven, said: 'He was an intelligent man but when I first went to sea with him he would never shoot the net on the port side. Other fishermen did. It's true that the turn of these single-screw boats made it easier to shoot on the starboard side because of the propellor thrust, but that had nothing to do with it. I have seen us with three nets out on the starboard side, two of them torn, and instead of shooting the port net, he would haul it round to the starboard side also. I would ask him 'Why are you making this extra work?' And he would say: 'Christ said to the fishermen on the Sea of Gallilee who weren't catching any fish: 'Cast your nets on the right-hand side' and that's what I'm doing.'

It seems that many of these superstitions may have had a Biblical origin for the Jews are said to have so abhorred swine that they could not hear the name spoken and in Leviticus, Ch. 11 many of the tabooed animals are listed as unclean. Yet other superstitions are explained as an attempt to bring order out of chaos, to reduce a world full of danger and doubt to an understandable and controllable unity. And they have persisted as in other precarious occupations such as mining and motor racing, right up to the present. A couple of decades back a boat which had not been successful for a week or two, instead of leaving Newhaven harbour directly was observed to sail round in a huge sweep while the crew ran around the gunwales with flaming paper torches 'burning the spirits away'.

Witchcraft never seems to have excited Newhaven as it did other places although a reference to it occurs in 1591 when some holes near the place, known as the Fairy Holes, are mentioned in the indictment of Euphame McCulzane who is stated to have attended a convention of witches there, and also at others called the Bruine Hoillis where she and many other witches with the devil in company put to sea in a riddle.

Newhaven had less call than most fishing communities to exorcise the forces of ill-fortune since it was among the most prosperous, with a constantly assured food supply. The 1st Statistical Account says: 'Such are the astonishing powers of reproduction in the generality of the finny tribe that perhaps no destruction of them that man can commit would greatly diminish their numbers. The fisherfolk usually have large families to the production of which the fish diet is supposed to be favourable, but the men prefer butcher meat when they can afford it, or oatmeal though of late many of them use potatoes. While children of other families in the parish average five to a family, the fishermen usually have six.'

In earlier times oatmeal was the staff of life and could be mixed with milk as porridge, with water as gruel or made into a paste to bake as bannocks though later the potato became more popular. Fish too small for sale would be fried by the bucketful. On the return from a successful trip the crew might meet in the skipper's house where a big cod would be boiled up and a pound of salt butter melted over it. Herring was a favourite meal. It was believed by doctors to be a common cure for sickness and was often prescribed with 'skinny tatties'

A primitive but evocative representation of the pier and its activities before the new breakwater was built to enclose the harbour. The busy passage of ships to and from Granton Harbour shows trade now by-passing the little port of Newhaven.

followed by 'soor dook' for a stomach upset. The Bass Rock provided solan geese and their eggs and the gannet fat was believed to have medicinal value in rheumatism. There was plenty of milk, butter and cheese to be got from the surrounding peasantry in exchange for fish and the fishwife on her country rounds would often come back with a pair of rabbits that had been snared or a bit of haugh or beef. And of course they kept poultry and fed them on fish offal. The normal drink was tuppeny ale, so-called because it cost twopence a Scots pint, equal to two English quarts. Whisky became more popular from the middle of the 18th century.

The Barley Bree

Up until the later part of last century, before the great religious revival and its associated temperance movement swept through Scotland, hardly anything could be done without the bottle being passed around though not all carried it this far:

> Betsy Miller, Betsy Miller,
> Sold her sark and drank the siller!

As one writer remarked: 'A man could hardly assure his neighbour it was a good morning without having to confirm the remark with a glass of whisky.' And no transaction was regarded as binding except it received its libation.

There were fourteen inns and alehouses in the village and most of them would open before breakfast.

Of course the big social events were the occasions when a certain excess was looked on as obligatory: It was a custom of the times that Scotland ordained for its people.

Peter Smith, the fisherman poet of Cellardykes, summed it up:

> A man that couldna take a gill
> Was what ye'd ca' nae man ava'
> In Dyker talk 'a bidly ba'
> In fact, drunk? Na, ye canna be
> Till the whisky ran oot o' yer e'e
> If they e'en gaed tae moor a boat
> They had a drap tae clear their throat.
> Hed what they'd ca' their 'Fowler's Drink'
> On Setterday nichts tae pair their clink
> What mony a hard-earned croon was spent
> An' markit doon for tar or pent.
> The women often ta'en a dram
> An' cowpit it ower like ony man.
> Aye, even their freens o' the black cloth
> Tae tak' their gless were naethin' loathe
> A story which I heard'm tell
> That happened in the Kirk o' Craill
> Will gie ye here an illustration
> The minister's name I winna mention
> He had amang his congregation
> An auld wife who for occupation
> Selt drink tae ony man wha took it
> Minister or man she never lookit.
> Ae Sabbath while he preached awa'
> He thocht he heard a snore or twa
> So looking ower where Janet sat
> He saw she was's blin's a bat
> While her neebor tried, tho' a' in vain
> Tae bring her tae her sense again
> Says the minister: Just let her be
> I'll wauken her, and that ye'll see
> Sae daudin' on the pulpit broad
> An' in a voice baith strong and lood:
> 'A gill an' bottle o' ale, ma dear!'
> 'Aye, aye,' she says, 'I'm coming sire!'

Newhaven was no different than the lave but the estimable James Wilson when Boxmaster hit upon a scheme which would capitalise upon the habit. It was at the time, in the 1860s, when Newhaven was trying to find the money for a new harbour which it was estimated would cost £1600. The Commissioners of the Board of Fisheries had at their disposal an annual sum for building harbours but they required the fishing community to show their willingness by raising a quarter of the required sum. The Leith Dock Commission generously agreed to put up £100 and this left £300 for the fishermen to raise. Mr Wilson

There were 14 taverns and inns to serve a total population of around 2000 when this picture was taken in 1843 (Hill and Adamson, courtesy of the Scottish National Portrait Gallery).

wrote: 'From the failure of the oyster and herring fishing and other causes it is quite clear to those acquainted with the place that the sum of £300 will not be raised except by some extraordinary means. The following plan is one that will thoroughly commend itself. There are about 300 on the roll of the Society each of whom with few exceptions uses at least one and a half gills of whisky in the day and there are as many women who use an equal quantity, making 300 gills per day. This, at 3d per gill amounts to £3 15s in the day, or £26 5s every week. In the course of 12 weeks then that would give a sum of £315, being more than what is required to secure an excellent harbour which would protect the boats belonging to the town and be a benefit to future generations. It is perfectly practical to raise the above sum in this way if the people would only for 12 weeks unite together for that purpose. It is perfectly safe to do so, for some, as healthy and laborious as any in the place, have never tasted intoxicating drinks for years. It will require self-denial but it is only for 12 weeks and when the object is so worthy surely a vigorous effort will be made.' There was a marked lack of response.

(The temperance movement found many fanatical converts in the fishing villages towards the end of last century, the early converts being regarded as distinctly odd, if not bordering on insanity. A grandfather of mine when told by the doctor to take a wineglass-full of medicine, solemnly bought a wineglass, measured the contents into a cup, then ground the glass under his heel.)

The occasions for unrestrained week-long celebration in the village were the penny weddings. A hundred years ago the ceremonies began on Monday with the bidding of the relatives when the young couple in full wedding dress, went separately with their supporters to call, with suitable libation, on their families. On Tuesday they would repeat the process by summoning their friends among the young men and women. Wednesday there was a procession through the streets led by the fiddlers and Thursday was given over to the feast called Feetwashing. The big day was Friday when there was the ceremonial bedmaking, and the separate procession of the groom and his supporters and the bride and her maids to the marriage-place, often the bride's home which was packed to the door, or the manse, the women in their bright striped gowns, the men in white trousers, velvet waistcoats and blue bright-buttoned coats. Before entering, the best man had to put down a heel of the bride's shoe, the bridegroom doing the same with his own shoe. Then followed a procession, very like the modern French custom, through the streets in couples, right round the village to the Peacock, led by the bride and the best man, whose hat was festooned with white streamers, and behind followed the bridegroom with the bridesmaids and all the other guests, sometimes as many as a hundred couples. Then after the dance in the Peacock, followed the bedding of the wedded couple with practical jokes the order of the night. When the bride entered her new home a napkin and a dish of bread were put over her head. On Saturday the groom was roused by his cohorts and made to prove his manhood by shouldering a creel filled with stones until the bride came out and redeemed him with a kiss. An old verse commemorates such weddings:

Weel Friday cam, the growing moon
shone beautifully clear
An' a' the boats wi' flags were drest
Frae Annfield tae the pier
An' Dr Johnston, worthy man,
Had twa-three hours to spare
So he toddled to Newhaven
An' spliced the happy pair
Wi' raisin-kail et cetera,
Began the wedding feast
An' there was roast and fried and bak'd
Before the party placed;
An' boiled and stewed and fricaseed,
Frae goblet, pot and pan,
But when the viands disappeared
The real fray began!

Though mutual attraction brought them together, it was a working partnership they formed. The motto which guided them was 'Marry for love and work for siller.'

They danced at the weddings but dancing was always popular with them. If the fishing was bad they danced for luck, if it was good they danced for joy. They also loved singing, it was like breathing to them, and they were born

From early days boats and the sea played a major role for youngsters - in the 1840s they would be at work before they reached their 'teens (Hill and Adamson, courtesy of the Scottish National Portrait Gallery).

raconteurs, Charles Reade describing them as 'musical and narrative.' There was the occasional exception like the deaf woman with a voice as flat as a pancake who was gently chided by the minister for coming in at the wrong time: 'Aye, minister, but the Lord likes to hear the craws as well as the nightingales.'

This joy in song led to the formation of the famous choirs of which there were three at one time. The first to be formed was the Fisherlasses' Choir in 1896 by Mr J Morrison Cooke, teacher at Victoria School which later became the Fishergirls' Choir under its conductor Miss Ritchie. The Fisherwomen's Choir, was formed for the adult women after the first world war by Mrs Ritchie (no relative) who was awarded the MBE for her services. Her daughters continued the work. The choirs achieved nation-wide success and made several trips abroad. The dresses are heirlooms, Miss Jean Noble who has sung in the choir most of her life having two beautiful shawls handed down in the family for over two hundred years. Some say few of the gentle chorister could now bait a mile o' hooks though they might charm a finny catch into the creel with their sweet music, of which Sir Hugh Roberton of the Glasgow Orpheus Choir said: 'These people are unique in their unspoiled naturalness; their faces lined with character, they sing straight from the heart. If I ever feel I am getting above the world I live in I shall go to Newhaven to be inoculated.' In 1965 the

Fisherwomen's Choir visted Norway and aboard the Norse Fishing Cruiser led the whole fishing fleet down the fiord to Trondheim for 'Fiskernes Dag'.

Doctors, Lawyers and Strangers

Despite their apparent excesses Newhaveners were ruggedly healthy, many living into their eighties and going to sea into their seventies. They didn't believe in taking time off work, holidays were unknown and if they felt under the weather they would go into Graham the chemist's. He had two big fancy glass bottles in the window and they would ask for something out of his red bottle or out of his green bottle, depending on what it was they had diagnosed for themselves. If it was a sore throat, they would wrap their stocking filled with hot salt round their neck or swallow a pat of butter rolled in sugar. For a chest cold, a porridge or bread poultice and for anything and everything, camphorated oil, kept in a green bottle on the mantelpiece, and in the spring a spoonful of sulphur and treacle to clear the blood.

Dr MacDonald was popular with them but they hesitated to consult him in case he would tell them to stay in bed. But he knew the mood of the place and his remedies were usually suitably robust. Mrs Ann Harley tells how he'd say: 'You've got pleurisy. Right, kaolin poultices, belladonna plasters.' That, and a clap on the back and you were all right. Her father, Tom Wilson, had had to consult Dr MacDonald once during the herring season, and he must have been bad for the good doctor said: 'A week off'. 'But doctor, the fishin's on'. 'If you don't stay off you won't be my patient any more.' There was no way out of it. Meantime up came his full crew and he gave them meticulous instructions. But for the whole week he sat and stared out over the water. 'Never again will I send for the doctor in the middle of fishing. I'll put the poultices on mysel'.'

Their attitude to lawyers was less ambivalent. If they were not exactly classified among the unmentionables, they were certainly to be given a wide berth. Mrs Colley illustrates the point: 'Newhaveners had their own pride. If there was maybe an illigitimate child, she would be adopted by some family in the village and maybe be called a wee servant lassie. They were all church-going and good living. This lad was adopted and when he grew up he knew he was illigitimate and he went out to Australia. In those days that was like going to the moon. When he left he said 'Remember, I will never forget you and what you people have done for me.' My granny was going out with her creel and in those days there was only rich and poor. And a lady said: 'Oh, Margaret, I have had an awful time. You see, my name is Seaton, that's my own name. Well there was somebody in Australia called Seaton and there is money been left but after my husband has spent a lot of money investigating it turns out it is to go to poor people in Newhaven.'

'Oh, Mum, my name is Margaret Seaton and I know who it is.'

'Then you will have a claim.'

So she runs home and tells her man: 'One of my customers says somebody has left us a lot of money but he can't remember their names exactly.' They were fair away with themselves. 'But then we will need to see a lawyer! And what if it wasnae him? We couldnae afford a lawyer. What will we dae? We canna risk it.'

Their dread of lawyers amounted almost to a superstition. A Newhaven man caught trawling inside the Isle of May was hauled up into court. He told the story afterwards: 'Sheriff Orr was the man that did the case. I ga'ed him the sign but he didnae respond. 'Twenty-five pounds', says he. 'Five pounds your honour?' 'Twenty five pounds,' says he. Sandy, I'll tell ye this, there's nae lawyers in heaven.'

They were equally suspicious of strangers, perhaps because in earlier times strangers often brought disease. Outsiders were referred to as 'blaggart strangers'. If you weren't a Bow-Tow you were treated with reserve if you came to trade and hostility if you came to pry. The origin of the name Bow-Tow for Newhavener is lost in the past and is given a variety of explanations today. Some say it's something to do with the boats being given a tow. There is a suggestion that it means those who live below the town. A retired sea captain thought it referred to the days of woodenwall ships when quite a lot of Newhaveners served in the Navy. To distinguish themselves to each other they would have a bow tied in their hat ribbon. An explanation from a Leither was that they didn't wear galluses and kept their breeks up with a bit of tarry tow. The most likely explanation came from Tom Hall. In Newhaven parlance a buoy is called a bow and a rope is tow. The man was the buoy or bow who supported the woman who was the tow or rope which descended to the net or the creel, and originally only when they were united could they be referred to as Bow-Tow but later the name became generic for Newhaveners.

Nicknames or bynames were very common in Newhaven as in other fishing ports. With only a limited number of surnames it was necessary that some form of distinction should be found. The Rev. Dr Graham used to say that of a dozen fishermen standing at a street corner the probability was that half of them were John Carnies and the other half William Fluckers. The Christian name of a Councillor Carnie was James and he lived to see his descendants of a third generation by which time there were four James Carnies. Other common names were Durham, Logan, Linton, Liston, Lyle, Noble, Paterson, Rutherford, Seaton, Wilson, Young. (None of these names would indicate a Flemish origin and some were those of families which had been prominent in the neighbourhood, so quick was the stepping down in social class among younger sons in this poverty-struck nation).

To avoid confusion the men when signing their names would add their wives' maiden name in brackets after their own, as for example, Alexander Noble (Carnie). But the same Alexander Noble was known around the village as 'Auld Currish' and that would be the only name he would ever get. 'Sometimes you never heard their real names,' said Rena Barnes. 'And you never called them Mr or Mrs, not even the children, unless they were outsiders. As a child it was auntie this or that even if they weren't relatives.'

As to Christian names, few had more than one and these followed a definite rule. The first son would be called after his father's father, the first daughter after her mother's mother, the second son after his mother's father, the second daughter after her father's mother, the third son after his father, the third daughter after her mother and if there were more children they would be named after uncles or aunts in order of age. So with such a paucity of names in use and reuse almost everybody had a byname. It started when they went to school. 'Somebody would call you a name. 'I'll fight you!' And your mother would say, 'He'd no right to call you that.' But it was all round the class and it stuck.'

Most people accepted it, but some didn't like to hear it in their presence. An old fishermen with the byname 'Tailie' (tallow) had a bit of advice on the subject for his grandson. The boy when he first went to school had to pass an auld wife sitting at her door who called after him 'Tailie!'. 'Juist you cry her 'Nervie' next time,' he said. Right enough, the next time she tried it, the boy turned round and shouted 'Nervie'. Her grin vanished and he never was bothered again.

Bynames tended to be of three types: those applied to a family to distinguish them from another family of the same name, those used to call a friend, and the derogatory type which it was safer not to use in the recipient's hearing. Some bynames got handed down from generation to generation.

What is strange is how apt many of these nicknames turned out to be, though some admittedly were a bit wide of the mark as for instance the rugged six-footer who was known all his days as Angel because his mother had been overheard using that endearment. Some earned their names the hard way like Lebe Burrell. They were having a dance down the pier and she got carried away with herself and birled off the pier. Some of them seemed to have no reason but some rhyme as for example, Doddaleedy, Hanse-me-dance, Rugstanes, and Easter Puff, but to enumerate further might offend susceptibilities.

The story is told of one fishing village where a new bank manager found the ledger accounts pencilled with such legends as 'Binky', 'Beeny's Tam', 'Wullie Cup' and so on. He rubbed them out and brought utter confusion to the records.

The population of the village grew relatively slowly during the nineteenth century in comparison to the rest of the country. In 1793 there were six hundred in the village and by the 1841 census this had increased to around 2000 but throughout the remainder of the century barely another thousand was added. Emigration principally to Canada and Australia creamed off many of the younger men and now the Free Fishermen's Society has members all around the world. One mass migration captured the public imagination when in 1889 a contingent of fifty young men was given an enthusiastic send-off when they volunteered as boatmen at Port Elizabeth, South Africa, the port finding itself overwhelmed by the gold rush traffic. Assembling in Newhaven, they marched in procession to Princes Street Station accompanied by brass bands and contingents of the local volunteers and Good Templars in regalia carrying banners and emblems. The Rev Dr Kilpatrick accompanied them by train to London, where they embarked. Although the majority returned at the end of their two-year engagement, a number chose to settle in South Africa.

In politics they tended in earlier years to be conservative though later towards the end of the 19th century they were of a Liberal mind, being represented in the earlier part of this century by Wedgewood Benn who did much for the village. There were no radicals among them. They were proud of their distinctiveness and regarded themselves, if not exclusively God's chosen people, at least closely related. They had a pawky humour and many of their sayings have passed into popular currency. There was a lot of practical sense in the philosophy, for instance of 'Keep yer ain fish guts for yer ain sea maw' or 'Set when there's nae work to be done standin'. They had little patience with critics and believed that 'Fuils and bairns shouldnae see things half done'. It was a hard life and they were 'Aye up before their claes were on'. There was no fortune for those who were 'Aye ahint like the coo's tail', for 'Siller doesna bide wi slovens'. They believed in themselves and they were proud of what they were doing.

CHAPTER 5

The Bartered Village

When the captains and the King departed on the eve of Flodden the village settled back into a decent obscurity. The great dockyard, its purpose spent, crumbled into decay and the sea, constantly probing at the sandy links, prepared to gather this last vestige of royal intent to its depths.

The village had now passed into new hands, for shortly before the launch of the *Michael*, James (whose wondrous schemes, from flying off the battlements of Stirling Castle to making gold from mercury, kept his pockets permanently empty) had sold it, house and harbour, port and pier and privileges, to the Corporation of Edinburgh.

The Burgesses of Edinburgh had watched jealously the rise of this seagate rival to their subject port of Leith, which since earlier times they had kept sair hauden doon, regarding it almost as conquered territory. On the pretext of an Act of James III Edinburgh claimed the power to make laws of its own for Leith, to refuse the unfreemen of Leith the right to trade, to appropriate the Shore Silver, (a duty on ships originally raised to upkeep the piers) and above all, the power of punishment, exile or death for all crimes committed above the high tide mark. It was enacted, among many other prohibitions, that all indwellers of the town of Leith, being unfreemen, might not buy codling, herring, salmon or other fish coming into the port, or salt or pickle the same nor send them away to England and other places. It appears that enterprising Leith had found a new venture in the salting and pickling of fish for export and Edinburgh would use its powers to say 'thou shalt not.' These powers it now proposed to extend over Newhaven.

The Charter of 1510, which is still preserved, conveyed to Edinburgh the new port of Newhaven lately constructed by the King on the seashore between the Chapel of St Nicholas in the north part of the town of Leith and the lands of Wardie on the West with all the rights and privileges hitherto enjoyed by that port.

Having achieved its end, Edinburgh pursued a policy of studied neglect, the only evidence it gave that it recognised Newhaven's existence was the appointment in 1511 of several men who were sworn upon the High Angels to keep the streets and shore clear of middens.

Thereafter through the centuries, Newhaven passed through a succession of servitudes, being in turn subject to St Cuthberts, the Canongate, North Leith, Leith and Edinburgh. But local government as we know it did not exist and ordinance swung widely between harsh imposition and careless disregard, the practical effect of which was that they were largely free of restraint. For a large part of the time the Church but principally the Free Fishermen's Society provided what local government there was.

A PART OF OLD NEWHAVEN.

The pantiles, characteristic of the roofs in the village, were originally brought back from the Netherlands as ballast (Courtesy of Mrs J Christie).

The lands on which Newhaven stood for long remained with the crown and were administered by a Baron Bailie appointed by the King. Later they passed into the hands of the Logans of Sheriffbrae, a cadet house of the Logans of Restalrig and later still into those of Ewan McGregor who in 1713 sold them to Trinity House. The latter built the farm of Trinity Mains from which the district of Trinity takes its name.

From the Charter of 1510 it appears that Newhaven had at that time one street, the South Raw with the sea coming right up to it and houses on the landward side. The earliest maps indicate that Newhaven village was on the shoreward side of a lagoon which had been artificially created by extending the arms of a bay until they formed almost a circle, which could be transformed into a giant drydock by closing the entrance. (A later pilot chart - of 1693 - shows that the great stone breakwaters had succumbed to neglect and the constant pounding of the seas, though traces of them are still shown as a hazard to shipping).

The houses, built of wood and thatched with turf, were crowded beside the public well on either side of the little stone-built chapel and were for the most part better than most other fishers' cottages since many of them had been built by Royal command to house the artisans at the dockyard. This village vanished in 1544 and it came about thus:

Henry VIII, pursuing his aim to unite the two kingdoms, had proposed a marriage between his only son Edward and the infant Mary Queen of Scots. But the Scottish people remembered that:

Closes running their crooked courses up from the shore to Main Street were a colourful part of Newhaven life. This is Wester Close, one of the larger ones (Courtesy of Sandy Noble).

> It is of the English nation
> The common kend condition
> Of truce the virtue to forget
> And reckles of good faith to be

They resented what they recognised as an attempt to annex their kingdom and told him of his proposals: 'There is not so little a boy but he will hurl stones against it, and the wives will handle their distaffs, and the commons universally will rather die in it.' Henry, in exasperation, embarked on his 'rough wooing'. He ordered the Earl of Hertford to make an inroad into Scotland and

New Lane, part of the 'New Town' of Newhaven, showing the outside stairs to the first floor houses and the yawls drawn up on the shore. New Lane was also known as 'Soo Raw' (South Row): 'Up Soo Raw for rags and bones, Up Soo Raw for saumon' (Courtesy of Mrs Greta Dyer).

there to put all to fire and sword. 'Burn Edinburgh,' he raged, 'raze and deface it when you have sacked it and gotten what you can of it, as there may remain forever a perpetual memory of the vengeance of God lighted upon it. Beat down and overthrow the castle, sack Holyrood House and as many towns and villages about Edinburgh as ye conveniently can. Sack Leith and burn and subvert it and all the rest putting man, woman and child to fire and sword.' The orders were carried out with zeal and Burton says : 'Unless we may find some parallel in Tartar or African history to the career of this expedition it will scarce be possible to point to any so thoroughly destitute of heroism or chivalry.'

The full brunt fell first on Newhaven. Buchanan says that without knowledge of any in Scotland a great navy of ships was seen driving towards the Forth. What should they mean? The Cardinal supped and said: 'They are come but to make a show and put us in fear. I shall lodge all the men of war in my eye that shall land in Scotland.' Still sits the Cardinal at his dinner. Men convene to gaze upon the ships, some on the Castle Hill, some to the Crags and other places eminent. There was one question: 'With what force shall we resist if we be invaded?' Soon after six at night were arrived and had cast anchor in the Road of Leith more than 200 sail. Shortly thereafter a boat put off and sounded the depths from Granton to east of Leith. Then at first light the

Main Street looking West at the end of last century, and showing the Free Church steeple, put up by the fishermen who fetched the stones from Fife. A fiddler plays for pennies thrown from an upstairs window screwed up in a paper poke.

galleys put their snouts to the shore near Newhaven.The great ships discharged their soldiers in the smaller vessels and all were put on dry land before ten o'clock. The first man that fled was the holy Cardinal like a valiant champion, and after him the Governor.

A Scots attempt to stem the landings was swept contemptuously aside. Newhaven was overwhelmed, its houses destroyed,though its piers were left intact, and Leith was won with the loss of only two men despite the great trenches that had been hastily dug. The English army on entering Leith found the tables spread, the dinners prepared, such abundance of wine and victuals besides other goods the like of which, they said, was not to be found elsewhere in Scotland, nor in England. (So much for Edinburgh's attempt to keep the Leith folk hauden doon). They broke down the pier at Leith and burned every stick of it and every house in the town, took two goodly ships, the *Salamander*, given by the French king at the marriage of his daughter, the other the *Unicorn* made by James V, into their fleet, which now put into Newhaven's pier where, says an army writer, 'we caused our ships loaded with our great artillery and victuals to be brought into the haven and discharged them at our leisure.'

Then they marched on Edinburgh which being built largely of wood blazed so fiercely for three days upon its hills that it did what the Scots could not and drove back the soldiery. Meanwhile the fleet engaged in destroying every ship and boat from Stirling to the mouth of the Forth on both coasts.

MAIN STREET, NEWHAVEN, 531.

Main Street looking East in 1903. The Victoria School is the large building in the background. The ornamental lampposts (not illustrated) survived until 1985 when they
were replaced by concrete posts.

The Rebuilding

Yet scarcely had the enemy done its evil worst and withdrawn than the work of
rebuilding began among the smoking rubble. With the fertile Lothians around
them there was no shortage of food, one traveller soon after commenting on
the wonderful multitude of oxen and sheep, though how the fisherfolk fared
without the means to drive their trade is not reported.

But by September 1550 Newhaven must have been restored to life for it was
then the scene of a brilliant pageant as 60 stately galleys and other ships
assembled in the roads to accompany the Queen Regent and her suite as she
sailed from Newhaven to visit her daughter Mary who had been smuggled to
France out of Henry's reach. She embarked for Dieppe along with a colourful
train of attendants including the Earls of Sutherland, Huntly, Cassilis, Home
and Marshall, the future Regent Moray, Lords Fleming and Maxwell, the
Bishop of Caithness and Galloway, the French Ambassador and a large number of fine ladies - probably the most spectacular gathering of quality that the
little port ever witnessed. They had come in procession along the road from
Leith where the Queen Regent had her palace on the Shore, its lower storey, a
continental piazza forming the Timber Bush or Bourse where much of the
commerce in this primary import and other merchandise of the Port was
conducted.

In the rebuilding of Newhaven a cheerful anarchy prevailed for the Dean of
Guild exercised his powers but seldom and this led to narrow lanes, crooked

closes with projecting stairs and enclosed spaces. Things were allowed to reach such a pass that at last in 1580 the Council reacted. 'Forasmuch as they understand that the passages leading between Newhaven and Edinburgh are gritumely narrowit by the nychbouris circumjacent and in many places enclosed, dyked up and wholly sealed up and cart gates stopped up by the setting up of stones that no carts may pass and the setting forth of stoops of stairs, the Provost Magistrates and Council propose visiting the area and where they find impediment, to cast it down.'

The pattern which now emerged of a broad main street with houses this time mainly on the North side and little lanes running down to the seashore and the pier, prevailed until the second half of the 18th century with relatively little change and by then Newhaven Main Street had taken on something of the appearance which characterised it until the recent reconstructions. A map made around 1750 shows the North side of the Main Street built up, a few houses on the South side, a villa at Hawthornvale and one at Laverockbank, and Mr Crouden's farm at Anchorfield. Fifty years later, by the beginning of the 19th century, the 'New Town' of New Lane, Annfield and Anchorfield had been built, separated from the village proper by extensive links and what later became the Fishermen's Park. There was a slight sense of distinction between the two parts of the village, the New Town regarding itself as rather better and that was where the pilots mainly lived. Those who later rose in the world and become trawler owners tended to move just outside of the village up to Stanley Road and Trinity, but that was a later development of the industrialisation of the fishing. The area inland of the village had become popular with rich merchants who had erected many handsome villas. There was a Mr Latta had Whalebank at the top of the Whale Brae, Mr Auchinleck had a house behind Newhaven and his next neighbour Mr Anderson of Laverockbank House. Then there was Sir Henry Moncrieff of Dennan Green. Wardie House was occupied by the Boswall family. Colonel Murray lived at Trinity Lodge, while Trinity Grove, said to be the finest private residence in Leith, was occupied by Mr (later Provost) Creech, an Edinburgh bookseller and publisher and afterwards by the Ballantines. Lady Bruce had a villa at the Citadel site, it was here that Lord Cockburn's father used to bring his family to spend the summer holidays and enjoy sea bathing, a very fashionable thing to do.

Step on another 50 years and by the middle of the 19th century the expanding population (which now exceeded 2000) had led to building on both sides of the Main Street, particularly on the seaward side where now the Free Church and Victoria School stood at opposite ends, separated by a string of inns, taverns and hotels. Around the corner in Craighall Road, seeming to hold itself in spiritual communion more with Trinity than Newhaven, stood Newhaven Church. The draw well at the pierhead was the social centre and opposite it there thrust out into the Forth the fine new pier. From then until the end of the century there was an acceleration landward of new streets and houses which engulfed some of the large villas. In this period Victoria Place, Willowbank Row, James Street, Ramsay Row were built and the new breakwater gave a sheltered harbour. There was a big sandstone building put up on Main Street where Tony Crolla's ice cream shop was later; it was called the Klondyke, having been built about the time of the gold rush and it was reckoned locally that if you got one of those houses it was like striking gold. Further along at Anchorfield, was another block of houses put up about the same time and known as Dawson City. A lot of Newhaven people went out to the goldrush.

Around the middle of last century the village is described thus: 'The place has an old-fashioned air and the red-tiled two-storey houses with outside stairs, the strings of bladders and the big boats drawn up on the shore or rocking in the harbour all give it a picturesque air which is lacking in modern wateringplaces. The Main Street extends 350 yards along the old sea margin and behind the ground rises southward to a bank crowned by a row of villas.'

About the same period James Bertram in *Harvest of the Seas* describes the village: 'Up the narrow closes we see hanging on the outside stairs the paraphernalia of the fisherman - his 'properties' as the actor would call them: bladders, lines and oilskin unmentionables with dozens of pairs of dark blue stockings that seem to be the universal wear of both maidens and mothers. On the stair itself if it be seasonable weather the wife and daughters repairing the nets and baiting the lines - gossiping of course with the neighbours who are engaged in precisely similar pursuits and today as half a century ago the fishermen sit by their hauled-up boats in their white trousers and their Guernsey shirts smoking their short pipes while their wives and daughters are so employed, seeming to have no idea of anything in the shape of labour being a duty of theirs when ashore. In the flowing gutter which trickles down the centre of the old village we have the younger idea developing itself in plenty of noise and adding another layer to the encrustation of dirt which seems to be the sole business of these children to collect on their bodies. The juvenile fisherfolk have already learned from the mudlarks of the Thames the practice of sporting on the sands before the hotel windows in the expectation of being rewarded with a few halfpennies. 'What's the use of a song for siller afore they have got their dinner?' we once heard one of these precocious youths say.'

It was around this time that the village became a popular subject for Scottish painters, Sam Bough and Keely Halswell in particular producing many canvasses which are now popular collectors' pieces.

The houses have gone through a gradual change, but except in the pantile roofs is there is little sign of the suggested Flemish influence, the Flemish using brick principally as a building medium. In the 16th century houses generally were still built of wood and in Newhaven several were two-storied. A century later some of the wooden houses had been replaced by cottages built of stones taken from the seashore (wood having become scarce and the city ordaining that building be done in stone) with walls no higher for the most part than a man and having roofs thatched with sods on which a feeble crop of smoke-blackened weeds struggled for a foothold, though here and there were roofs covered by the new red pantiles which were now being brought in from the Netherlands as ballast. Later still, all the houses were stone-built (it was said that 'there was hardly a hoose in the toon but had a kirkstane built intil't) with red-tiled roofs and mainly of two storeys with outside stairs. Travellers spoke of the cleanliness sweetness and wholesomeness of the interiors of the fishers' cottages, with their whitewashed walls, scrubbed furniture, clean bedding and freshly-scented flowers presenting a picture of tidiness. The open fireplace carried a swee for cooking and beside it stood the creepie, a low stool which served as a chair. A big double-bed was hidden in a recess closed in by doors or curtains. The furniture of the living room was completed by a table, press and a corner shelf with its array of ornaments brought home by seafaring sons. A little deep-set window was filled with a coarse greenish glass.

A glimpse into a fisher cottage about the middle of last century showed a change in degree rather than kind: 'A low-ceilinged room with the evening glow slanting through the small-paned window and falling on the brown nets heaped in the corner....The big bed with its brown and white curtains was filled with bedding and looked inviting though somewhat airless. Before it was a great brown kist which held the best clothes of the family. Above the dresser or long kitchen table were rows of shelves on which were arranged innumerable piles of plates of many patterns. On the mantelpiece were stoneware figures, brilliantly coloured, of shepherds and shepherdesses in Arcadian costume and sailors and their sweethearts in an apparently parting embrace. A staring green parrot dwarfed the branched coral from a tropic sea and works of art which represented the human form divine. Nor were pictures wanting to enliven the walls. Some were engravings of sacred subjects such as Jesus blessing little children or raising the widow of Nain's son or bearing the cross through the streets of Jerusalem. In the place of honour above the fireplace hung a highly-coloured picture of the whole royal family from the Queen down to the youngest princess. Besides these were family photographs which did scant justice to the really good looks of those represented.'

Through the half-open door might be caught a glimpse of 'ben the hoose' which boasted a handsome bed and a magnificent chest of drawers with spiral supporting pillars and a table with a crimson velvet cloth. On the latter were disposed the family bible and most of the household library of religious works, the rest of which found accommodation on the hanging shelf beside the window. A bright coloured rug made from odd bits of cloth and flannel adorned the hearth stone. Scrupulous order and cleanliness characterised the abode.

Up to a fewdecades ago an 18th century villager, time-warped into modern Newhaven, would not have felt himself strangely misplaced. Recently, however, there has been a change. In *Newhaven - an Oral History*, Sarah Dyer records the dramatic recent events. 'Land has been reclaimed, extending Leith Docks and providing space for flour mills and warehouses. New Lane was demolished and rebuilt to a certain extent in the same style as it was originally. The area between the Main Street and Park Road from Ramsay Row to the Whale Brae has been demolished and a modern development put in its place. Finally, all of North Newhaven from the Peacock Inn to the Marine Hotel has been completely rebuilt in the original style, making use of the original buildings where they still existed, with outside stairways and narrow closes. These buildings have been harled and painted white however, whereas the original buildings were for the most part in the natural stone.'

Perhaps the huge iron anchor which has been placed artistically at the foot of New Lane epitomises the changes. Taken by many to be an anchor from the *Great Michael*, it resembles more a standard Admiralty mooring anchor of World War I vintage, salvaged from the shipbreaking yards of Inverkeithing. Above the anchor are the group of Saltire Award-winning flats and houses, attractive in a modern way, a representation of what used to be.

Opposite them where the Hally stretched to the sea, is now land reclaimed for industry. It is one of a series of ironies that have punctuated the village history that after centuries of fighting against erosion from the sea, the links should have been submerged at last beneath a flow of concrete from the landward side.

CHAPTER 6

Memory be the Guide

In the process of change much has vanished. Esther Liston, Newhaven's last fishwife, told Sarah Dyer: 'The Hally (a stretch of links to the East of the village) belonged to the fishermen and they used to pull their boats up there. If they'd've left juist one boat on it it would have still belonged tae the Free Fishers but there wisnae a boat there and that's how the Leith Dock Commission could take it. They juist put a fence round it and later they could reclaim all that land. Now it's a' concrete. We used tae play hide'n'seek at the Hally, hiding in and out of a' the boats there. What they ca' Lindsay Place now, that's what we ca'ed the Hally. And there is one corner just at the side going doon to Croan's, Newhaven Place, one wee bit of it. That used to be St Andrew's Square but it's Fishmarket Square now. Long ago before Croan's and a' that there was only the one place that did the fish, Dow's, and they had a long piece of concrete that they used to dry the cod on and the salt for the salt fish. It was spread out and the sun beat on it.

'And the Fishermen's Park, that's gone now too. That's where they used to tan their nets and the women would bleach their clothes. We use to aye go to Maggie Thingmay's to get a pail of water, Maggie Rumple, that's Dalrymple. It was easier than going home.'

Rena Barnes described how the washing was done: 'They washed the clothes, rinsed them, spread them out on the grass in the Park and their sheets and pillow cases and underwear was all white. They lay there all day whether it was rain or snow or what and after that they washed them through again. And then they dried them afterwards, put them on a pulley across the close. But they had a whole day's bleaching. Now it was better if they got the sun and the rain - they needed both and that made them lovely and white. If there was no rain they used a watering can, watered them like flowers - all the fancy knickers. If there was any worn yins they didn't put them out.'

The Fishermen's Park was a noted feature of the old village. A problem in the village in the early days was the lack of a suitable place for the drying and tanning of the nets The drying had to be done on masts resting across two boats on the beach or on the old harbour wall. So the Free Fishermen's Society after long negotiation with the Admiralty had obtained a long lease.

On and off over the years there has been a boatbuilding yard in the Park, the last boat being launched from there and pulled through the streets to the harbour by the whole population - even the school children - in 1928. There was a sailmaker's shed there too. 'We just called that Turner's Shed and that was just opposite the school. We used to play there on the steps before we went in and after we came out.' Turner was the son of the local schoolmistress and made all the sails and rigging for the local boats. In the Park was the Coal Fauld

A watercolour painting of 1815 by W Smeall, showing Newhaven from the East. (Courtesy of George Liston).

Gas lamps lit the streets and closes and the children would make the rounds with the lamplighter at dusk. (Courtesy of Edinburgh City Libraries).

Annfield Beach and Promenade were favourite picnic places but land reclamation later pushed the seas back (Courtesy of George Liston).

Annfield in the 1880s, looking west with horse-drawn trams plying the promenade. (Courtesy of Mrs Greta Dyer).

where the nets were barked - dipped in tar and alum to preserve them. Another local enterprise there was the Smiddy, up a wee close. 'It wasnae really a close at all, just a lane,' explained James Watson, 'and at the top there was a wee blacksmith's shop run by a man cried Johnnie Calder.' It was up that close the fish were cured and the kippering done so the Park served a variety of functions.

Annfield today, now some distance inland, thanks to land reclamation, yet otherwise
little changed in external appearance.

The Whale Brae is popularly believed to have been so called because,
according to one account 'ane little whale' beached itself and was dragged up
there though other reports talk of a large school being stranded. In 18th century maps an area called The Whale is shown and there was an inn called The
Whale there which was the terminus for London coaches. Early in the 18th century, there was a glass factory on the Brae. Admiralty House, now demolished,
was built on Whale Brae in 1813 by the naval authorities whose headquarters
it was during the Napoleonic War. The Commissioners of the Navy had
petitioned Edinburgh Town Council for the entire three acres of the Fishermen's Park from Anchorfield in the East to Whale Brae in front of Jessiefield
though they did not propose to oust the fishermen who used the park. The
building was later used as a private house and here George Cupples, author of
The Green Hand and other novels, died in 1891.

Adjacent to Whale Brae was the Willbowbank area which is said to have got
its name from a legendary willow tree. The following is a free translation
of the legend:

The Willow Tree

High on a green and mossy bank that overlooks the sea
Timeless as tide, there flourishes a weeping willow tree
Seeming to droop her leafy head in an eternal sleep
Landmark to fleets of little ships come homeward from the deep.

Oft when at night the landsman chiel lays down his head in rest
Silent she broods o'er harbour bar where little ships abreast
Hoisting their sails in evening breeze and Borealis light
Skim out like gulls before the wind into the gathering night

Onward they glide, companions yet, each light and open bark
Lost to all else save neighbour's light, beyond a wall of dark
Holding their course in gathering wind, huddled from driving spray
Guided by fires that beckon on to distant Isle of May

Savage the storm and sudden that comes roaring from the North
Wild now the waves on every hand that rage across the Forth
Clutched at by wind and waters wild, blinded by driving rain
Few but despair to have the sight of their dear home again

Brave hearts, stout craft, we're floating yet for all that's come and gone
Our fathers lived through nights like this, so shall each father's son
So come what may this stormy night we yet shall live to see
The lights of auld Newhaven and the mighty willow tree

Blessed be the hoary willow tree that heaves now on our sight
Neath us our hard-won finny freight, above the morning light
And God be praised, we'll win our bread as blythely and as free
While leaves shall flourish verdantly on yon old willow tree

'Tis said a spaewife prophesied 'When that tree shall decay
The open seaboat fishing trade shall also die away'
And o'er the Forth great ships shall ride full of their finny prey
But sail those ships so boldy boys, that won't be in our day.

In days of old, the story goes, where stands that great tree now
The bank was bare of root and trunk, there waved no leafy bough
And on the flower-strewn bank there stood a lovely fisher lass
Her bonny bairn weel-happit in a creel upon the grass

While yonder on the cresting waves her lad's sail flies away
Yet as she looks her heart is filled with gathering dismay
For the Western wind's now Northing and the waves roll to the land
And the moaning sea announces that a stormy night's at hand

And sudden, fierce and furious the blast comes ravening in
And thunder roll and lightning flash join in the hellish din
His tiny bark is swallowed up, his nut-brown sail is drowned
O'ercome with anguish and despair she swoons upon the ground

Beside her sleeping bairn she lay while rain gave way to snow
And the lovely wife and blooming bairn were smoored far far below
They ne'er awoke, they ne'er were seen and as months slipped away
Their sad remains were covered o'er within that crumbling brae

But in the spring when bluebells grew the osier creel set free
A sturdy shoot from which there grew a mighty willow tree
That weeps in sad remembrance of a lovely fisher girl
With her bonny bairn in osier creel that lies beside her still.

D

The tenement known as 'The Klondyke', built at the time of the Gold Rush (Courtesy of George Liston).

The West End of Newhaven between the wars, showing the Marine Hotel and the tram to Granton.

For more than 70 years trams trundled along Newhaven Main Street in a variety of forms, first as horse-drawn, then cable-cars and latterly electric like this, one of the last to run. (Courtesy Edinburgh City Libraries).

Just over a hundred years ago the tree was still there, at the end of Willow-bank Row, protected by an iron railing.

Opposite Park Road was Jessfield Terrace. It was referred to as Pilot's Avenue, since it stood high over the Fishermen's Park and gave a good view of the ships plying in the Forth. Over a dozen pilots were in residence there in the period between the wars.

At the westmost end of Newhaven was The Cut or the Grassy Bank. It is also known as Craighall Road but not to Newhaven people. In 1822 the Edinburgh civic authorities anticipating that George IV on his visit to Scotland would disembark at the new Chain Pier had constructed a broad new thoroughfare in a direct line from the seafront. Alas, he landed instead at Leith after a great fuss was made. The visit, brilliantly stage-managed by Sir Walter Scott and recorded by Turner focused the romantic attention of the nation on things Scottish. There is a graphic description of the scene: 'So soon as the Royal Barge came within hail of the pier the Royal Standard was hoisted on the lighthouse; an immense cheer accompanied by the waving of hats and handkerchiefs burst from the multitude. The noise at once subsided into perfect calm, as if the breathless interest of the people, the palpitation which had endured to a degree almost painful, had for the instant choked all power of utterance. The Royal Barge passed the pierhead when three young men as pipers struck up some national airs. The King bowed and a great cheer rent the air.'

Stanley Road was the terminus for some tram routes to Leith and to Pilrig (Courtesy of Mrs J Christie).

Newhaven Silver Prize Band had a national reputation in the early years of this century. It did not survive the First World War. (Courtesy of Edinburgh City Libraries).

The historic stone which some say commemorates the fishermen's sallies against the scattered ships of the Spanish Armada, though others have a more prosaic explanation. It has been built into one of the new houses on Main Street in approximately its original position.

Later, as the King passed through Newhaven, a fishwife ran forward with a glass of whisky and a piece of cake on a tray. The King graciously accepted the whisky. A fisherman sitting on a wall caught the King's eye. 'God bless me, he surely kens me,' cried the man, and fell off the wall.

At the other end of the village to The Cut, the road to Leith was often washed away in storms and in such conditions the point at Annfield could be so hazardous it was known as the Mantrap. In 1767 representations were made to Edinburgh that the road was in a very dangerous state owing to the encroachment of the sea and it was proposed to change its course further inland. This would mean cutting through a piece of ground at Anchorfield which was claimed by a Robert Davidson whose house stood nearby. He wanted £36 to

Modern Newhaven has a tidy appearance though it has lost much of its character. Great Michael Close commemorates the area where the great warship was built.

give up his rights but on investigation it was found that he hadn't any, he had simply fenced off that part of the links. So instead of getting his money he was taken to court and fined. In 1774 an exceptionally high tide swept away a great part of the bank from the Citadel to Newhaven, damaging many houses. Trinity House gave £20 towards flood relief. Little was done and in 1789 a young woman going from Newhaven to Leith fell over the precipice into the sea and within six weeks the same catastrophe had befallen four others. In 1797 the storm bulwark at Newhaven was completely destroyed and large boulders were rolled up onto the shore, many of them split as though with gunpowder. A minute of Edinburgh Town Council of 1810 records that trouble was still being experienced from the sea washing away the road. John Glover, wright of Leith, who owned a tenement of houses near Anchorfield, was given permission to take stones from the beach to make a bulwark against the encroachment of the sea, the previous one having been swept away.

The Road to Town

The road to Edinburgh was up the Whale Brae and thence to Bonnington, across the river and up to Broughton and the Canongate. The footpath through open country as far as Bonnington from Newhaven was known as Whiting Road. Down to the early years of the 18th century there had been stepping stones at Bonnington but later a wooden footbridge was built largely

The award-winning development at the East end of the village.

for the convenience of the fisherwomen. Beyond the ford another footpath led through the countryside to Broughton Loan. In the minutes of Edinburgh Town Council in 1763 it is noted that this common highway to Newhaven had existed for centuries since ever Newhaven had been inhabited and had been in daily use by people on foot or horseback without interruption until 1762 when Mrs Rannie, a tenant in the lands at Bonnington on the north side of the Water of Leith at Bonnington Mills attempted to stop Whiting Road coming out on to the new turnpike road by digging deep ditches across it. But she had to fill them in again when the Newhaven folk took their objections to the Corporation. An earlier minute records that in 1732 the bridge at Bonnington to Newhaven had been almost carried away by a spate and £5 was granted to the poor fishermen towards its repair as otherwise they would be forced to reach Edinburgh by way of Leith. The bridge was not completely repaired until 1747. Whiting Road was converted into a carriageway towards the end of the 18th century and in 1812 the road between Pilrig and Bonnington was made suitable for vehicles.

Up at Edinburgh's East End if you go down the Waverley Steps from Princes Street you may see a bricked up area opposite Platform 1. This gave on to a tunnel which ran under the Waverley Market, under St Andrews Square and appeared three-quarters of a mile downhill at Scotland Street. This was the route of the Edinburgh, Leith and Newhaven Railway, and according to the *Railway Record* of the time probably no railway in history encountered so many difficulties - it was seven years before a train ran. A ceremony was held at the Chain Pier in 1838 to mark the laying of the foundation stone of a Newhaven terminus. The distinguished guests in great spirits drank a bumper to the project while the workmen made do with a plentiful supply of Greig's Best March Ale. But nothing the company could do was right and costs escalated, fraud and falsehood were alleged and the folk of Trinity demanded compensation to the tune of £40,000 though eventually settling for a tenth of that. 'One of the hollowest bubbles ever blown' said the *Railway Times* as the company abandoned Leith and Newhaven ends and concentrated on Trinity. During the building of the tunnel four workmen were drowned. Eventually it was completed and trains were pulled through from Waverley on a wire rope before being coupled up to a locomotive at Scotland Street. And despite all this, the little railway proved a great success, for with the opening of Granton Docks it was extended there in 1846. (When this was being built a skeleton was unearthed together with Spanish coins of the time of Philip II. Was he a seaman from the Armada, many of whom had collected at Newhaven and Leith to await passage home? Was he murdered in a brawl and buried surreptitiously to avoid trouble with the authorities?)

As the main railway route to the North the line became very profitable and resulted in the world's first train ferry being built to carry trains over the water to Fife. It operated until the Forth Bridge was opened in the 1890s. The ferry was called the *Leviathan* and was 400 tons burthen and 167 feet long, the lines aboard her running from end to end. She could not operate in bad weather which resulted in the passengers often being put up for the night at Granton Hotel.

The railway proved a blow to Newhaven for it diverted the highly-profitable cross-Forth ferry service to Granton and the gradual extension of the railway system made it easier for other and distant ports to reach the capital quickly with their fish.

After twenty years of profitable operation the tunnel was closed in 1868 when a new line to Leith was built, and was subsequently used to grow mushrooms. It was considered as an air raid shelter during the last war. Recently, with the rebuilding of Waverley Market it was partly filled in at the Princes Street end.

The Village Shops

There was a great variety of shops in the village, none more characteristic than Jeannie Falconer's which sold coconut-covered toffee from a tiny low-ceilinged room in Main Street, tucked under one of those outside wooden staircases. She was famed not only for her toffee apples and toffee brittle but for her other delicacies of a quite different kind - twopence worth of 'liar' which might be cold but was preferred freshly cooked and hot and wrapped in paper like a fish supper. This was in fact cow's udder and like most offal was not only nourishing but cheap. Jeannie bought bread at the Co-op and got the dividend

The skyline of the modern village (Courtesy of George Liston).

that was 3s 4d in the pound. She would get her dividend then she would sell it at the right price. All her business was done wi' pencil and jotter. You went in to pay for it on a Saturday. And you could go in there for a couple of ounces of bacon instead of going to the store.' It was also the school tuckshop. She sold the famous Polisman's Gundy, a stick of soft rock, covered in shredded coconut and sherbet dabs and ha'penny luckybags.

'Everybody that had a window on the Main Street would have a wee shop, maybe sweets. One of them had a notice 'Paraffin ile and other sweetmeats'. They would make a farthing here and a farthing there. Folk just bought as they needed, a wee bit every day, maybe a bag of vegetables, or maybe if they were flush, a forpit o' tatties. Teeny Knight had sweeties but she used to take in mangling, a farthing an item for blankets and sheets. Ironing was a problem and she had a big old-fashioned mangle with a table for pushing the stuff through.'

Then there was Store Johnny. He had a cellar full of chandlery for the boats. Mrs Colley recalls a grocer called Geordie Miller whose shop was in the centre of Newhaven. 'He would have this row of biscuits in glass cases. You would hear the plink of glass. What was going on there behind the biscuits? This would be the men getting a drink. They say he died a millionaire.'

One of the most popular families of shopkeepers was the Crollas who had come fom Italy in the 19th century. They had a reputation of helping out with tick in hard times. Tony Crolla who now runs a grocer's, tells how in his father's time you could take a piece of fish into the chip shop and have it fried for tuppence and with another tuppence get enough chips to give you a good fish supper. 'Try doing that anywhere today and see what the reaction would be.'

The Stone Plaque

Except for the ruins of the Chapel of St Mary and St James there is nothing of antiquity in the village beyond the mysterious stone plaque set into the wall of one of the houses, a large abutment sculptured with a pair of globes, a quadrant, an anchor and a three-masted ship of war flying the Saltire at each masthead. It bears the inscription 'In the neame of God. 1588.' The endearing and irrepressible Mrs Cupples in *Newhaven - Its Origins and History* has a ready explanation: 'On that ever memorable day just 300 years ago now (1588) a grand and signal occasion came to Newhaven: It began with no small alarm: Armada. During some little time of anxious preparation Scotland, protesting sympathies strongly with Queen Elizabeth, from Newhaven and from every other Scottish harbour squadrons of active little vessels had been getting fitted out and manned by fishermen and seamen who now chivvied and annoyed the scattered fleet. Fishermen of Flemish descent sailed out in retributive enterprise. In commemoration they erected a massive stone tablet formally placed on high between two substantial houses on Main Street facing seaward through the open place called St Andrew's Square where numerous fishermen of all ages are generally to be seen walking their very short turn of three steps and overboard.'

(The Armada, on its way to Holland to pick up troops for a landing in Galloway, was pursued up as far as the Forth by the English fleet but was then scattered and destroyed by storms. The survivors generally were given a friendly reception in Scotland.)

Mrs Cupples describes the Newhaven stone: 'The monument itself is surmounted with the outspread Scottish thistle with the national motto *Nemo me impune lacessit* engraved on the scroll and the date 1588. Immediately beneath is figured a three-masted galley of unweildy and foreign aspect with a Romish cross on the penant at each mast head. Next comes a transverse band showing this legend: 'In the neame of God.' Underneath this again are various quaint symbols well carved, a quadrant, an anchor with a pair of compasses and a marlin spike. The Latin motto *Per vertuti sidera terram mare* - Valour guided by the stars can traverse both land and sea.'

Another tradition locally is that it was set up later to mark the house where Mary Queen of Scots had spent the night following her flight across the Forth from imprisonment at Loch Leven Castle.

More mundane is a third tradition that the stone was unearthed from Cramond Burn and simply built into the wall for decorative purposes.

There are possibly two stones. The ship portrayed is a typical three-masted armed merchantman of the period, flying the Saltire at each masthead. The other part of the stone bears resemblance to the arms of Trinity House as does the Latin legend. Perhaps this part of the stone came from property in the area owned by Trinity House who had acquired extensive lands around Newhaven. Other stones with similar dates and inscriptions are built into the present Trinity House in the Kirkgate.

CHAPTER 7

The harbour

Though Sir Louis Gumley, Lord Provost of Edinburgh, once described Newhaven as the jewel in the city's crown, it must be admitted that precious little care was spent on it.

Under the Charter of 1510 the Burgesses of Edinburgh were bound to uphold the pier and bulwarks but their interest slackened once they had staunched the competition with Leith. In 1518 the Abbot of Holyrood and the Queen took legal action against the Burgesses for failing to upkeep Newhaven harbour but without success and for nearly half a century little was done and almost the first item of expenditure relating to Newhaven in the Council minutes concerned the hanging of four Englishmen, the Captain and the crew of the *Kait of Lynn* for piracy by stealing a cable and four pistols from a ship from Stettin then lying at Leith.

Hatred of the English after the Hertford raids had become almost paranoic and whether or not the men were guilty of the charge of piracy was regarded as a mere irrelevance:

> Item, for cords to bind and hang the four Englishmen at Leyth and Newhaven - iijs
> Item, geven to George Tod, Adam Purves and ane servand to make ane gibbet at Newhaven in haist and evil wedder - vjs
> Item, for garroun and plansheour naillis - xxd
> Item, for drink to them at Newhaven - vjd
> Item, for twa workmen to beir the wrychtis lomis to the Newhavin and up again, and to beir the work and set up the gibet - xxd

(A more common and economical form of execution was simply to stake out the condemned man between high and low water marks and let the tide do the deed.)

It may have been that on her departure the Queen Regent drew attention to the neglected state of the pier, or it may have been that Edinburgh in its continuing battle of wits with Leith had decided to favour Newhaven. Whatever the reason, Edinburgh at last honoured its obligations to the Royal treaty, a sum of £500 'usual money of this realm' being spent from the Common Good Fund in 1554 to repair the ravages of time. Sir John Wilson was master of this work which was suspended over the winter and begun again once the gales had subsided. It was common in mediaeval times for shipping and related activities to cease over the winter months and there were even ordinances to this effect. In 1557 the Provost Bailies and Council ordained that Alexander Park, treasurer and Sir William McDougall, Master of Works, inspect the work carried out and form an estimate of the cost of further repairs. Timber for the

Newhaven Harbour and the Chain Pier from Wardie with Inchkeith in the left background and the Forth abustle with traffic (Courtesy of Edinburgh City Libraries).

The harbour in the 1870s showing the characteristic yawls, mainly single-masted and undecked, having the Fife line of vertical stem and stern. The harbour rail was used for drying the nets.

The old harbour light, replaced when the new lighthouse was built in the 1870s. It still stands over the harbour today. (Courtesy of George Liston).

pier was brought from Norway and a further sum of £500 was spent, yet owing to the meanness of the Corporation it never got a thorough repair and was always patched up in a temporary manner, their conduct being so skinflint that their own contractor protested that he would not be responsible for any fault in the work.

There is no record of subsequent repair and the great bulwarks, beyond the ability of a few fishermen to maintain, slipped down into the sea. It seems the fishermen themselves were responsible for building and upkeeping what became known as the Western Shore Harbour, a primitive stone pier and slipway which protected the shore from the worst of the westerly gales. The shore was a clean and attractive one with fine gravel and gentle slope seawards. It was a useful place to pull up the fishing boats as well as a great attraction to holidaymakers and bathers and later many bathing boxes were set up along the shore in the summer.

When the piers at Leith were being lengthened and Victoria Dock was being built many loads of clay and shingle were carted away with the result that the beach near Annfield was ruined.

Early in the 19th century, the fishermen's primitive pier was used as a basis for a new slipway for a ferry service to Fife and later the authorities developed

The New Lighthouse, lit first in 1878, at the harbour mouth.

it by building on the East side of it a high pier to accommodate steamboats. It seems they tried to keep the fishermen from using this new pier at first but gave way under a chorus of protest on condition that the fishermen were civil and accommodating to the ferry passengers. The head of the pier was only four feet back from the houses and the road to the pier was by St Andrew's Square which at that time was known as the Back Yard. Later a new road was built to Cramond and this, passing the head of the pier, considerably widened the space between the houses and the pier.

Near the head of the pier on the north side of the old Draw Well was the Life House where the lifeboat was kept. When the Ferry Pier was constructed the trustees built a strong slip to the sea from St Andrew's Square. The Life House fell into disrepair and a new one was built where the Victoria School now stands. But according to the records of the Society both house and boat in time 'got liberty to go to waste.' In any event, a lifeboat was probably superfluous as in time of need every fisherman in the village was ready to turn out.

The pier and harbour after the breakwater had been completed. (Courtesy of George Liston).

The harbour in recent days sees little fishing activity though pleasure craft find a mooring there.

The fishmarket continues to function even though the fleet has departed (Courtesy George Liston).

Ambitious plans to extend Leith Docks as far as Newhaven which would have given the village a fine new harbour were proposed in 1818 but as the cost would have been in the region of £300,000 the idea was dropped.

When Granton's extensive docks were completed in 1844 the river crossing station was finally removed there, and the ferry operators tried to sell the stones of the Newhaven pier adding insult to injury but this blatant piece of self-interest was thwarted when two Newhaven men set off for London with the support of Leith Dock Commission and convinced the authorities that as the Ferry Pier had been built on the site of the old harbour the stones could not be removed.

The New Breakwater

So the fishermen fell heir to the Ferry Pier but it afforded them little shelter and none in Northerly winds so that in a gale they had either to risk serious loss or take their boats to safer moorings at Granton or Leith. After many years of fruitless effort by the Society to get assistance in the erection of a proper harbour they decided in 1864 to build it themselves and to appeal to the public for support.

In their petition to the public they claimed that the new railway to Granton prevented them hauling up their boats beyond the reach of the breakers and to find protection for their fleet they would themselves build a breakwater to the West of the new pier, bringing stones in their boats from quarries on the Fife

An aerial view taken around 1975 showing the harbour and some of the new buildings south of Main Street (Courtesy of 'The Scotsman').

shore. But besides this they required the services of a builder and this meant money. The public, they said, would benefit from the new harbour because large quantities of fish were daily brought to Newhaven by boats from all parts of the Forth for the Edinburgh market. And the oyster-fishing would be left to poachers if the Newhaven fleet were scattered.

They claimed: 'The boats of Newhaven number a fleet of about 200. The families dependent on the fishing number above 300 and the population living in Newhaven number upwards of 2,000. The proposed new haven would continue the existence to a large number of individuals which would be lost to them without it. The petitioners cast themselves and the lives of their wives and weans on the charitable consideration of the Community.' Without that support the first winter storms would destroy the fleet and bring ruin to the fishermen and their families. The appeal met with a good response and for two years boat-load after boat-load of stones was brought by the fishermen from Queensferry and the breakwater at last rose above the surface of the sea. But money to buy more stones ran out and the work came to a stop. Gradually the half-built breakwater slipped back into the sea.

Disheartened but not disuaded the fishermen continued to press their case.

Granton Harbour and Pier around 1880. Much of the commercial traffic deserted Newhaven when the fine new harbour at Granton was built and connected to the railway.

In 1872 they petitioned Leith Dock Commission: 'We are frequently exposed to great and dangerous risks when overtaken by storms on returning from our fishing grounds. We are consequently obliged to run for shelter up the Firth and our perishable cargo of fish is on such occasion completely lost.

'We are now changing the class of seagoing boats from the open shallow water vessel to a regular fishing smack to enable them to live at sea during stormy weather. Such vessels draw considerably more water than the ordinary boats and so render the necessity for a deep-water harbour more urgent.'

Again the appeal fell on deaf ears. Then at last in 1874 they found a sympathetic listener in the M.P. for Leith Burghs, Mr Donald McGregor. He promised to ask Parliament for £10,000 to help. There may have been some cynicism when news of this was brought back to Newhaven but less than a month later a civil engineer attended by three fishermen was seen taking soundings and measurements for the new harbour.

On Saturday 15th April 1876 the laying of the foundation stone of the new west breakwater took place amid great rejoicing. The streets and pier were decorated with flags of all colours, the deep-sea boats were dressed in style, the Draw Well and the Barometer Tower were cleaned and painted as was the ancient stone in Main Street.

After the ceremony had been completed upwards of 100 gentlemen assembled in Victoria School where a dejeuner of cake, oysters and wine was provided. There were many laudatory speeches. The Rev Dr. Fairbairn said this was the most important event in the history of Newhaven. The fishermen were among the most honest, energetic and industrious in the country. Bailie McNab, Leith, who was reckoned an authority on the subject, said that Newhaven had arisen in consequence of the breakup of a fishing village on the Isle of May by Henry VIII and the settlement at Newhaven of one of the Guilds of fishermen who had previously inhabited that island and who had afterwards founded what was now the Free Fishermen's Society, which was the oldest industrial society in Scotland. The Rev Mr. Graham talked about the village's historic connection with the *Great Michael* whose measurements he gave as 80 yards by 30 yards. George Flucker, representing the fishermen, responded and said that hundreds of families in Newhaven 'with rejoicing would be half-fou the nicht' (laughter). It was not uncommon to see a man or woman half-fou in Newhaven and upon an occasion like this their joy might lead them to take a little stimulation.

It was a gala day and a great procession formed, preceded by men carrying the flags of the Free Fishermen's Society along with two fishing boats, gilded and dressed with gay ribbons with six men rowing and one steering, as well as a splendid model of a full-rigged ship. Then came the Boxmaster with his silver medal, the Preses with the Society's silver cup and the youngest member of the Society with a silver trowel and silver mortar bucket. The procession was joined in Leith by 400 Masons, Free Gardeners, Odd Fellows and Foresters all in their particular regalia. After the laying of the stone under which coins, a newspaper and an almanack were placed and over which a fishwife scattered flowers, the procession marched up Leith Walk, along Princes Street and back by way of Granton. In the evening there was a grand soiree in the Madras School. Mr. McGregor was presented by the Society with a silver trowel ornamented with a design of boats in the harbour and a bible. Mrs. McGregor was given by the women of Newhaven a grand doll, four feet high, dressed in fishwife's dress with creel and basket on her back and cured fish in the basket. The expenses in connection with the affair are noted in the Society's books: Trowel and bucket - £10 12s 6d; band and pipers, £13 8s; bottle and coins, £1 2s 6d; poles and deputations to Edinburgh, £1 12s 4d.

The harbour when completed in 1878 was 500 yards long by 300 yards wide, with an entrance 70 ft wide. The East Pier was 750 ft long with a lighthouse at its western returnhead. It was 3½ acres in extent and could accommodate three times the number of boats belonging to Newhaven.

Euphoria was shortlived however. The following year, the Dock Commission tried to recoup some of its outlay by imposing harbour dues of £1 per annum for the boats under 30 ft and £2 for those above that, pilot boats to be free unless engaged in fishing. The fishermen refused to pay on the grounds that the work was not finished which was true as the entrance had not been completely cleared of stones. So the Commission sent a tug with 33 policemen aboard to Newhaven to attach the fishing boats. When they tried to seize one of the bigger boats in the harbour a melee started and the Deputy Commissioner was thrown into the sea. The fishermen who in the past had used words so eloquently to gain their end seemed to feel that the point needed some physical underlining. But shortly thereafter two fishermen were flung into the harbour to join him and the rest of the Newhaven men conceded a 2-1 win to the Commission. The tug set off for Leith with the boat in tow. The owner had no other recourse but to follow on foot and pay up the £4 demanded to get his boat back and thereafter the other fishermen paid up too. Two fishermen, John Wilson and William Liston, got 30 days apiece in jail, one for throwing the Deputy into the water, the other for striking the Superintendent. The general feeling was that maybe they had gone a bit far in making their point. James Wilson, Boxmaster of the Society, wrote that the crew responsible for the start of the trouble got clear by paying the dues and he went on to state that before the Dock Commission built the harbour they had intimated that they would be charging dues and the Society had agreed to pay these. But the Leith Burgh Pilot thought the Dock Commission had over-reacted in a ridiculous manner and should be censured. They said there should have been 'A little more wisdom and a little more tact and prudence and a complete absence of that extraordinary naval attack on this hard-working and industrious community by the steam flotilla from Leith under the direction of the Dock Officials, who had never been brought up to this rough course of warfare and to say the least of it came out of the inglorious struggle worse than second best. Seeing the dislike of the Newhaven men to pay taxes of any kind it would have been better for the Dock Commission to be patient with them.' They agreed it was wrong of the Newhaven men to resist payment but pointed out that three large boats had been damaged on the stones left in the harbour mouth by the Dock Commission.

Finishing touches were made to the pier in 1889 when the Dock Commission put up iron stairs at the hammer head as well as mooring rings. They also raised the pier in the middle, separating the west slipway from the eastern quay, which did not meet with universal approval. There appears to have been no further argument about dues.

Well into the present times Newhaven Harbour retained its picturesque air. A newspaper writer claimed in 1936 that no Holywood mogul ever conceived a setting so striking as this commonplace reality of Newhaven at work, its boxy little harbour packed with the lovely little ships of the inshore fishermen, one of the breeziest sights in Scotland, while on the piers, amid great heaps of ice, coopers knocked up boxes as quick as a flash and small boys and gulls vied for the discarded fish, and on the streets fishermen in their long white boots and blue jerseys clumped about like a picturesque species of amphibian, and the old men sat in the sun in St Andrew's Square and talked of the past.

CHAPTER 8

Changing Fortune

Pictures of old Newhaven give the impression of a village fixed like Brigadoon in a timeless dream. The reality was somewhat different for the spin of fortune's wheel that more than once brought Newhaven into national prominence and the description by Russell as the wealthiest fishing comunity on the Forth, on other occasions brought the pinch of poverty. But throughout the ups and downs fishing remained the principal preoccupation - even when smuggling proved a profitable diversion.

When Edinburgh gained possession of the village there were both east and west extensive grassy links sprinkled with flowers such as sea pinks, sea-holly and gilly flowers, all resistant to the wind-tossed spray, but the encroachment of the sea on the one hand, and the tide of building on the other, in the course of time swept these away. In 1573 Edinburgh received 30 merks for the use of Newhaven Links as grazing ground; 20 years later the city received one fifth of that sum owing it was said to the encroachment of the sea, though in 1615 there was still extensive grazing, for a minute of the Corporation notes the let to Alex Dick of pasturage of Wester Links Newhaven betwixt St Nicholas and Wardie Brae, but he was not to break the ground or cast feall (turf) or divot of the links or alter the marches. With nightsoil gathered from the streets of the village, orchards flourished and the sandy soil yielded crops of pease, though great flocks of geese did much damage.

When Newhaveners talked of the Links they meant the ground lying north of the Park between Annfield and the pier and on these links the boats were laid up as required though in gales they might be pulled up between the houses. Much later possession of the Links was transferred from the village to Leith Dock Commission who exacted a 10s rental 'for that ground where the big boats and yawls do lye.'

The links were the scene in the latter part of the 16th century of an abortive attempt at salt-panning. Most of the villages around the Forth had these salt-pans and smoke from the coal fires drifted along both shores. The pans were operated on a dreadful form of exploitation, almost of slave-labour by the salt masters who owned the pans. They paid the saltmakers no wages at all, but provided them with coal to heat the pans in return for which an agreed quantity of salt was given. If the labourers managed to produce a surplus of salt, which they usually did, they could sell it. These saltmakers who were described at the time as 'creatures of infinite poverty and miserableness, rather brutes than rationalls' were tied to their place of work and could if they ran away be brought back and punished. The master's salt was usually exported either to England or to Scandinavia and the Netherlands and roof tiles often brought back as ballast. The makers' salt was sold to cadgers and other poor

111

An early fishmarket on the pierhead before the new buildings were erected by the Leith Dock Commission.

people who carried it about in creels on horseback up and down the country, selling to fishermen to preserve their fish and landsmen to preserve their meat. About half of Scotland's salt came from the Forth pans about this time.

In 1567 a letter came from Mary Queen of Scots and her spouse James, Duke of Orkney, Earl Bothwell, bidding the Provost and Council of Edinburgh to let three London merchants, Cornelius de Wris, Anthony Hickman and John Achulay, have part of the common land at Newhaven for making salt for 50 years. The Council agreed to do so and the three set up salt pans 'for the making of Great Salt, together with biggins, house, stone, timber and dykes thereto'. The enterprise did not prosper - perhaps because it was unpopular with the fisherfolk? - and the town repossessed the land and biggings and sold it to Alexander Park, Dean of Guild. One suspects a certain degree of financial jookery-pookery for here is Park within months offering to sell it back to the magistrates on payment of £300 Scots to be paid within St Giles Church between sunrise and sunset on 12 days' warning. (The churches were often used as places for financial transactions). He must have got his £300, for Eustacchius Roche, a Fleming, who had previously been among other things a tax-collector and who had had several unsuccessful ventures in lead mining, came forward with a proposal to make a superior kind of salt by a new cheap process. He had the Royal authority for his venture, having promised to assign the Crown ninety percent of the profits, retaining only ten percent for himself. For

A fine catch of cod carpet the pierhead market in the 1880s while buyers haggle with salesmen.

a rent of £20 a year he was given the old salt pans 'and all the righteous perti-nents lying beSouth Newhaven' plus permission to build another eight to ten saltpans and as many furnaces as he fancied. In the same year (1588) the Council gave a tax of the lands and houses at Newhaven, formerly set to Englishmen, to a foreigner who is none other than our old friend, E. Roche: 'thinkis expedient, agreis and condescendis to sett to Ewstachius Roch, Flemyng, siclyk taks of the lands and howsis and rowmes at the Newhavin as wes sett to the Englishmen of befor, of the lyke yeiris and dewteis payand to the guid toun in the name of entres, the sowme of twenty-foure pund.' Once again the saltmaking foundered for writing in the next century Thomas Tucker reports that only ruins of the salt-works remain. It is probable that Roche was principally interested in the taxes he could extract from the village.

Another enterprise at Newhaven which had a chequered career was the ropewalk. The first one was established by James IV as part of his Royal doc-kyard to provide cables, warps and rigging for his ships. (The remains of this ropewalk - which was where the Peacock Inn now stands - were said to have survived until the middle of the 18th century). In 1626 Patrick Wood received permission to establish a ropery on the Links and built wooden houses for his employees. In a Latin manuscript of 1640 mention is made of the ropewalk at Newhaven. In 1668 a bailie of the Burgh of Canongate got a monopoly for all Scotland in ropemaking and took over the ropeworks from Patrick Wood. About 1688 James Deans, another bailie of Cannongate, took over the

The new fishmarket buildings gave a boost to the flagging fortunes of the village. The daily fish auction attracted buyers from all over Central Scotland (Courtesy of Mrs Greta Dyer).

ropewalk but it failed for want of encouragement. In 1692 his son Thomas endeavoured to restart it with the support of the City Council and this was more successful. In 1742 the factory was amalgamated with a Leith ropery and the Newhaven works closed in 1760 with the expiry of the lease.

These enterprises were all additional to the fishing and fish retailing which at this time brought considerable prosperity to the village. It must have been a place of some note for in 1681 Charles II raised to the Scottish peerage Charles Cheyne of Cogenho in Middlesex with the title of Viscount Newhaven. There is no evidence of what commerce Cheyne had with the village, though there has been a Cheyne family in Leith since the time of Robert the Bruce. The title became extinct in 1728.

The village had a modest reputation as a place for sea bathing even before the building of the Chain Pier (which was described as the finest bathing station in Scotland) and the 1st Statistical Account of 1793 refers to strangers having houses erected for holiday purposes. Many bathing machines were sited on the beach and one proprietor had the temerity to open for business on the Sabbath and was promptly fined by the Kirk Session. But Newhaven never achieved the reputation that Portobello enjoyed. In an article in the 'Scots Magazine' A.C. McKerracher describes a visit of Jules Verne to Portobello to view these bathing machines. He was surprised to find that the men were segregated some 50 yards from the women. Despite this avoidance of propinquity the effect must have been somewhat undone as the gentlemen walked quite naked into the sea, oblivious of the nearby ladies. Jules Verne and his friend with more modesty came out backwards to the great hilarity of the

Fisherwives were among the principal customers at the fishmarket, carrying their purchases in creels as far as Lanark and Falkirk. (Courtesy of George Liston).

female bystanders. Edinburgh's coast had quite a reputation for its seabathing, though some claimed that the climate in April and May tended to be damp and foggy due to an East wind. (But an 18th century survey of the number of days on which the open-air ropework at Newhaven could be operated compared with a similar enterprise at Greenock showed that Newhaven had 80 more days per annum of dry weather than the west coast port).

Ferry Terminal

A more successful venture and one which brought great prosperity and national prominence to Newhaven for nearly a century was its development as Scotland's largest and busiest ferry and packet station. Though Queensferry presented the shortest and safest sea-route to Fife, Newhaven had always served Edinburgh as a crossing point to the 'Kingdom'. A proclamation of 1715, directed at Newhaven by the Government, showed that the passage was not always used for approved purposes. The proclamation declared that the Government had been informed that certain fishermen, boatmen and others residing within Newhaven were carrying over in their boats to the other side of the Forth persons that were rebels or others obnoxious to the Government. The Water Bailie strictly forbade this and offered a reward of £40 for informers, with no names mentioned. The proclamation was to be broadcast by tuck of drum in the Main Street. In the '45 uprising there was less Jacobite support south of the Forth than there was in Fife and what ferrying there was of the Prince's men was done largely out of commercial considerations.

A later ordinance from the Water Bailie prohibited Sunday ferrying across the Forth. This title of Water Bailie was later replaced by that of Admiral, but the former title was perhaps the more appropriate, for the Admiral had no fleet or ship or even flag. His function was limited to exercising his local government powers in the court. The Lord Provost of Edinburgh stood over all as Admiral of the Firth, and the Provost of Leith was Admiral of the Port.

It was the passing of the Turnpike Act of 1751 which brought the Newhaven ferry service into prominence since it transformed the network of tracks meandering between settlements - muddy tracks fit for cattle or panniered ponies or rough sledges - into a road system which allowed the development of the stagecoach and opened up a communications web with Newhaven near its centre. Now it took only an hour to come down from Edinburgh by stage coach. There quickly developed regular ferries to Aberdour, four daily to Burntisland, four to Pettycur, and three daily to Kirkcaldy and Dysart. You could go either cabin or steerage, there being a saloon for first class passengers at 2s a trip as against 1s 6d for the deck, and stage coaches ran every day from Edinburgh to suit the arrival and departure of the different boats. A parcels company carried goods between the capital and Newhaven. As well as the bigger boats there were a dozen pinnaces vying for the trade and they would often try to tempt passengers off the bigger boats by offering a cheaper fare, which sometimes led to a free fight.

With the coming of steam to the Forth in 1812 - and it was in this part of Scotland that the world's first practical steamship the *Charlotte Dundas* was developed by Symington - there came a great increase in trade for Newhaven since the 'broad ferry' as contrasted with the Queensferry Passage now offered an attraction for trippers as well as travellers. The *Comet* was brought through from the Clyde in 1813 for a time, and Henry Bell ran a regular service to Stirling from the Chain Pier. The London and Edinburgh Steam Packet Company had sailings every Wednesday and Saturday and the UK Steamship Company had a London sailing every ten days. Voyages were often wearisome, 50 hours being reckoned a quick passage but they often took a week or considerably longer, the boats sometimes being driven to the coast of Holland.

Another company had steamers on the Newhaven to Aberdeen to Inverness to Orkney route. If you were in a special hurry there were two ocean greyhounds, the *Brilliant* and the *Velocity*, with 100 hp engines which left Newhaven every Monday, Wednesday and Saturday at 6 am for Aberdeen, calling en route off Elie, Anstruther, Arbroath and Stonehaven. The *Brilliant* went on to Inverness. All the mail from the North of Scotland came down through Fife by coach to Pettycur, thence by ferry to Newhaven and on again by coach to Edinburgh. In 1821 the *Scots Magazine* reported that a gentlemen had left Belfast on a Thursday, reached Glasgow the same evening, embarked on board the *Tourist* steamer at Newhaven on Friday and arrived at Aberdeen that night. It was commented that had this been reported 50 years earlier it would have been difficult to get people to believe it.

Many travellers have described their crossing of the Forth from Newhaven, not always in the most complimentary terms. Defoe writing in the early part of the 18th century said that the ferry passage to Burntisland was no less than seven miles; sometimes they met with bad weather and the passengers were so often frightened that he knew several gentlemen that would always choose to go round to the Queen's Ferry and he commented that he could well understand how it was said that there was never a Laird in Fife but once a year he would give his estate for his life.

Despite this, accidents were not all that frequent and the Burntisland magistrates boasted of 'not one of their great boates having drouned these hundred years'. The most spectacular disaster recorded was in July 1633 when Charles I crossed from Burntisland to Newhaven in 'grat jeopardy of his lyffe' and one of the boats accompanying him foundered through overcrowding and there perished 35 domestic servants. A large quantitiy of the King's silver and household goods went to the bottom in the foundered yawl (divers please note) and the chronicler foretold great trouble between the King and his subjects, a prophesy unfortunately fulfilled. The fare at this time was 1s for a man and his horse and for a single person one groat.

The Town Clerk of Edinburgh described how in 1814 he took one and a half hours to Kinghorn. But on his return a week later he managed the journey in a small pinnace in only 50 minutes, a very good passage. He noted that shortly afterwards a kind of cutter was introduced, a large open boat very like the Newhaven fishing boats but with two masts and sloop sails, not the square sails of the fishermen. The hinder part was seated round for passengers with a locker in the middle which served also for seating when required. About this time one of the ferries carried a musician who used to sing on board, accompanying himself on a small portable harmonium. He was a fine figure of a man though blind.

The Town Clerk (James Laurie, who claimed to have made the crossing 700 times) wrote: 'In or about 1821 I went to Kirkcaldy one Saturday for fun. There I met with a party of botanists one of whom was an old school fellow George Arnott, now professor of Botany at Glasgow. We dined together at Kirkcaldy and then rode to Pettycur and shipped back on board a cutter. It was calm when we sailed and so continued for some time but a gale came up and gave us a most tremendous tossing. I was sitting on the corner of the locker and Arnott was sitting facing me and every lurch the boat gave the sea lapped over us, striking me on the back of the head and Arnott in the face. We could not better ourselves for every seat was occupied all round and we were kept fully one hour in this most disagreeable predicament. The gale fell before we got across though we were driven considerably to the eastwards and we came quietly into Leith after a passage of two and a half hours. All the time of our trouble the skipper sat quietly and steadily at the helm as if there was nothing the matter and his men lay down in the forepart of the boat under shelter of the upraised windward side.

'Much about the same time one of these cutters the *Wemyss Castle* was upset in a squall and went to the bottom in the middle of the Forth. How many people were drowned I don't recollect.

'After that three small steam boats were provided for the ferry by the Ferry Trustees, hieing between Newhaven Burntisland and Kirkcaldy. Landing or shipping at these places was often disagreeable if not dangerous for when the tide was out the passengers were landed or shipped by means of small boats sometimes overcrowded and over very rough water and not seldom we were landed at Kirkcaldy on men's shoulders.'

Famous Inns

The ferry encouraged the development of several famous hostelries, one of the earlier ones being The Whale and it was from here that the *London Fly* would depart daily at two o'clock of a summer's morning, doing the journey in the remarkable time of four days. Another was the Boatie Row Tavern which held a licence continuously for over 200 years. About this time too, the famous Peacock Inn was established. Thomas Peacock, an Edinburgh vintner, attracted by the ferry traffic, petitioned the Council in 1767 for a feu of part of the links and some cottages and established the inn which quickly built up a reputation for its fish dinners which it holds to this day. The Peacock consisted originally of a few one-storey cottages with windows facing the sea front upon which in stormy weather the waves from the Forth made the living conditions uncomfortable. A hundred years later the redoubtable Mrs Clark added another building in Peacock's Court where were served 'Real and Original Clark's Newhaven Fish-Dinners'. Under its present proprietor, Peter Carnie, a Newhaven-born businessman with extensive other interests, it has been completely rebuilt and its reputation stands higher than ever. It has an unsurpassed collection of Newhaven mementos and pictures including nearly a hundred of the famous early Hill and Adamson calotypes.

At first the pier was only a slip to take the ferry pinnaces at various states of the tide but later to accommodate the steamboats the high bulwark on the Eastern side of the pier was built. It was at this latter pier Sir Walter Scott, just two months before his death at Abbotsford, landed on his return from Italy following a vain search for health.

There was considerable commercial traffic too from the new pier, not all of it welcome. Defoe had remarked on it during his tour of the kingdom and deplored it - the shipping out of large quantities of gunpowder. Just previous to his visit, he said, a storehouse of gunpowder had caught fire and exploded, wiping out a whole street of houses and causing many deaths. For many years thereafter trains of horse-drawn wagons loaded with gunpowder were brought to Newhaven, often standing for days in front of the houses awaiting shipment before the traffic was finally stopped.

So busy did the little port become that a Captain Sir Sam Brown of the Royal Navy had another pier built in 1821 by private enterprise, the Chain Pier, the cost being £4000. It was used for steam packets carrying passengers and their luggage between Newhaven and Stirling, Alloa, Grangemouth and

The Peacock Inn, famed since the 18th century for its fish dinners, continues to deserve its high reputation today.

Queensferry and was known rather dismissively by the locals as the baggage pier. It was hoped that George IV would land here on his visit to Edinburgh but Leith ruled otherwise. The pier passed to the Alloa Steam Packet Company in 1840 and about a decade later became a favourite resort for Edinburgh bathers, the charge being one penny for entry. A special train was run from Waverley at 6.15 in the morning to Newhaven for bathers. At the end of the pier was a gymnasium and it was a grand thing after trying to swim to the Newhaven stone pier 500 yards away and back to come up and swing on the parallel bars or try some other piece of equipment in the gym. During a great storm in October 1898 a great part of the structure was washed away leaving only the end and the shore approach. The wild weather drove three small ships ashore in the vicinity that night.

A journey from the Chain Pier when it was at its most fashionable saw, on a midsummer afternoon, a little group of fashionable ladies and their beaux join the stray dogs and small boys on the Pier to witness the departure of the paddle-steamers *Victoria* and *Ben Lomond* for Stirling. While the ladies stole glances under their parasols at the desperate-looking pilot of the *Victoria* their gentlemen standing boldly close to the edge, spoke knowingly of the faster lines of the *Ben Lomond*, which they freely wagered would be first to Stirling.

Then with a shout and a bustle and much waving of hankies both ships were off. The *Ben Lomond* had a dozen lusty performers by way of a band while the *Victoria* had but a flageolet and drum, though three small boys standing on a box over the wheel helped to swell the din in the *Victoria's* favour. Occasionally in the upper river the vessels were abreast and their paddle-boxes touching, so narrow was the dredged channel, then the *Ben Lomond* would forge ahead. When this happened the flageolet and drum would be refreshed and encouraged with ale while the pilot of the *Victoria* was cheered on to fresh endeavour by the passengers. Then came the big moment. The *Ben Lomond* was slightly ahead as a sharp bend in the river was approached but the *Victoria*, having the inside berth, managed to close and then, with a sharp swing of the helm she collided which had the intended effect of driving the *Ben Lomond* on to the bank and the next moment the *Victoria* was by herself proceeding full steam ahead for Stirling.

At last the ferry trade outgrew the inadequate facilities at Newhaven and the building by the Duke of Buccleuch of magnificent new docks and piers at Granton, brought gradual decline once more to the village. It is natural in simple communities that there should be between neighbouring villages a degree of antipathy but the Newhaveners' dislike of 'Godless Granton' had in it the added spice of justification for once more the village declined into a simple fishing community.

The Fishmarket

But again fortune sought out Newhaven. In a pamphlet on *How to prevent further decay and again resuscitate the ancient village of Newhaven* printed in 1870, Dempster, The Ancient Mariner, wrote: 'How has the mighty fallen might be exclaimed of this one-time rising and prosperous fishing village.' He told how once all the fishing ports of the Forth had brought their catches to Newhaven that the local fishwives might sell them to the surrounding countryside. 'The whole field, both in city, town and for miles around was theirs. Newhaven at that period not only rose in importance as a thriving village but its community managed to live both cheerfully, comfortably and luxuriously.' But the coming of the railway and the steamboats reduced its fortunes by giving other fishing villages the opportunity to send their catches further afield to more profitable markets.'

The population of Newhaven, he wrote, was nearly 2500, the greater number being members of the fishing community. Several families were becoming so poor and impoverished from the great scarcity of oysters together with the loss of the retail trade which had been a source of enjoyable employment which brought wealth and comfort in its train, that the previous winter a subscription had had to be raised to purchase coal for them. The *Scotsman* had stated that 32½ tons of coal had been distributed among 71 families of the poor of Newhaven. His solution: Erect a wholesale fish market at Newhaven at the waterside. Fish could be sent by rail to this market which might develop into a Scottish Billingsgate. Such a wholesale fishmarketing system would encourage capitalists to build large decked vessels for all-weather deep-sea fishing and by this means he believed the Newhaven men might bring in £100,-000 worth of fish a year.

The Ancient Mariner, Henry Dempster, was a true original and although not a native of Newhaven he lived there for many years. He had always been fascinated by boats and as a boy was frequently climbing about the riggings of vessels in the harbour or dancing about on the roofs of houses, sometimes standing on his head. He became a pilot in China and India but gave that up to pursue his inventions which ranged from an aromatic smoking filter for pipe-smokers, through a new kind of sailing ship appropriately named *The Problem* (which sank) to fishing boats with great tanks for holds, so that the fish might be kept alive, and much else. Alas he died in the North Leith Poorshouse. He was very much against 'creel-hawking' as he called the fishwife trade, and a great proponent of the fishmarket.

There had long been a fishmarket at Newhaven, but it was a small village affair, with fish laid out on the harbour stones, a cheerful babble of voices between auctioneers and customers and the gigs of customers, patient donkeys trembling between the shafts, standing by. Even earlier, in the 15th and 16th centuries, the main market had been at Edinburgh just beyond the Tron, down towards Holyrood, where a great balance for weighing goods was kept. It is recorded that a fishwife who gave short measure was condemned by the Magistrates to stand in the market there with a string of herring around her neck and a notice of her offence pinned on her chest. And when Kirkcaldy of Grange, the Captain of Edinburgh Castle, bombarded the High Street in the cause of Mary Queen of Scots, a canonball landed smack in the middle of the fishmarket, scattering the crowd. Shoals of fish were blown sky-high, ending on surrounding roof-tops and people flocked from nearby houses to seize the rest while confusion lasted. Another canonball landed among them leaving five dead and about 20 badly wounded.

Regularly a boat's crew would bypass the market and take their catch to the Shore at Leith which in the 19th century had a vivid and colourful life all its own. R L S. used this to effect in *Treasure Island*. Ex-soldiers and naval men in bucket stirrups and tarpaulin coats sat in drinking dens eking out an existence telling tall tales of dangers past or press gangs dodged. There were dance halls and dens of vice under water level between Burgess Street and the Signal Tower where smuggled liquor was cheap and brawls were frequent. Through the crowded street wandered a band of Italian bear trainers playing bagpipes, a solitary juggler, a wild sailor called the Dog Robber, half seas over and trying to dance with the bear then pricking the bagpipes with a concealed knife, causing a riot as he went down cursing under a charge of enraged Italians. And looking on an Irish fiddler who had a handy knack of defending himself in a brawl by using his fiddle as a club. The arrival of the Newhaven fishboats was signalled by the Burgh Bellman going from street to street and folk with pails bags and baskets would scramble for bargains. Among the crowd was Big Meg Stuart at whose shop opposite you could buy a cod for 6d or a bucket of sprats for 3 d. The Bellman had a donkey cart and he and his wife would buy up a load of fish and take it round the lanes. In an argument his wife would make her point by walloping him over the face with a haddock. Another peculiar feature of the waterfront about this time was a band called the Fogey Haulers, a class of men who made their living by hauling small smacks and clippers in and out of Leith harbour with ropes. They had a harness and worked five or six in a line, straining at the rope for all they were worth. They had their headquarters in one of the pubs on the Shore. They added to their livelihood by harbour searching for coal dropped from the quays and were often to be seen in long boots, deep in the mud retrieving the coal.

More than two decades went past and the Ancient Mariner had sailed on his last voyage before his scheme for a fishmarket came to fruition. An area of ground to the East of the pier was filled in and on it on 5th December 1896 Leith Dock Commission formally opened the fishmarket. The ceremony was performed by Mr James Currie, owner of the Currie Shipping Line in the presence of a large crowd after which the sale of fish went ahead and the notables retired to the Marine Hotel for breakfast. The market was an immediate success and inaugurated a further era of prosperity for the village for it attracted the trawlers and all the ancillary industry of servicing them. The market was described as a fine wide place open to the sea with sliding doors and alive with business-like yells of 'Here you are now, bring your money' and of white-coated salesmen intoning to the crowd of buyers: 'twenty-forty-sixty-eighty...' while the fish, packed tight in their boxes stared glassy-eyed and impassive at the roof. Five or six hundred buyers would be there and about a third of them Italian chippies. The fish came from all over - Kinlochbervie, Wick, Eyemouth, Seahouses and sometimes North Shields.

CHAPTER 9

Caller Ou frae the Forth

Boswell would have got a dusty answer if he had offered his learned friend a dish of the famous Newhaven oysters during their Edinburgh sojourn. But he might have got a quotable quote because Dr. Johnson detested oysters. He once compared them to children's ears in sawdust.

But the good Doctor was very much in a minority. A couple of centuries ago oysters were big business. Thirty million oysters a year were dredged up from the Forth alone by local fishermen, the bulk being sent out by sea to London or Holland.

They had always been a staple food of the poor. Sam Weller said: 'Ven a man's werry poor he rushes out of his lodgings and eats oysters in reglar despration.' Now they had become fashionable too and the well-to-do would rub shoulders with the lower orders in candle-lit taverns where the centre-piece on the board was a great bowl of raw oysters in their own juices, accompanied by jugs of porter to sustain a night of singing and dancing. After the eight-hours bell sounded in Edinburgh's shadowed High Street and lamplight formed pools in the caverned closes, the fisher lasses' street cry, 'Caller ou-ooh', its haunting upward lilt like the first notes of a song, would tempt the homeward bound quality to stop and exchange with the sparky fishwife some snell repartee and small silver for half a dozen Natives in their shells, freshly prised open and dashed with salt and pepper and breathing of the sea.

Caller, Scots for fresh and moist, suggesting the newly gathered fruits of the sea, and 'ou' for 'ousters' as Newhaven folk sounded it, inspired Ferguson to a long poem in their praises:

> September's merry month is near
> That brings in Neptune's caller cheer
> New oysters fresh
> The halesomest and nicest gear
> Of fish or flesh
>
> When big as burns the gutters rin
> If ye hae catch'd a droukit skin
> To Luckie Middlemist's lou in
> And sit fu' smug
> Owre oysters and a dram o' gin
> Or haddock lug
>
> When auld Saint Giles at aucht o'clock
> Gars merchant loons their shoppies lock
> There we adjourn wi' hearty fouk
> To birle our bodles
> And get warewi to crack our joke
> And clear our noddles.

125

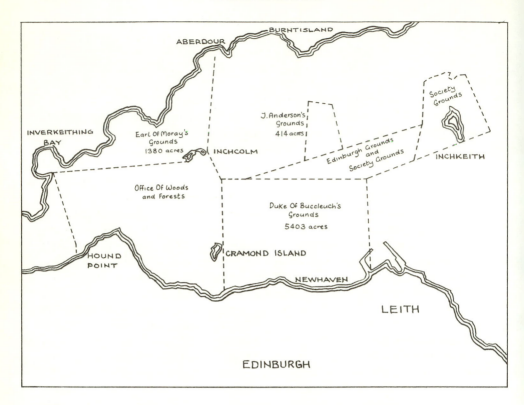

The oyster beds of the Forth off Newhaven, which in their best years yielded a harvest of thirty million oysters a year, most of which were exported to London and Holland.

Newhaven had for long a monopoly of the best sources of this caller cheer in the green scalps on the breast of Inchkeith and the Beacon grounds lying off the Black Rocks which they claimed through charters from James VI and Charles I. Keeping the unmarked boundaries of that monopoly against neighbouring villages of Prestonpans, Fisherrow and Cockenzie, who had the adjoining fishings, involved sea battles over the centuries. There was a constant tally of black eyes, dinged ears, duckings and the frequent capture of a boat and the crew, who after a good meal were sent to walk home. A letter dated 1774 from Sir Walter Scott's father, requested the return to Fisherrow of seized dredges, 'and oblige your humbel servant, Walter Scott, W.S.'

Robin Black in the *Short History of the Free Fishermen's Society of Newhaven* says the trouble reached a peak in 1788 when 24 Fisherrow boats invaded the scalps and there was a battle royal with the local fishers resulting in the capture of two Newhaven boats which were towed away to Burntisland. But the Newhaven men using the night for cover rowed over the water, slipped into the harbour and towed them back again. As a result of this continual off-shore sparring the High Court of Admiralty in 1791 conducted an inquiry into the ownership and control of the oyster scalps in the Forth. The result was greatly gratifying to the Society because the Judge supported the traditional belief that though they didn't own them, they had the exclusive right to dredge the City scalps, a privilege conveyed on them by James IV.

That judgment brought peace for 20 years but then war broke out afresh. A Society minute of 1812 noted: 'Took 12 boats belonging to Prestonpans and Cockenzie in the Westward of the Island of Inchkeith and put them to shore as they were trespassing on the City oyster bank. October - took three boats belonging to Fisherrow and also three boats belonging to Cockenzie and Prestonpans. This day several of the Society were much hurt at the capturing of these boats.' The crews were detained in Newhaven for several days at a time and were always kindly treated and well fed before being sent home. Usually a court case would follow which sometimes resulted in imprisonment. Sometimes the City would help to police the scalps by sending down Magistrates to board a tug with members of the Society in chase of the poachers, and when this happened the invading fleet would turn and flee. On one occasion, relates Robin Black, one Fisherrow boat wasn't fast enough and was captured and taken in tow. The rope was cut but men from the tug jumped into the water with a chain which they made fast to their capture, although its crew strove to beat them off with sticks, clubs and fists. The skipper of the offending boat got 60 days' imprisonment.

Though the struggle was in earnest there was less of malice than of boisterous bravado. The admirable James Wilson, whose selfless work for the village as Secretary and Boxmaster of the Society was only later recognised, records that on one occasion 'the 'Pans fishermen collected all the fishermen, carters, workers in the saltpans and other men in the towns of the South Bay and came west right off Newhaven in Leith Roads, well armed and all ready for war. I cannot say the number that were gathered together but there was a great number. I believe there was not a boat belonging to all the towns in the bay that was left behind.' It can be imagined what consternation this armada must have caused in Newhaven, but it appears to have been all a great show-off for after sporting themselves for a time they all went home. The last clash in this forty-year war ocurred in 1856 when after several days of poaching by a 'Pans fleet, the Society hired a tug and captured one of the boats. The Pans crew, after being refreshed with meat and drink were handed over to the law, but some friends bailed them out and they slipped down to Newhaven and made off with their boat in the night. 'This case,' said Mr Wilson, 'was the last and now at this present time there is peace and goodwill and agreeableness between the Newhaven fishermen and the fishermen dwelling in the different towns in the South Bay of the Firth of Forth.'

The City Scalps

Legal fights with Edinburgh and other proprietors who claimed ownership of the scalps or beds around Inchkeith were on the other hand bitter, protracted, humourless and expensive, upwards of two thousand guineas chinking into the pockets of the legal fraternity from the coffers of the Society during the 19th century. The devoted disinterested work of the Society in this fight is well told in its official history.

Edinburgh based its case mainly on a series of Royal charters, from Bruce onwards, the principal one being granted by James IV. From then on, once a year, the Magistrates and Councillors drove down to the Parliament Square at Newhaven and there they drank their claret before being rowed with a good deal of pomp and ceremony out over the water to inspect, as best they could, their property on the sea bed full fathoms five below, except, of course when a North wind blew, returning no doubt to a celebrated fish tea at the Peacock or some earlier local hostelry.

But for nearly 300 years, apart from passing a stream of regulations relating to the scalps between 1663 and 1697, and a subsequent spate between 1742 and 1790 defining the close season and the size of oysters that might be taken, but generally aimed at procuring supplies of the best oysters for the Edinburgh market, they left the fishermen to their own devices in maintaining and cherishing the scalps, the whole cost of this farming falling on the fishermen. Being long accustomed to this loose rein and as free men whose ancestors had from time immemorial worked the scalps, the Newhaven men came to believe that Edinburgh's claims were false and that they alone had the right to the dredging.

This belief was reinforced by the ruling of the High Court of Admiralty in 1794. Oysters by now were at the height of their popularity and Edinburgh realised that the scalps had become valuable property. The Judge Admiral ruled, as was said, that though Edinburgh had exclusive property in the scalps, yet this ownership could only be exercised through the Society.

But a man convinced against his will is of the same opinion still, and Edinburgh never accepted the ruling as the end of the story. There must be a way in which they could benefit from this source of wealth on their doorstep.

So it was a great shock to the Society when without warning in 1815 Edinburgh demanded an annual rental and thereafter continued to jack this up yearly. It seemed to the Society that court or no court, the Corporation was showing a strong desire to put the Society off the scalps altogether. 'Why they should seek to do so,' says Robin Black, 'is difficult to understand, because their charter of overlordship specifically charged them with maintaining 'all the rights and privileges of the folk of Newhaven'.'

The Society now were guilty of an error in tactics which was to cost them dear - they allowed Edinburgh to see the full riches which might be exploited: The year 1834 saw a glut of oysters far beyond the capacity of the local market to absorb so the Society asked the Council if they might export some of this surplus to England. The Council agreed and 24 cargoes of excellent oysters were quickly despatched, the number of barrels in these cargoes amounting to 14,075, each barrel containing about 1400 oysters at 7s a barrel. After all costs this left a surplus in the village of nearly £5000, a truly astonishing sum.

'An Oyster Cellar in Leith' by John Burnett, F.R.S.

There can be no doubt that this bonanza resulted in the bombshell decision of 1839 when the renewal of the Society's lease was refused and the City awarded the fishing to an Englishman, George Clark, on a 10-year lease at the colossal sum of £600 a year.

There was a great outcry but the City remained obdurate. The City justified their decision by saying that the Newhaven men weren't looking after the scalps properly. It served their interests poorly however, for Clark began a plunder on a grand scale. He brought up 70 dredging boats from Essex which dredged from morning till night and shipped big cargoes of oysters of all sizes down south, leaving Edinburgh with almost none. He refused to pay any rent, and sued the Corporation because they couldn't keep the Newhaven men from continuing to fish the scalps which they did very effectively, selling large cargoes to Clark's English rivals, and though he employed a tug to patrol the grounds, the fishermen had their own spy system to warn of its approach and they were never caught.

His ruthlessness and Edinburgh's greed having begun the rot that finally destroyed the industry, and having banged all the heads together, Clark after a single season disappeared from whence he came. The City ruefully admitted that 'Since entering upon his lease Mr Clark dredged for oysters to such an extent and in such a manner that the scalps would soon have been left unproductive while meantime the Edinburgh market was inadequately supplied.' The Corporation and the Society decided to patch up their quarrel.

This they did through the Court of Session which reaffirmed Edinburgh's vested rights but continued: 'These rights have always been exercised in the manner most beneficial to the public, the oyster beds having been protected and cultivated by the Society, preserving the spawn or seed of the oysters and by limiting the extent of fishing of each man to 600 oysters per day.' The City, despite the rents it gathered could not be said to have helped in that conservation.

After that there was relative peace for more than 20 years but legal warfare broke out again in the late 60s with further assertions by Edinburgh that the Newhaven men were despoiling the fishing. Both local ministers rushed to the defence of their parishioners. Dr. Fairbairn of St Andrew's Free Church wrote: 'The men generally have fished in a proper fashion. If some went wrong it was a deficient gauge which was given to them. They know how to keep their ain sea maws and are too wise to kill the goose that lays the golden eggs. The Society's office bearers are intelligent men and fully apprised of the right method of fishing. The affair affects the interests of the 300 families in the community.'

He continued: 'I now see how the City has been brought to the belief that the Newhaven men destroy the young oysters. It was stated by the Granton Pier Master and his subordinates that they frequently saw lying on the Granton beach young oysters the size of 4d and 6d. No doubt they did. But what is the explanation? These were parasite oysters stuck so closely there is no breaking them off.'

Edinburgh determined on a major legal onslaught on the Society's rights and to 'reduce, retreat, rescind and annul' all previous agreements. This time they succeeded and the Society were at last reduced to the role of tenants. But it was a Pyrrhic victory for the grounds were now approaching exhaustion.

The Duke's Scalps

If the struggle with Edinburgh was a cause of bitter worry, the simultaneous fight to retain the fishing on the Duke of Buccleuch's scalps on Newhaven's doorstep, between the village and Queensferry, was characterised by moments of high drama punctuated by hilarity. The right to fish these scalps off Granton was first awarded to the Society in 1572 but permission seems to have been intermittently granted and withdrawn over a period of a couple of hundred years. But in 1788 it was granted to Newhaven men and it remained generally with them until 1867 when on calling one day to pay the annual ground rent the Society's officials were told that the scalps had been let to James Anderson, an Edinburgh fishmonger, for a period of 15 years.

Outraged, the Newhaven men resorted to open poaching. Anderson hired a cutter and tried to chase them off the grounds but as of one accord the boats turned on the cutter, there was a tussle and the cutter men retired hurt to Granton harbour.

But one day as they were at their dredging the Newhaven men were surprised to see a steam tug with Anderson and the police aboard bearing down on them. Overwhelmed by the approach of this Gilbertian apparition, they decided on flight, buoying their dredges and abandoning them, then pulling hard for the shore. The tug singled out one of the boats as prey and steamed purposefully to cut it off. 'Then,' said Mr Wilson, 'one big boat and a yawl from Newhaven, both well-manned, went off to the rescue. All the other boats turned to support this effort and when the party on the tug saw the menacing approach of the whole fleet they hurried back to the safety of Granton harbour. Elated by their success, the fishermen went west to Mickery and ordered all the English who were fishing for Anderson to clear out and get off to Granton.

The Newhaven men openly fished the scalps next day but as they came ashore a cabman told them there were detectives among the crowd at the pier and pointed them out. A group of women standing near the pier overheard him and ran off, banging on doors and windows for reinforcements. Then while the men debated what action to take, the women rushed to the pier and, Mr Wilson says, knocked down a detective who ran for shelter in a house. 'But he was dragged out and went away with a sack of sore bones.' Another detective was chased up the street by the women 'and what he got he knew best himself.' The third pretended he wasn't there but just as he thought he had pulled it off, his hat was jammed down over his eyes and down he went. He picked himself up and ran off pursued by a mob of women and children. 'There was no more of them that day,' said Mr Wilson. But four days later Anderson's men were back on the scalps, this time guarded by a gunboat! Not being able to trump that ace, the Newhaven men cried quits for the time being.

The newspapers had got hold of the story and published embroidered accounts of what had happened, accusing the Newhaven men of being pirates and hoisting the black flag. The fishermen explained that the flags used for their lines were all black and that when boats went out one of these flags was hoisted. But the chatter about pirates persisted and, said Mr Wilson, 'it was some time before the Black Flag was done.'

The Duke had shown some concern for the livelihood of the Newhaven men and had made it a condition of Anderson's lease that he should employ them to dredge for him. He circumvented this requirement by offering the Newhaven men ls 6d per hundred to dredge for him while offering other fishers 3s. In this ploy he attempted to involve Dr. Graham, writing to him: 'It is His Grace's desire that all the fishermen of Newhaven be employed to cultivate and improve the ground and I am prepared to offer them a fair remuneration for their work and give every man and boy full employment and you may rest assured that they will find in me a True Friend to themselves and I am confident that they have in the Duke of Buccleuch as firm a friend as ever they had. I will be most happy to wait on you and explain my intentions towards the men.

Meantime I regret to learn that although I have warned them, several boats were seen upon the ground today dredging. I have secured the names of every man and boat and should they persist I shall have no alternative left but to allow the officers to apprehend them.' A further letter said he had told the Duke what he had written and was now requested to say that ONLY all those crews that agreed to assist him in improving the ground THIS SEASON would be allowed to dredge on it in after years and it would depend entirely on the future conduct of the fishermen towards him as to the date of His Grace allowing them to have the grounds again under their control.

He found no takers for the Newhaveners told the Duke: 'We are all free fishers, not servants of your tenant. His object is to agrandise himself by securing a monopoly of oyster scalps in the Forth. We planted the seed beds which he is now ravishing. We and our ancestors have been cultivators of oysters all our lives and fully understand the mode of cultivating and improving the scalps and are better acquainted with these methods than other men.' Anderson, they said, was using steam-driven iron dredges weighing 60 lbs whereas the Newhaven men's wooden dredges weighed less than half of that. It was all the difference between using a harrow which properly steered and planted the seeds and a heavy plough which uprooted and buried. Anderson they said, was working from Monday morning till Saturday night turning up the subsoil as if it were the bowels of the earth hauling as many as six dredges to a boat. The soil would not bear a heavy weight on it; for example when an anchor was cast on the scalps and uplifted, a dredge coming upon the upturned soil brought up nothing but sand and mud. If his Grace had had in mind to destroy and ruin the scalps he could not have found a more effectual way.

Public opinion did not support them. Anderson was an effective propagandist in his own cause and constantly wrote to the papers presenting his case. Anonymous letters were received alleging the fishermen were taking immature oysters. It was generally felt the Newhaven men had been on to a good thing for long enough. The *North Briton* (organ for the Duke) said primly: 'We cannot shut our eyes to the fact that they have not in times past made the most of the splendid bargain they enjoyed and they have been outbidden by more enterprising men.'

These more enterprising men would ruin the scalps by overfishing, said the fishermen. Their words proved prophetic for within less than 30 years the Duke's beds were a desert. Clark too had left a similar record of reckless damage on the City beds which led to their decline and exhaustion. The International Fisheries Exhibition in Edinburgh in 1882 had exhibits in the oyster section from France and England but none from Scotland. As late as 1897 the question of restocking was seriously considered but nothing came of it. Another blow came during the Great War when gunboats were anchored over them and ash from their boilers effectively smothering most of the remaining scalps.

The Society's records carry the story of the fishings back as far as the 16th century. But long long before that there were fisherfolk camped on the shore in turf huts working the scalps and line-fishing the cod and haddock. Perhaps among their early customers were the Romans who had built a road as far as Cramond and who were known to have sent oysters back from Britain to Rome in wooden tubs packed with snow. By the beginning of the 16th century when the little enclave was given a name by James IV there was a colony of fishers and James is recorded as sometimes spending the day with the oyster dredgers, gathered at the Whale Brae or out on the water as they rowed for ten hours at a time over the scalps, towing their heavy wooden rakes and singing their interminable songs which gave tempo and ease to the work of the oars. As the boats had to move steadily while the dredge was pulled along the seabed at the end of the towrope at a constant angle of 35 degrees, the best way to keep the oars steady and the rope taut was to set the rhythm to a song. David Herd, 17th century accountant and song collector, said it would appear the fishermen sang to the oysters to charm them into the net. The Second Statistical Account noted: 'Long before dawn in the blackest season of the year their dredging song may be heard afar off and except when the weather is very turbulent their music appears to be an accompaniment to labours which are by no means unsuccessful.'

These songs were different from other more literary songs of the Scottish Lowlands. They were not polished verse but were mostly improvised as sung and forgotten as quickly. Charles Reade in *Christie Johnstone*, says: 'The song in itself does not tend to above 70 stock verses but these are the nucleus round which the men improvise the topics of the day giving preference to such as fringe on the indelicate.' A few verses sung afterwards around the fire to amuse the bairns have been preserved as children's street songs:

> Katie Bairdie had a coo
> Black and white aboot the mou'
> Wasn't that a dainty coo?
> Dance Katie Bairdie

Scott in 'The Antiquary' recalls a more literary song:

> The herring loves the merry moonlight
> The mackerel loves the wind
> But the oyster loves the dredging song
> For they come off a gentle kind

The fishermen believed 'they winna tak unless ye sing' and so they charmed them into the net, expelling the sound in a kind of musical ejaculation as they rowed:

> I rade to London yesterday
> On a cruket hay-cock
> Hay-cock, quo' the seale to the eel,
> Cock nae I my tail weel?
> Tail weel, or if hare
> Hunt the dog frae the deer
> Hunt the dog frae the deil-drum -
> Kend ye nae John Young?

> Willie Tod, Willie Tay,
> Cleckit in the month of May
> Month of May and Averile
> Good skill o' reasons,
> Tentlins and fentlins.
> Yeery, ory, alie!
> Weel row'd five men,
> As weel your ten.
> Come buy my oysters aff the bing,
> To serve a shireif or a king,
> And the commons o' the land,
> And the commons o' the sea
> Hey benedicete and that's good Latin.
>
> There's an auld carle sits by the sea
> Wi' a white caun'le on his knee
> Says you're ane and I'm fower
> Were ye ever at Aberdour?
> Aberdour's a bonny place
> Peer lees upon the green
> Quo' the haddock to the eel
> Crook ye yer tail weel

Or this variation:

> Says you've a Chevy I've a Chase
> I've a bonny blue gless
> I've a dog amang the corn
> Blawin' Willie Buck's horn
> Willie Buck has a coo,
> Black and white aboot the mou'
> They ca' her Bellavintie
> And she lept ower the Brig o' Dee
> Like any Covenantie
>
> Hay hoo, Hairy Hairy
> Mony a boat sailed the Ferry
> Mony a boat, mony a ship
> Tell me a true note
> True note, true song
> I've dredged ower long

As the boats were within sight of the womenfolk they sang:

> Meg and Mag and Jess and Jane
> Oh, how they leugh when we get fish
> But how they girn when we get nane!
> See them waitin' on the green
> Gin we dinnae try we shall be seen.

An old oysterman recalled long afterwards: 'There were four of us in the boat and we were away in the morning wi' daylight comin' in on a winter day. We went east four or five hails (hauls) wi' the oars then workit back. That's if it was a fine day. But if it was sail, there was nae singing except maybe an auld man singing to himsel'. We'd come back with thiry or forty baskets o' clams.'

Out there at the height of the season which ran from September to April might be up to 90 boats, each on its allotted beat and kept on station by observed landmarks:

Fleming's Ink Works til the gas works
Dredge ye weel and fill yer creel

And fill their creels they did. It was not unknown for a boat to dredge 9000 in a day. Yet it was not the harvesting of the largest but the very smallest that was detrimental. The very method of fishing, particularly by the later commercial exploiters, brought up large quantities of seedlings adhering to the mature shells. The London merchants offered fancy prices for these seedlings which they fattened in artificial beds down south. At Billingsgate, moored along the wharf known to costermongers as Oyster Street, were the cluster of smacks, a forest of masts and tangled vines of rigging, their decks thronged with men and women presided over by salesmen in white aprons, their holds piled high with oysters which men with shovels loaded into peck measures and emptied into sacks, the finest of oysters. Yet many owed their origin to the beds of the Forth. Transplanted and fed for years in the artificial beds on the Thames, then scrubbed and burnished, these polished aristocrats commanded twice the price of their rude northern cousins.

The price of oysters has fluctuated widely over the centuries. In Ancient Rome they were weighed against gold. In the thirteenth century they were a ha'penny a hundred, a day's pay for a labourer. Towards the end of the 18th century schoolboys would buy a dozen for a ha'penny for their lunch, and barter a kiss with the fishergirl for the thirteenth. By the 1830s when there was a glut they were selling at 6d a bowl and the price often included the bowl. English merchants now appeared at Newhaven and took away several full cargoes of the surplus at 7s a barrel. But next year they would offer only 5s, arguing that they had lost many dead the previous year. They took away 14,000 barrels worth £3,500. And the year after when they came back they complained again about their losses and offered only 4s. The fishermen protested they were being cheated, but the merchants would not yield. In despair the Society tried to control the supply by imposing a limit of 400 per man but some fishermen refused to fall into line. Yet even self-interest yielded in the end and a Union was formed by the Society which brought order out of anarchy. When the English merchants came back again they were chagrined to be met by a united front and prices rose to as much as 43s a 1000 for large oysters. The highest price ever reached was £1 per 100. From the profits the Society was presented with four new flags, ten flag poles, 12 log batons for use in processions and the model boats 'were gilded and got wooden men in them with masts and oars all at a cost of £8 8s 6d.'

Sailing before the wind for hundreds of years the folk of Newhaven, self-centred and self-contained, enjoyed a comparative comfort and continuity of life and work that was the envy of their neighbours. They owned their houses, their gear, their boats, their freedom. Why then is there today a desert where the scalps were? A museum where there was a village? A harbour empty of workboats? A church whose bells once inspired the music to *Caller Herring* now silent? A people who for half a thousand years kept to the confines of their own parish now scattered abroad?

It would be easy to blame the over-exploitation on the City fathers and the Duke of Buccleuch but that would be only part of the story. The European flat oyster whose fecundity would cover the seabeds of the world in a couple of generations if its spat were unchecked, has a legion of eager foes. It has been estimated that only one seed in more than a million survives, what with shrimps lying under the parent shell waiting for the ovulation and fish gobbling them up in the free-floating stage. And when the spat does attach itself to a rock, a bit of seabed rubbish, the back of an indignant crab or more usually another oyster, it becomes prey to a fiendish queue of itinerant appetites. There's the scuttling crab with a pebble in his claw, ready to pop it into the parted shell so he can get in there to feed, the boring worm that mines his way through the shell, the mussel that builds his town on top of the oyster, suffocating him in the basement. But more sinister is the starfish, that by unrelenting strength over a period of several hours, wrenches open the shell of the weakened oyster, inserts his own stomach into the parted shell and digests his meal at leisure.

Starfish can be kept in check by drawing over the beds a string of mops in which they become entangled. The spat can be given a sure anchor by returning spent shells to the seabed and undersized oysters can be returned to the deep. And most effectively the beds can be rested when they show signs of being overfished. All of this good housekeeping the fishermen practised over hundreds of years and kept everything in balance. Their Lordships of the Admiralty Court said so. No one else kept the beds in good order, cared for the seedlings and guarded the scalps from hurt. Not that the fishermen were entirely blameless but their exceses were modest compared to those of the hard-headed men of business who in the 19th century took over the harvesting of the beds for a quick return.

But Anderson and Clark and to a lesser extent the fishermen themselves were only instruments of an inevitable process for as with hunting economies generally, the demand finally overtook the supply. The Forth, though the largest, was only one of many British oyster centres which during the 19th century failed.

The Times in 1868 carried a leader on the subject: 'From Prehistoric Man to August 1868 is a long stretch of time - from July to eternity the Americans are wont to say when they speak of such intervals. And what has been done in that period? Why all the oysters in our seas have been eaten up. There are no longer as good fish in the sea as ever came out of it. The oysters are gone and no wonder. About five weeks ago in the excavation of a salt marsh on our southern coast there was discovered a skeleton of a man buried in the fashion indicating the highest possible antiquity with a thick layer of oyster shells all around him. Whether he had killed himself with oysters like King John with peaches and new ale, whether he was renowned like Dando for oyster eating above his fellows or whether he had been smothered at his own request in the food he liked best nobody can say. But this much is plain that races as old as Lucustrian Man ate oysters as fast as we do. That was the beginning of the consumption. It ended in 1864 when 700 million oysters were devoured in London alone and the result is that oysters are now 3d apiece and hardly to be got on those terms. The fact is that the wild oyster is pretty well as rare as the wild horse. It was a bold man who first ate an oyster. It will soon be a lucky man who can follow his lead.'

Not everyone accepts that over-fishing ruined the scalps. Tom Hall, a Newhavener who after being a naval officer, captain of a minesweeper and trawler skipper, was captain of the Forth River Purification Board's ship *Forth Ranger* for many years, has made a long study of the subject.

In a letter to *The Scotsman* in 1970 he gave another cause: 'To someone walking on the seafront or sailing the Lothians shoreline the sight of large expanses of water and beaches polluted with the more buoyant outpourings of Edinburgh's 15 sewer outfalls, may be distressing enough, but the filth that the casual onlooker observes is only one aspect of the long-term destruction which escalates daily to the point of no-return.

'In a supposedly unenlightened age the law at least required that Edinburgh citizens cry 'Gardyloo' before ejecting household wastes to the world at large. In 1970 Edinburgh, despite her cultural pretensions, ejects her entire untreated sewage to her adjacent and vulnerable shoreline. No one cries 'Gardyloo'. The once-prolific fauna and fish life of the Lothians shores are incapable of verbal protest and can only give notice of awareness of its presence by involuntary extinction.

'In the past before pollution we had an area from Cramond eastwards to Gullane Point fed by three rivers, heavily oxygenated and rich in nutrients ...which gave rise to the huge oyster beds that over a century ago almost entirely covered the area, oyster beds which were among the richest in Europe.'

'There are no oysters in the Forth now. Some apologists blame over-fishing but this is not so. The fishermen farmed the oysters, taking no more than the natural yield, pruning and transplanting. In any case no fisherman will fish below an economic level of return and in a healthy environment the process of recovery sets in once this level is reached... Our one-time ecological affluence is now submerged in effluence.'

Anderson, a century earlier, in the midst of his commercial excesses foresaw the total depletion of the Forth. 'Do you think the ova of various fish could be hatched in Granton Quarry?' he wrote to the Society. 'The ova could be obtained from various steam trawlers from fish quite ripe on the trawl. I am of the opinion millions could be hatched of various kinds and preserved until able to protect themselves and then allowed to escape. During summer tons of herring ova could be got from the boats now being sold to farmers for manure, and sent to the quarry and brought to life and restock our Forth as it was.'

The French, who were most successful in turning a hunting into a farming phase used oysters from the Forth for much of their seed-stock. Another irony was that Dutch traders who had been short-changed by having barrels of oysters partly filled up with mud and had dumped the lot in the canals, now found themselves with native scalps.

Oyster farming isn't something new - the Chinese were doing it two thousand years ago. Generally, however, it has been associated with pearl culture. The Romans had a theory about pearls: they thought they were crystallised tears of angels. So where are the angel-tears from the Forth? Alas, the pearl comes not from the edible oyster but from a cousin more akin to the humble mussel. The edible oyster does indeed produce a pearl, but it is a mockery which turns a muddy colour and crumbles to dust in time. The pearls for which Scotland was celebrated up to the 18th century, which once formed a staple trade and which are treasured among the Scottish Crown Jewels, came from fresh-water mussels in the Tay, the upper Forth and the Ythan. The pearl fisheries of the River Tay were so prolific that they yielded £10,000 between 1761-4 and commanded top prices on the London market.

Like its cousin the oyster, the mussel-pearl has fallen victim to over-exploitation. And in another respect these two are alike: You have to be rich or reckless nowadays to enjoy either and to be able to sing as John Rydon does in *Oysters with Love*:

> Let us roister with the oyster,
> In the shorter days and moister
> That are brought by brown September
> With its roguish final 'R',
> For breakfast or for supper
> On the under shell or upper
> Of dishes he's the daisy
> And of shellfish he's the star.

CHAPTER 10

Fishing Ways

The noo wharever neibors meet
In hoosie warkshop or the street
By rich and puir by auld and young
One word the noo is on each tongue -
The herrin'

'Tis heard in Jenny a'thing's shop
In yon braw pailace ca'd the Co-op
Mentioned by banker, doctor, teacher
And whiles is muttered by the preacher,
Herrin'

(Peter Smith, The Fisherman Poet of Cellardyke)

The coming of the herring shoals was to the inshore fisherfolk of last century the most important event in their calendar, a wayward and unpredictable harvest that could spell the difference between prosperity and poverty in the year ahead. The eager frenzy with which the predators fell on the shoals is told by Christie Johnstone:

> 'I was at Inch Keith the day,' said Flucker. 'I played a bowl in the water and I catched twaree fish. I'll let ye see his gills and if ye are a richt fishwife ye'll smell bluid.' Her brother opened his jacket and showed a bright little fish. In a moment all Christie's nonchalance gave way to a fiery animation. She darted to Flucker's side.
> 'Ye hae na been sae daft as tell?' asked she. Flucker shook his head contemptuously.
> 'Ony birds on the island, Flucker?'
> 'Sea-maws, plenty, and a bird I dinna ken: he moonted sae high, then doon like thunder intil the sea and gart the water flee as high as Haman, and porpoises as big as my boat.'
> 'Porpoises! foolish laddie - ye hae seen the herrin' whale at his wark, and the solant guse ye hae seen at her wark: and beneath the sea, Flucker, every cod-fish and dog-fish and fish that has teeth is after them; and half Scotland wad be at Inch Keith Island if they kenned what ye hae tell't me.'

Yet though they lived on the brink of these richest herring grounds, the fishermen of Newhaven for hundreds of years paid scant heed to the silver hoards, regarding the herring more as bait for larger, line-caught fish. For the herring, because of their erratic voyaging, provided no dependable living.

Herring spend most of the year in the open sea, swimming near the surface of the deep cold waters. At spawning, they move in tremendous shoals close to the land the female travelling on her side and rubbing her body against weed or rock until she deposits her eggs - up to 50,000 of them. The male swims close behind and fertilises the eggs with his milt and the eggs adhere in jelly-like masses. After spawning the fish disperse only to come together later in large shoals on the feeding grounds. It is this concentration for spawning or feeding that presents the fishermen with his best chances.

The shoals lie on the seabed beyond the reach of nets until, in the 'merry moonlight', they rise to feed, the great dark expanse of the ocean showing a shining, shimmering cloud, like fire burning under the waves, a phosphoric light that speeds over the waters, marking their erratic progress, attended by bowing whales and plunging gannets. The surface assumes an oily look from the gasses released and a strong, characteristic odour taints the air. That is the signal to shoot the nets.

Tradition says that in 1793 Thomas Brown a local fishermen was line-fishing for haddocks and poddlies near the shore at Donibristle when he was amazed to find his boat afloat in a sea of herring. He scooped them up in pails-ful. The fisherfolk of Queensferry hearing the strange news quickly cast their nets and were rewarded with rich harvests - though they are said to have ignored a similar occurrence 20 years earlier when a mainsail which had fallen overboard off Inverkeithing was brought up full of herring. Very soon up and down the Forth the herring hoards were being netted in miraculous abundance.

And so, says legend, began the great herring fishing of the Forth which became known world-wide through the song composed by Lady Nairne to express the feelings of the Newhaven fishwives. The music drew its inspiration from the pealing of the bells of St Andrew's Free Church, Newhaven, and from the melodic cries of the fisherwomen of the village:

> Wha'll buy my caller herrin'
> They're bonny fish and halesome fairin'
> Buy my caller herrin'
> New drawn frae the Forth
>
> When ye were sleeping on your pillows
> Dreamt ye aught o' our puir fellows
> Darkling as they face the billows
> A' to fill the woven willows
>
> And when the creel wi' herrin' passes
> Ladies in their silks and laces
> Gather in their braw pelisses
> Toss their heads and screw their faces
>
> Wha'll buy my caller herrin'
> Oh ye may call them vulgar fairin'
> Wives and mothers maist despairin'
> Ca' them lives o' men.

Baiting the lines was a long and arduous job often involving the entire family, where several miles of hooks required cleaning, baiting with mussels and folding between layers of grass to prevent tangles.

A Silver Harvest

There is approximate confirmation of the date when herring fishing began in earnest in the Forth from the lst Statistical Account. The entry for the Parish of Queensferry says: 'It began at the end of the year 1792 opposite to this and in a part of the Forth outside the bay at Inverkeithing. During the season a plentiful supply was sent to the coastal towns. Next season the herrings were still more plentiful. Little was done about preserving or barrelling them, no salt or barrels being available. From the middle of October until lst March you could count 80 to 100 boats almost every day and the herring was found in great abundance from Burntisland to above Bo'ness. A single boat could take 30 to 40 barrels which were sold at £8 to £10. A great number of herring busses from Glasgow came via the Great Canal and had a most successful fishing. Vast quantities were cured and sent to the foreign market. About 6000 barrels were taken at Queensferry alone. The retail price was 6d per 100. It is the general opinion that the herring have frequently been here before but never fished for.' This great silver harvest came every year for four years, then vanished again to appear erratically until the 1830s. After that, says Mr Wilson 'the herring are now caught many miles from land, the boats taking from nine to 12 hours to go to the fishing grounds whereas in former times an hour or half an hour was all that was required.'

Newhaven's interest in the herring was awakened late because a superb abundance of white fish and rich oyster beds took all their skills and their cobbles, though sometimes used for journeys of daring distance, were essentially inshore boats and only later as nearby grounds were exhausted, were larger boats built.

Much earlier there had been extensive herring fishings in the Forth though these declined later with the erratic movement of the shoals. Earlier in the 18th century Defoe in his *Tour through the Whole Islands* says: 'Queensferry - and here I must take notice of a thing which was to me surprising, I mean the quantities of herrings taken and that might be taken in these seas. There was at that time a fleet of between 700 and 800 sail of Dutch busses coming into the Firth loaden with herrings. The Scots themselves have taken a vast quantity for they said they had had a very good fishery all along the coast of Fife and to Aberdeen. The water of the Firth was so full of fish that boys passing at the Queensferry in a little Norway yawl tossed the fish out of the water into the boat with their bare hands.' There are records which show the herring were prolific in the Forth between 1710 and 1725 after which they vanished without warning. They appeared on the East Coast again in large numbers half a century later.

The Dutch Invasion

The first authentic records of Scottish herring fishing relate to the West Coast when merchants a thousand years ago shipped great quantities to the Netherlands. The herring fishings of the North Sea began to be exploited in the late Middle Ages when following a variation in submarine tides, caused it is believed by an exceptional alignment of sun moon and earth, the fish moved out of the Baltic into the North Sea and the Swedish towns which had grown rich on the herring harvest were suddenly bereft. Holland was quick to exploit the new-found riches which the great underwater waves had washed to her doorstep. By the middle of the 14th century Dutch, Flemish and German vessels were regularly engaged in fishing off our coasts and during the following century they became such a menace that James III ordered that boats, nets and all other necessaries for fishing should be found by coastal burghs. In 1493 James IV ordered that all such burghs were to build vessels of 20 tons to be employed in fishing and that all idle men and sturdy beggars were to be pressed into service as crews. It was to no avail, for the Dutch had established a supremacy over the North Sea herring fishing. At the beginning of the 15th century they were employing a splendid little craft, a buss, twin-masted with bluff bows, of about 20 tons which carried a crew of ten men and three or four cobbles which were lowered overboard to net catches far beyond the ability of any other vessel. They had larger vessels which followed their fleets of busses and cured the fish, this curing process having been discovered by a certain Willem Benkelen of Sluys who died in 1397. They had also discovered the art of gutting, salting and packing the herring while still at sea. In 1600 their her-

The fishing round was not at an end when the boats returned to harbour. There were nets to be mended then tanned in boiling vats in the Fishermen's Park.

ring fleet was estimated to number 5000 and the industry was said to employ 200,000 people. In 1603 they are said to have sold herring alone to the value of £4,759,000 to other countries. Not only their success was an aggravation; they would come ashore and pretend they did not know the Scottish laws. The Magistrates were asked to send them a proclamation warning them not to profane the Sabbath by drinking, singing and dancing.

The Dutch herring busses would assemble annually in the Shetlands and follow the herring shoals down the East coast into the mouth of the Forth. James V, trying to find the solution that had evaded his predecessors, started colonies of Fife fishermen in the Hebrides where the Dutch had established themselves, but the Islanders preferred the Dutch and decapitated the settlers and sent their salted heads back to the King in a barrel. James VI tried again, banning the fishing off Scottish coasts without a permit. The Dutch brought along armed convoys to protect their fishing fleets and continued to fish what they called their 'goldmine'. Charles I ordered the Dutch to be driven from British waters, Cromwell's Navigation Acts of 1651 laid down that only herring caught in English ships could be brought into the country and Charles II ruled that no salted or dried fish could be brought in by foreigners. More effective was the introduction by Charles I in 1718 of a bounty system by which fishermen were rewarded for their catch by cash. Bounties were paid for every parcel of white herring of 32 gallons exported of 2s 8d, for full red herring (ie smoked entire and ungutted) 1s 9d per barrel, for empty red herring 1s per barrel. The building of fishing vessels was also rewarded by bounty. Yet it was not until the Dutch ceased to be an important maritime nation following the battle of Camperdown in 1797 that the Forth fishers, now awake to their natural wealth, had the opportunity to develop the herring fisheries to the full.

Further down the coast there had been native herring fishings since early times. In 1299 thirteen hundred red herring were mentioned among the King's stores at Berwick. In 1577 an exact record by the parish minister of Dunbar tells us that a thousand herring boats congregated there drawn from many towns and villages nearby as well as some foreign boats to take part in the annual 'drave' or drive upon the vast shoals that frequented the area. It was a kind of annual gold-rush and was attended by all excesses and moral and social deviations characteristic of such events. Herring roads radiating from Dunbar inland to the thickly populated Lammermuir and Merse districts are still traceable, along which long convoys of horses laden with panniers of herring were led by cadgers to feed the townsfolk. A crossroads on one of these roads was known as the Haudyaud, a resting place for the women who carried great baskets of herring on their backs. Yaud, an old horse or cow, was the contemptuous term used towards these poor women.

One particular drave is well remembered for a sudden storm scattered the great fleets of fishers and fourteen score were made widows in one night. The recording minister attributed the disaster to their setting off on a Sunday. It is maintained in certain parts of Scotland that the reason there is no herring fishing in Dunbar and Stonehaven today is that the men used to fish on the Sabbath.

Most of the herring caught were sold cured to Russia, Germany and other continental countries and some were exported to America. Scotland had a virtual monopoly of this trade which declined after the first world war. Before 1914 the herring industry was exceedingly prosperous, about half a million crans, nearly 40 million herring, being landed every year and about three-quarters of that going, pickled in brine, to Europe. Between the wars, though, not only was the foreign market lost, home consumption fell by about half and even of that market a large share was held by imported fish under a trade pact with Norway. Ships were scrapped or sold abroad as the industry wallowed in the trough.

The Fishing Year

But in the 1790s, with the coming of the herring shoals, dawned the era of Newhaven's best prosperity with a general pattern of winter oyster dredging and line fishing for haddock and cod, and summer net fishing for herring. But the pattern was never static and throughout the coming century varied as the silver hordes vanished and reappeared, as the oyster beds were gradually exhausted and as new methods of winning the harvest were discovered. In

The kippering sheds in Fishermen's Park provided occupation for the womenfolk.

addition to the summer fishing, there was also, though of less consequence, a winter herring fishing around November and December, and crab and lobster fishing in late spring.

The real excitement was the herring. Towards the end of May preparations were made for the ten-week season, starting, in the early 19th century, with the Shetland drave and following the herring down the coast. In the later 19th century it would start with the Irish herring fishing to which only the larger boats went, that is those from 39-45 ft. Kinsale, Howth and Ardglass, reached via the Forth and Clyde Canal, were the largest centres of the fishing, the boats being away for five or six weeks sometimes using Ayr as a base. On their return they made for the East Coast herring fishing at Aberdeen and Stonehaven, following the clockwise movement of the shoals, some of the boats doing their fishing under the bounty system. Meanwhile the smaller boats went to the May Island for line haddock fishing, bringing their catches back every other day to Newhaven. The crews consisted of four men each of whom had 800-1000 hooks on his line. When the big boats returned from Aberdeen and Stonehaven they often joined in the haddock fishing around the May in 17 to 22 fathoms. This continued as long as the state of the weather would permit, generally ending some time in October when the big boats would go down to Yarmouth or Lowestoft leaving the smaller boats at the May until Christmas. If the fishing had been poor elsewhere they hoped that the Yarmouth 'drave' would restore their fortunes for a boat could make £70 in a week - nearly £4000 in present terms - giving each of the seven-man crew a share of around £14, and a few weeks of that would ensure a comfortable year ahead.

There were lean years too, though fortunately few, when the fishing failed. Sometimes it was the weather that was against them. In 1829 Thomas Young as Boxmaster wrote to an Edinburgh merchant that boisterous weather had rendered the supply of line-caught fish very scarce. The large fish in such weather went offshore into deep water. What fish there had been had been sold to the families from Edinburgh at the bathing quarters. He would try to get a good turbot for the council's dinner. In 1870 the Society wrote to the Lord Provost asking for a remission in rent on the oyster beds as the late fishing at Dunbar had proved the most disastrous that had ever been in the memory of the oldest inhabitant, so disastrous that nearly all the men had to leave Dunbar in a state of debt not getting enough to pay their lodgings. The whole sum total realised among 300 men was only £100 or 6s 8d each for six weeks' work. The magistates did not see their way to granting the request. John J. Wilson, a trawler skipper for nearly half a century said: 'The market was the thing. You could come in loaded with fish but not get a market.' Harry Dempster wrote: 'During the months of May and June I have seen Newhaven pier literally covered with dead fish and few buyers when you might have taken them away for little or nothing.'

An important activity for the smaller boats was the sprat fishing in the upper Forth, which Newhaven men took a large share of, using fine-mesh nets. But villages nearer the sea got no share of this harvest and argued strongly that in the netting, the Newhaven men were taking large hauls of garvies, immature herring, which was ruining the stocks. So loud was this protest that an Act of 1861 outlawed sprat fishing with fine nets. The Newhaven men were so hard-hit they contested the Act in the Court of Session in 1869 and lost. So they paraded the streets of Edinburgh and formed up in a mass outside the windows of the Fisheries Board and demanded to be heard. A naval cruiser, H.M.S. Lizard was ordered to seize all nets found but the fishermen gathered on the quay and the women armed themselves with stones. The commander said it would not be possible to get the nets unless his men were armed and he could not answer for the lives of the fisherfolk. The tension was allowed to ease and gradually the sprat fishing was resumed.

Men not engaged at the line or net fishing went back to the oyster dredge. The date of starting oyster fishing never varied: it was always 1st September and the closing date was 30th April when the Society's flag was hoisted at the pierhead. Mussels were taken too and used for line bait or were sold to Moray Firth fishermen who came down in their boats and took away full cargoes.

Line Fishing

Until the coming of the herring fishing the bulk of the fish caught at Newhaven were on hook and line in inshore waters, Defoe noting: 'There are great quantities of white fish taken, and I took notice the fish was very well cured, merchantable and fit for exportation. There was a large ship at that time came

Drift-netting, which largely superceded line-fishing required bigger boats to follow the wayward shoals of herring. Getting the nets ready to shoot aboard a steam drifter in the 'fifties. (Photograph by Paul Shillabeer, F.R.P.S.).

from London on purpose to take in a loading of that fish for Bilbao, Spain. There was also a great trade in it to Norway, Hamburg, Bremen and the Baltik.' The hook and line method went back to prehistoric times; nor had the gear changed much over that span, medieval fish hooks being indistinguishable from those used today. Until recent times fish continued to be caught in this way by the smaller boats and those Newhaveners who still can recall the earlier years of this century will tell you of the gruelling work of these methods.

Bait for line-fishing was mainly mussels and the village was fortunate in having large mussel beds at hand; these were fished either by a dredge to which a strong net was fixed and which was towed behind a small yawl, some fishermen doing nothing but mussel fishing around the Martello Tower; or by the girls gathering them at Granton in creels while the tide was out. This meant that they might have to rise at two in the morning, more often between four and six, and they could be heard setting off for the beds a mile away in the early hours, their clear young voices singing psalms or the popular Moody and Sankey hymns. In winter they might have to break the ice to get at the mussels. Lugworms, two feet in length, were a preferred bait when chopped up, but required much arduous digging to capture. Returning hours later they would shell the mussels with special sharp knives and they would be able to deal with two and a half thousand mussels in a morning, and set about baiting several thousand hooks on the lines for the following day's fishing. The men didn't take much part in baiting the lines but for the women and girls it was a major part of their work and even young boys would be pressed into service to redd the old bait from the line and re-bait from a basin or bucket full of mussel-tongues, an art now lost of concealing the hook. The youngest members might have to be roused from falling asleep on the job which having started in the early hours, might sometimes go on until eleven o'clock at night. It was important that the lines should run out freely without tangle, so they were coiled in a basket or scull, each coil being separated by a layer of grass which had been gathered from the Fishermen's Park or raided from the tended gardens of Wardie and Trinity to the complaints of their owners, by the younger members of the family. When it rained the baiting would be done indoors - 'Nae fancy polishing thae days,' said one old fishwife. 'I can mind an auld woman that used to sit at Lamb's Court and sell the mussels that werenae used for bait. She sat there with an auld tin basin, brown outside and fawn inside, fu' o' mussels and buckies and partans.'

(Mussels were so prolific they were sold to other fishing villages. One record showed 30 boats from Peterhead and other parts calling to load mussels, some having to wait three or four weeks for a load.)

Haddock were found not far from land so the smaller boats could be used. The haddock lines would have from 700 to 1000 hooks about two feet apart, each on a dropper or snood of horshair, and be about half a mile long. The bigger boats would have seven to eight lines to a boat, each man looking after his own line. Before the trawling the fishermen might expect to find seven to eight hundred fish a haul. Fresh fish landed at Newhaven had to be hurried to town in creels on the women's backs to be sold in time for the evening meal and all this for pence for as the industry grew and the supply of fish increased, prices slid. Haddock which in 1790 cost 7s 6d at Newhaven were selling 75 years later for only 9d each. In 1865 haddock for curing were 9s to 12s per 100. Weighing an average of 6 lbs these fish were split open and smoked over oak shavings or better still peat fires which gave them the special flavour of finnan haddies, so-called because the cure was first introduced at Findon near Aberdeen. This work was again done by the women of the village, the smoke-house being at the top of the Fishermen's Park.

The use of ice to preserve the fish came in about 1780 and was first reserved for salmon. When the great herring draves in the Forth began, cargoes were packed in ice and sent down to London by fast sailing vessels. About the middle of last century, it became the practice to bring ice across in large quantities from Norway.

Although the technique for cod fishing was similar to the haddock fishing, it was more arduous, the bigger boats having in later times to sail or row up to 30 or 40 miles to the grounds. The great lines, as they were called, had only 160 hooks but they were 1000 feet long. Seven or eight of these would be tied together to make a line stretching over a mile.

A typical Scottish drifter, in this case from Peterhead, setting out for the fishing grounds, mizzen sail set to steady her course. (Paul Shillabeer).

Arriving at the fishing grounds around dawn, they would drop a greased lead to find if there was any herring spawn for if there was, the cod would be there grazing. Overboard would go the bladder float with its flag, anchored by a large stone, then as the boat was sailed or rowed forward, the line was paid out and another buoy, also anchored, would be thrown over. Back they would row to the first buoy and lifting the line the fish would be gathered into the boat. They liked to shoot their lines on a lee tide and haul in on a weather tide, keeping broadside on so that as the boat lifted with the swell the line was eased aboard and saved from breaking should there be a heavy catch. When landed at Newhaven in the middle of last century, cleaned, split and lightly salted and packed in barrels holding 24 fish, cod might fetch between 40s and 55s a barrel. Nothing was wasted - the guts and heads being sold for manure and the livers and roes sent off to the English markets. Cod liver oil, a cure-all remedy, was also useful as lamp oil and for lubricating the leather seaboots. Apart from cod, these great lines brought in a catch of ling, skate, halibut and turbot, some of enormous size. A halibut caught in 1828 was 7ft 6 ins long, 3 ft wide and weighed 320 lbs.

Gradually as the century progressed, under the influence of the herring fishing, there was a partial turning away from line fishing towards netting and this had the effect of easing the burden on the women and children of the awful drudgery of baiting.

A revision of the bounty system at the beginning of the 19th century made the herring fishing much more attractive and lent impetus to the move towards net fishing and bigger boats. Drift netting, a very ancient form of fishing, is virtually the only method by which surface-swimming fish such as herring and pilchards and mackerel can be caught in great quantities. The drift net is an underwater curtain of netting hanging a couple of fathoms below the surface in a straight line often over a mile long. It is suspended from buoys or corks and is attached to the boat by a rope. The fish swim into the nets and are trapped by their gills in the mesh.

Crews on these boats consisted of seven or eight men usually close relatives, and the boat might be collectively owned, or owned by the father with his sons working as crew. Usually they got equal shares, with one share going to the boat for upkeep. There was often a youngster aboard, learning the trade and doing the cooking.

Drift Netting

It is almost dark in the little harbour as the fleet prepares to set out. Except at the pierhead, there are no lights but the glow of cooking fire from each hull, silhouetting the oilskin-clad figures as they bustle about stowing their gear, casting off and setting to the oars. Clear of the harbour the squeal of block and tackle heralds the hoisting of the sail, and the little ships which have been tossing in the chop, steady as they lean to the breeze while skippers adjust their course by the stars. Behind them the village lights dim to extinction. Each crew is carried along in a firelit circle, an untidy world of ropes and nets and buoys and ballast. The steady thrumming of the sheets and the music of the bow-wave are drowned now as first one voice and then another takes up the favourite 23rd Psalm, to be joined by neighbouring boats. Soon the voices die and the music of the sea resumes on the long journey down towards the distant fires of May.

The dawn is almost breaking when a crewman spies sounding whales on the bow and all eyes scan the surrounding seascape for that erratic quicksilver shadow that tells the presence of the herring shoals. With a slithering hiss and the splash, splash, splash of the buoys the nets are shot, all six of them, two hundred and forty fathoms in all and then another 20 fathoms of warp is let go as a swing rope, all this taking half an hour of wordless bustle while the little ship sails slowly ahead. Now she is brought round head to the wind and lies nodding to the great sea anchor which bobs away towards the horizon. (In a blow it often happens that a skipper decided to ride the seas for a night or two attached to his nets rather than risk hauling them in. 'Making the sea a friend' was how they said it). Ballast is moved to the stern to keep her head up should there be a sea running, the mast is lowered and a watch is set as the vessel drifts with the tide and the crew coax up the fire for a brew of tea and stamp about the boat to bring life to their frozen limbs or shout remarks to the

Hauling the nets at the end of the drift could bring a silver harvest to fill the hold. (Paul Shillabeer).

nearest boats. Again the favourite hymns spread through the fleet, and far over the sea can be heard 'Jesu, Lover of My Soul' or 'Rock of Ages'.

As the sun edges up the warp is occasionally hauled in as far as the first net to see if fish are about. One of the crew says he can smell the herring and now a buoy disappears, and then another. They buoy the end of the warp and cast it overboard and set off down the net to discover that buoy after buoy is either drowned or barely showing. They are both elated and apprehensive as they haul back to pick up the warp. Two take the head rope and two the yarn and the hauling begins. In comes the first net with barely a spattering of silver, then with much puffing and cursing and heaving the great white mass of the second net is coaxed to the surface and over the gunwales, a river of liquid silver which the other crewmen shake clear of the net and into the bilges. Wet through, glistening with scales and heaving till their hearts are bursting, they bring in net after net until it is almost a relief to find the last no more than part-full.

The nets stowed they begin the long beat up the Forth against the headwind, knowing that their catch will be valueless if not soon brought to port. The traditional hymn sung now after a good catch was 'O God of Bethel'.

On arrival a sample of the herring is taken up at once to the market, the catch and gear unloaded and a beginning made again on the interminable round.

Drift netting was a more leisurely form of fishing than the trawling which later became the major method of taking fish, yet it still required a full commitment for even while ashore the fisherman's task was not done. The nets needed constant mending and tanning or barking and this was done mainly in the Coal Fauld next to the Fishermen's Park on Saturdays in great boiling vats with a strong solution of alum and tar which helped preserve them from the salt water. This was something of a social occasion when the village gathered to gossip. Then the nets had to be dried and mended before being put back aboard ready to sail after midnight on Sunday if the weather favoured them. The weather played a great part and they had developed a special sense in reading it. They knew the moon as a friend. If the wind started to blow before a full moon it would blow until the moon was full. A new moon on its back meant wind and a halo round the moon meant bad weather coming. 'There was so much they knew about it,' said Mrs Anne Harley. 'My father (Tom Wilson) would say: 'The moon is not right, you are wasting your time'. The moon had a lot to do with the herring fishing, and the tide had to be running. and there was the season of the year. There was some people used to go up and down the Forth at night looking for fish, and the minute they found the fish out went the lights. 'Black boats' they called them. Imagine being out there with no lights! But that didn't worry them. That was their workplace. I would say they were very seldom caught in a storm because they could see it coming up and if they saw it was more than they could cope with they would reach into another harbour. But one of my grandfathers had a boy lost in the Eyemouth disaster.'

The Newhaven men later in the century tended to favour the Danish seine net. The purpose of this net is to encircle the fish, both ends of the net being drawn back to the boat and the bag of the net traps the fish. The whole process takes not much more than an hour and it is repeated again and again throughout the day. By this method a supply of really fresh fish can be got quickly back to port, and this suited the Newhaven economy with its well-organised selling network and ready market. The authorities however took a dim view of seine netting in inshore waters as they claimed it was akin to trawling and this resulted in a Newhaven skipper appearing in court in 1890, but the method continued to be used.

Boat Design

The Scottish fishing boat evolved from two contrasted types, the elegant sea-kindly Viking ships, and the blunt utility of the Fife coast build. At the height of its synthesis, the Zulu, it was described as the noblest fishing craft ever designed in Britain and one writer described a fleet of Zulus thus: 'It is truly one of the finest sea sights of modern times to see this great brown fleet come marching up out of the horizon and go leaning by you at a ten-knot speed, the peak stabbing the sky as it lurches past some 70 ft above the water. The sense of strain and power is not so produced by any work of man at sea.'

A trio of East Coast drifters. (Paul Shillabeer).

Newhaven boats until the coming of the herring at the end of the 18th century were small and lightly built of larch with overlapping planking, designed for inshore fishing as were most boats in the Forth estuary. They began to increase in size during the first quarter of last century as longer voyages were undertaken to follow the wayward prey. Most Newhaven families owned two boats, a smaller one, an open yawl of 15 to 24 ft with a breadth of 5 to 8 ft using 12-ft oars and a mast with lugsail stepped far forward being used for oyster dredging and inshore line fishing, and the bigger Fifies of up to 12 tons, and 30 ft in length that could venture further out in pursuit of the erratic shoals. The bigger boats were open yawls with a single mast and a high dipping lugsail with upright and fairly sharp bows and sterns with no rake, and clinker built of overlapping planks, good seaboats which with their long keels were not easily broached. By the middle of last century they averaged about 36 ft in length, 13 ft 3' beam and 4 ft 3' depth with a carrying capacity of 17 tons, clench built and copper fastened. Fitted with mast and lugsail they cost £80-85 ready for sea. Unlike the graceful craft of the North East, which were mainly provided by the lairds to a crew of employees, the Newhaven boats, purchased by the fishermen themselves, were uncompromising in their workaday homeliness, yet they were superb sea craft and to see them shouldering home in a blow was a splendid sight.

Until the middle of the century few boats were decked or even half-decked.

The crews were exposed to wind and rain and sea. Following the erratic shoals with sail and oar in open boats was a precarious fortune and a hard life especially as the fish often vanished for weeks, and even when caught getting them back to port against adverse wind and tide could prove hazardous. But the men refused to consider decks, saying that they would impede the use of the oars and make the boat top heavy with a big catch aboard and fishing with lines was easier from open boats.

Both local ministers, the Rev Dr Graham and the Rev Dr Fairbairn, argued strongly for larger, decked boats. Harry Dempster, the pamphleteer, also urged the building, by interested capitalists, of larger boats which the men would operate as employees. His idea was that not only should these boats be decked, they should be fitted with a sea-filled well in place of a hold in which the fish swim about until they were got to market. Otherwise, he said, 'now the oyster scalps in the Forth are getting so barren many of the Newhaven fishermen ought to emigrate to some part of the coast near the German Ocean where they would be in a more favourable situation to prosecute the white fishing trade. The fishermen are labourers and there are plenty of prime fish in the North Sea, had the men the proper description of vessels to go and capture them; and if it can be shown there is a sufficient amount of fishermen's labour at Newhaven to bring into that village every year £100,000 sterling, surely that ought to be a matter for consideration by all shopkeepers and other tradesmen with whom fishermen deal by purchasing their goods.'

Gradually, despite the men's resistance, and thanks mainly to the work of Dr Fairbairn, the fleet was rebuilt with larger decked vessels. He rightly judged that it was best to make the fishermen do as much as they could reasonably be expected to do and then to supplement their efforts. Whenever a crew came forward with a certain proportion of the money Dr Fairbairn got the remainder advanced to them. It is said that he commissioned the remarkable early photographs taken of Newhaven fisherfolk by Octavius Hill as a way of raising money for the boats. At the time he died in 1879 he had the satisfaction of seeing that, in addition to the 170 smaller boats at Newhaven, 33 boats of this new and improved type had been provided at a cost of £250 each and as much more for the fishing appliances. In the '80s there were such 45ft boats as the *Success, Murdina, Methuen, Elizabeth Carney, Elizabeth Fairbairn*. Later there came the 50-60 ft boats. They had crews of 7 men. At their largest late in the century Fifies reached a length of 75 ft and 25 tons deadweight. One of these big sailing Fifies has been preserved by the Anstruther Fisheries Museum and is to be seen in the harbour there.

Steam began to be introduced into the bigger drifters in the last quarter of last century, at first to work the winches then as an auxiliary to sail and the absurd long thin funnels between the masts gave them the name of 'pipe stalkies'. Then with the coming of paraffin engines the characteristic features of the modern Scottish drifter began to emerge, the single flush deck, the bold shear, the straight stem and deep counter stern and the small superstructure.

Newhaven Harbour in busier days (Courtesy of 'The Scotsman').

The first paraffin engine was fitted into a Newhaven boat in the early years of this century, the *Guide Me* of 36 ft owned by James Inglis. Mrs Harley tells the story of her father Tom Wilson having one of the first Kelvin engines fitted. 'He had two boats and for a long time after he didn't sell the sailing boat. When they got the engine they knew nothing about it and they were sitting there with the book. Someone had read the book so they made him the engineer. They sent for a mechanic and they were all sitting there watching him and asking about this and that. At last he said: 'I know this much, I will never get another job here.'

'My father owned fishing boats and his father before him and his father before that. There was an article in the *Scots Magazine* where he was quoted as saying: 'I'll never forget sailing with my father to the fishing. He was at the tiller and I was at the sheet. I can hear him now - 'Steady, steady, an inch, an inch, an inch, and a wall of water rising up in front of me, the boat lifting, water dashing across my face, my eyes full of it and the taste of salt in my mouth.''

There had been a boat-building yard at the Fishermen's Park off and on during the centuries but often the bigger boats were built at Port Seton. The last boat built at Newhaven, by James Ramsay, was the *Reliance* in 1928. She was pulled from the Park on a great cart by the whole village, including the school-children, given a holiday for the occasion, helped pull on the ropes and the juggernaut squealed its way through the flag-decked streets to the slipway, four hundred years on from the launching of the *Great Michael*.

A diesel driven drifter, The Girl Olive of Fraserburgh. (Paul Shillabeer).

The Coming of the Trawl

'My father was on the trawlers. He wouldnae let me go near them - said it was-nae a life for a dog, let alone a human being. But there was money in it.' James Watson, like many of his generation, turned away from the sea, becoming instead a fish salesman.

'We only saw my father at weekends,' he said. 'He would sleep mostly. I didn't see much of him except lying about the house waiting. My biggest recollection of him is getting him wakened. It's hard if you have been brought up in the welfare state to imagine the conditions that these people worked under. They went 200-300 miles out and were away a week at a time. After the war (1914-18) the North Sea was teeming with fish because before that it had been one huge minefield and the trawlers didn't get to fish in the North sea. Most of them were commandeered as minesweepers and the crews joined up because of their knowledge of the coast.

'There was no electricity aboard the trawlers - jist paraffin lamps. A trawler net is down for four hours and these boards scrape along the bottom and move the fish up into the net, and they are steaming along trailing these out like a parachute. They sail round hoping it won't tangle with some old wrecks or rocks and lose their nets. And they leave a man on watch to steer a course and there would maybe be about nine aboard the trawlers at that time. What they had to do was snatch sleep while the trawl was down. You were supposed to be able to turn sleep on and off and I dare say a lot of them never even got their clothes off. They took off their sea boots and oilskins and got their head down and tried to snatch some sleep and then they were roused, it didn't matter what time it was, night or day. You would be up on deck hauling in the net on a

Motor fishing vessels moored in Newhaven Harbour (Courtesy of 'The Scotsman').

cold cold night and the fish were winched aboard and the net was winched aboard and the fish were emptied into what was called a pond compartment where they were separated into different types of fish and put into baskets, baskets of herring and haddock and cod. These baskets were put down the hold where another member of the crew boxed them with a certain amount of ice. They kept this up for a week. I don't think they even got their faces washed. They came in on a Saturday and they had to help in cleaning up ready for the next trip with clean boxes and six to eight tons of ice. Then they would get their share and by the time they got home it would be lucky if it was 4 o'clock on Saturday. They might go to a football match and have a drink. Of course they didn't get up at seven or eight the next morning. I've seen me half a dozen times in the bedroom trying to waken him. They were greatly religious - they never sailed on a Sunday. That was their existence.

'There was money in it but I would not say there was a lot unless you were a skipper. You went so long and you went to a school and took certain grades. The mate was paid so much in the pound of the value of the catch, the skipper a bit higher. Last figures I heard was 1 s 3 d for the mate and 1 s 6 d for the skipper. The rest of the crew was paid so much a day plus a bonus of say ld in the pound value of the catch. But I would say that by and large taking Newhaven as a whole they were a little better off than the labouring classes of say Leith. There was always that little bit spare. They were never on a shoe string. I would not say there was any genuine poor. I would say my upbringing was very comfortable. They even sent me to music to learn the violin which you would not have expected in a house where the man was making 25 s a week. That was a good wage. A labourer would not be making more than a pound a week. Then the trawlers brought a certain amount of prosperity because you had a lot of ancillary industry. You had to service the trawlers, carpenters, engineers, chandlers' gear, nets, they were big heavy nets.'

It was a dangerous life, too, ten times more dangerous than mining. James Watson recalls: 'Being washed overboard was always a danger. If you were caught in a storm you just had to ride it out. You were too far away to try to get back. I have heard my father say that with some skippers you were never scared no matter what the weather was like. Maybe the skipper had that personalty, he didn't show fear. Other ones you were scared because they showed it. Most of the accidents happened when they were dumping ashes because most of the boats burned coal. If you burn coal you have to clear out the fires during a quiet spell. They filled up drums when they got a chance and tipped them over the side, carrying them on their shoulder. The rail was only three feet high. If you were about to pitch it over and the ship gives a roll you might be caught off balance and go over the side. Quite a few have been caught that way. The only thing to do is to let the bucket go. It was not a life at all. Nowadays with the advantages of electricity and radio telephones so that you can talk to your wife or the owner sitting maybe 300 miles away, it is different.'

Another danger, said John Wilson who was at the trawling for 50 years, 43 of them as skipper, was guiding the wires on to the winch when hauling in. 'You had a long iron bar and had to stand in front of the winch and if you were unlucky you could get pulled into the winch if your foot slipped.' He was proud of the fact that he had never lost a man. 'The reason was Newhaven skippers went on the deck when they were taking the trawl in so they saw the weather and they knew when to stop when the waves got a certain height. Some of those from Grimsby and Fleetwood, you could tell they couldnae keep their feet in a sea.

'The miners growl a lot. My God, they did not growl when they came with us the two three times they tried it. I don't know one that stayed to draw their pay. They would sooner be down the pits.

'The furthest East we would go was 250 miles out into the North Sea from the May Island and then we might go about 90 miles North-East of the

Fishergirls followed the herring fleets down the coast and could gut, salt and fill a barrel in eight minutes. (Paul Shillabeer).

Shetlands and going West, 250 miles out from the Outer Hebrides. The boats were mostly 125 ft long and were owned by Carnie and Gibb of Granton, or Paton or the biggest owners, Devlin.'

Trawling brought the industrial revolution to the fishing industry. Coupled with steam power, it increased the catches enormously and provided great public benefit, a source of cheap, abundant food for the new urban masses. But a steam trawler cost £4000 and that was well beyond the pocket of the most affluent fisherman. So it subjected many of the fisher folk to a wage servitude they had not known. It was a harsh and brutalised life that robbed them of their pride in profession, a scavenging kind of fishing. And it robbed the remainder of their livelihood by clearing the fish stocks from the inshore waters. 'What really hammered Newhaven,' said John Wilson, 'everybody got into the trawlers where they could get a steady wage.'

Trawling didn't start in Scottish waters until the last third of the nineteenth century though oddly enough, a record in the Society's books shows that as early as 1793 a Government grant of £25 had been given to Newhaven fishermen towards a scheme for fishing with a trawl. This may have evolved from use of the oyster trawl, but there is no record that it succeeded.

When late in the 19th century trawling became established it immediately aroused great antagonism among local fishers. The first steam trawlers were

Boat maintenance on the slipway (Courtesy of George Liston).

old paddle tugs converted for the job and from then until the end of the century steam gradually replaced sail. As a method of fishing, its opponents claimed, it was ruthless, effective and indifferent to the future welfare of the stock, scouring the bottom to produce hundreds of boxes of fish where other methods would produce dozens.

The Free Fishermen's Society booklet says of it: 'The coming of the steam trawling to the Firth of Forth had from the beginning such consequences on the fishing that the fishermen all along the coast objected strongly to the new method of fishing. In particular the trawling system threatened the whole of the line fishing.' An entry in the Secretary's record dated 1880 states that the line fishing had been a failure for several years and that 'I myself have not been at the line fishing for eight years past.'

Newhaven became the focal point of protest, the Society and the Church playing a leading role. A petition was organised and collected 190 names in the village before being sent to all fishing villages along the East Coast. This was presented to Parliament but was rejected. But three years later the Newhaven fishermen became so alarmed by the rapid increase in trawlers and the damage they were doing that they determined to try again. Meetings were held in every village and fishing town along the East coast. Three representatives from each centre were to be sent to a big conference at Newhaven. Unfor-

The last boat to be launched at Newhaven (four hundred years after the first) is pulled through the streets by the villagers on its way from the Fishermen's Park to the slipway. (Courtesy of Peter Carnie).

tunately the organisers weren't quite up to the occasion and Newhaven got only one day's notice. Most of the men were away at the West Coast fishing but a messenger from the Society managed to round up a fair number and the meeting took place in the Free Fishermen's Hall. Most of the delegates wanted the total abolition of trawling but the Newhaven men took a more realistic view. They suggested territorial limits and no trawling after sunset, arguing that Parliament might be prevailed on to accept such modest demands. There was strong disagreement and the Newhaven men, not being able to carry the day, refused to accept nomination to the committee. However the Newhaven view prevailed at a subsequent meeting of the committee in the Society's hall, when a resolution was passed to ask Parliament for a Commission of Enquiry and ban trawling within five miles of the Coast. Parliament promptly refused to do either.

This unexpected rebuff had the effect of rallying the ranks. Within weeks the Newhaven men appointed two of their number accompanied by Dr Graham and Colonel Cadell of the Grange to go to London with representatives from other ports and lay their case before the President of the Board of Trade, Mr Chamberlain. They met that august gentleman the following day, together with 16 other Members of Parliament but no whit abashed, and wearing their customary working clothes, each of the 16 fishermen spoke to their case to such effect that Mr Chamberlain said they had a very real claim to the consideration of the Government, not only because of the intrinsic importance of their industry but because they were among the most industrious and loyally disposed subject of Her Majesty (cheers). A Royal Commission was appointed immediately to look into the entire trawling problem.

This Royal Commission met at various Scottish ports. In Edinburgh five men from Newhaven were sent to speak before it. Each told stories of wanton damage. John Wilson said there had been 35 cases recently in the Forth of trawlers damaging fishermen's lines. A St Andrews fisherman said his nets had been carried away and he had followed the trawler to Aberdeen but got no redress as the skipper simply said he had found no nets in the trawl.

Professor Huxley, a member of the Commission: Don't you think an association for the protection of the fishermen would answer?

John Wilson, Newhaven: No. It would simply be an association for the collection of funds to carry it on. Stripped of its technicalities such an association exists to pay lawyers bills.

Professor Huxley: It would be cheaper to lose the nets!

Another Newhaven man Watson Carnie, said he had been fishing at the Finkie Hole near Inchkeith. The place was formerly so abundant it was known as the California but now it was like the Walls of Jericho - there was nothing but desolation.

John Young of Newhaven told the Commission that so injurious had been the effects of trawling in the Forth that the fishermen might now as well shoot their nets in the streets of Edinburgh as within ten miles inside the Isle of May. The trawlers were forcing the fishermen to go further and further from home.

James Donaldson of Dunbar said that if the trawlers belonged to poor fishermen the gentry about the town would very soon do away with them. The Chairman commented that if trawling were done away with the supply of fish to the poor would be drastically reduced.

The indiscriminate nature of the trawl was well-described by one writer: 'The strange and gasping creeping things and crawling life that now spread on the deck, torn from the deep to die, a legion of little brown and yellow crabs like ants from a nest began to thrust out of the mass and hurry sideways... horrors crawled here, strange nightmare things without faces whose eyes were perched on stalks, whose ways and motions seemed awful... Many of the frail strange creatures were dead before they returned to their element...'

Since 18 months later nothing had been heard of its findings, a meeting was held in the Fishermen's Hall to form an association for the protection of the fishermen's interests in the face of steadily increasing trawling. The meeting agreed to form the Newhaven Fishermen's Protection Association and a petition was immediately sent to the Home Secretary praying that the trawlers be kept outside territorial waters and certain banks in the North Sea and coasts around Scotland. The meeting also decided to raise a fund to help members who lost their nets or lines through the action of trawlers. Shortly after, the Royal Commission issued its report. It concluded that there had been a falling off of flat fish and haddock in territorial waters but exonerated the beam trawl

Workers at the Granton net factory of Thomas L Devlin and Sons. The work was increasingly popular because of the steady wage.

of damage to the fish spawn. It contained certain useful recommendations: That a central Fisheries Authority be created to oversee the industry; that the Scottish Fisheries Board be given powers to make bye-laws to regulate trawling; that efficient steam vessels be provided for surveilance purposes; that steam trawlers should also carry their numbers on their quarter; compensation arrangements for damage to gear by trawlers; and the formation of an efficient sea police. Most of these recommendations were subsequently carried out.

Simultaneously the Newhaven men helped score a further success, being members of a deputation which met the Board of Fisheries in London as a result of which a bye-law was issued banning trawlers from the Firth of Forth, St Andrews Bay and Aberdeen Bay.

In this fight to save the fishing from the devastation of these new methods the Newhaven men played a leading part; not for the first time their determination and eloquence carrying the day.

The victory however was late, much of the damage having been done. Newhaven boats now had to travel further and further to the fishing beds as the stocks retreated under the trawl while villages far from their markets but nearer to the open seas, were now able to get their catches off to the consumers by rail.

Though it continued to earn its living from the sea, the village now existed largely as a distribution centre, the trawlers operating mainly from Granton.

CHAPTER 11

Jinking the Gaugers

It was the boast of Captain George Malcolm that on each successive voyage he and his crew could so disguise their lugger the *Good Intent* that no exciseman's spyglass could discover her true name. So on an Autumn evening towards the middle of the 18th century as he beat up the Forth against a fresh westerly, five days out of Gothenburg with a cargo of tea, most profitable of the contrabands, he felt reasonably safe against detection. To mak siccar he tacked boldly past Leith as though making for Bo'ness then at dark fell back and dropped anchor off Newhaven, all lights doused.

At once the ship's boat slipped quietly under the stern and made for the beach at Annfield. In the bow Harry Gardner, merchant of Leith, saw two lamps in the window of Adam Rutherford's cottage - all clear - and minutes later felt the boat ground on the shingle to be drawn up the beach by silent helpers.

It was midnight before Rutherford, who had been abed, had rounded up the crew of his fishing boat including the brothers John and James Flucker and four others whose names have not survived, and by two o'clock they had the entire consignment of thirty chests, six casks and four wax bags of tea safely on the beach, women and children having been roused to help, for a fierce haste was the spirit of the enterprise and the whole community had to be party to it. From the shelter of the sea wall a line of packhorses was led on to the shore, the boxes and casks loaded in special slings and then, each horse roped to the one ahead, the plodding procession clopped up through the narrow closes to the place of concealment above the village. Meantime the *Good Intent* weighed anchor and sounded her way up through the Queensferry narrows towards Bo'ness to run the rest of her cargo and load another of tobacco salt and coal for Holland.

Adam Rutherford, one of my mother's ancestors, did that night what was of his time and of his country. That the record survives among a thousand like adventures, resulted from a women's quarrel. At a party in Rutherford's cottage in the small hours the brandy flowed free and they opened one of the boxes of fine tea and decanted it into pillowcases to be shared around while Harry Gardner boasted of his voyage and the money he would make. Ann Watson of Coalhill, Leith, jealous of her friend, Gardner's wife, later told the story to Shadrach Moyse, a Commissioner of Excise and poor Harry was locked up in the Tolbooth but there is no record of any proceedings against Grandpa Rutherford.

All 18th century Scotland was involved in the enterprise of jinking 'thae blackguard loons o' excisemen and gaugers that hae come down on her like locusts since the sad and sorrowfu' Union.'

167

'What is in the wind this dark night? asks a Newhaven fisherman in *Christie Johnstone*. 'Six Newhaven boats and 20 boys and hobble-de-hoys, hired by the Johnstones at half a crown each for a night's job.'

'Secret service!'

'What is it for?'

'I think it is a smuggling lay,' suggested Flucker, 'but we shall know all in good time.'

'Smuggling!' Their countenances fell, they had hoped for something more nearly approaching the illegal.

After all, smuggling was part and parcel of the fisherman's profession and had been for as long as there had been excisemen. Asked in the 18th century: 'How in the name of wonder do you get sustenance?' a fisherman replied: 'We smuggle a little.' In the early days it had been the export of wool and fish, then during the Reformation the export of lead stripped from the roofs of churches and the import of Catholic priests, books, pictures and relics (for a purely commercial consideration), later tobacco and tea and wines and brandy, then after the Union when the great upsurge took place, a more sinister cargo of contraband arms for the Jacobites.

It was a great game, a patriotic duty and the profit was good. People must have their brandy and tea and tobacco and little of it was to be had except it came by stealth. It is true that the Kirk in General Assembly thundered against the great impiety and monstrous wickedness of such methods, which led to 'horrid lying and dissimulation with beastly drunkenness, fighting, slaughter and blood and lessening not a little His Majesty's just revenues' but the thunder had a hollow ring when so many ministers supplied smuggled wine for Communion, a social drop of illicit spirits for Session meetings, and the use of the manse cellar for a brandy hole. In the popular mind the smuggler was a hero, a benefactor, an honest thief who robbed no one but the Revenue and that, as Charles Lamb said, was an abstraction that he had never greatly cared about.

Fishing villages were at the circumference of this spider's web of intrigue and deception. Though lairds and merchants might provide the cargo and the ships, it was the fisherfolk who supported the network with crews for the luggers, lightermen for the silent running of cargoes and lookouts, storemen and despatchers ashore. The Kirk was barely attended on fast days if confidential news came of a lugger lying off-shore and the penalties resulting were for breaking the fast, not for breaking the law. The poet Crabbe describing this role, tells of villagers standing under the cliffs

> To show the freighted pinnace where to land
> To load the ready steed with guilty haste
> To fly with terror o'er the pathless waste;
> Or, when detected in their straggling course,
> To foil their foes by cunning or by force;
> Or yielding part (which equal knaves demand)
> To gain a lawless passport through the land.

Edinburgh Town Council in 1744 deplored the part played by fisherfolk in the 'scandalous and destructive though prevailing practice of smuggling to the detriment of the health and morals of the people' (and, of course, the revenue of the Corporation), resolved to discourage the immoderate and universal use of such destructive commodities as tea and brandy. People, they said, should be drinking ale and whisky. 'Fishermen,' they remarked sourly, 'do now prefer smuggling to fishing.' In a report to Parliament in 1783 George Bishop made a plea for lower duties to lessen the rewards of smuggling in which, he said, a hundred thousand horses, a fifth of the Kingdom's stock, were solely employed, eating their heads off in grain that might more profitably be used in distilling whisky. He declared that but for smuggling fishing could be carried on as it should be and 'would provide such a numerous race of hearty sailors as would make us superior to all the world by sea and our poor be better fed, clothed and employed in carrying fish to foreign markets which would be a great encouragement to trade.' The French could do nothing of privateering in the North Sea without British sailors, most of whom had been smugglers and fishers. Though nature had been very bountiful to us as no other part of the globe had such quantities of fish on their coast, yet through neglect the Dutch were plundering these riches to the extent of a million pounds sterling a year. 'Fishing and smuggling will never flourish together.'

The Firth of Forth dominated the contraband trade and among the fishing villages around the Forth Newhaven held its share of an enterprise where the gain on a single voyage would recoup the losses of many on more mundane business. But Leith was the notorious centre with a regular fleet of smuggling luggers and yawls attached to the port. All the year through and in all weathers little ships crossed the North Sea taking out coal, salt, wool and fish and bringing in brandy, gin, wines, silk, costly china, tea, tobacco, spices, oranges and lemons, playing cards, hand mirrors. boxes of sweets and whatever else the better classes, the lairds, the magistrates, the merchants, the clergy and their ladies might fancy to order from agents who regularly rode by. The respected Edinburgh bankers, Cotts and Co kept a man in Rotterdam whose business consisted in furnishing goods for smugglers to run and hardly a shop window in the Kirkgate or Edinburgh High Street but carried a display of contraband goods.

An English Reformer

From the late 13th century when Customs staffs were first appointed the English Crown had worried over the problem of collecting export duties in that nation. And for just as long traders had exercised their minds to avoid paying them. There is a record of a merchant at Hull in 1394 going to great trouble to smuggle in a small barrel of honey and a crate of 200 oranges on which the total duty was less than threepence. But after the Union of the Crowns, the English discovered a livelier conscience about Scottish misdemeanours which it is true the Scottish Parliament had never done much to suppress. In 1656 they sent Thomas Tucker up to Leith to introduce some order into the Scottish scene.

He found 'the people on the other side through poverty and an innate habit of their own to be cross, obstinate, clamorous and prone to apprehend every action an oppression or injury and again to repel both, either with noise or force.' He would have continued his first tenderness towards them had he not been forced to depart from it, 'not by levity or inclination to disquiet the people, but from the just necessity of compelling them to submit to the law.' A people, he believed, had to be brought to the discovery of truth.

He was certainly the man to do it. In his own words, there was no diligence wanting for the improving all ways possible the interests of the public. Before his coming 'there was nothing of either method or form to be discovered.' He brought a filing system to office documents that previously had been loosely flung about, drew up a table of standard imposts to replace a multitude of different rates, set up a new tax on salt, divided the country into collections and appointed tax farmers (who paid a set fee then collected the taxes to themselves), staffed all the main ports with customs officers, ordered the searching of all shop premises and inventories taken of the goods, placed a garrison on Inchgarvie to stop all ships and guard the upper reaches of the Forth.

These ordinances were not met with universal acclaim and resulted in at least one riot. In 1664 a quantity of English twill had been smuggled into Edinburgh over the walls and a warrant was granted to search all the shops. which were ordered to close at once, Sir Walter Seaton, principal Customar ordering sentries posted at each door. The merchants were so enraged that they rushed his house at night, burned his books and sought him out vainly to kill him'. The Captain of the Castle came down with soldiers and fired on the mob, killing an apprentice.

Tucker set out on a round of all the stations and creeks of Scotland to survey the whole picture. He remained unimpressed. 'The barrenness of the country, the poverty of the people generally affected with sloth and the lazy vagrancy attending and following their horses up and down rather than in dextrous improvement of their time, hath quite banished all trade from the inland parts and drove her down to the very sea side where that little which is still remaining (and it was never great in the most proud and flourishing times) lives penned and shut up in a very small compass chiefly in the east alongside the German Ocean.' The rest of the country was mainly inhabited by the Old Scotts or Wild Irish who spoke Ober Garllickh and lived by feeding their cattle up and down hills, fishing fowling or plain downright robbing and stealing.

Much the same picture was painted by John Knox over a century later in *A View of the British Empire*. Scotland he saw as 'a bleak narrow country composed in general of rock, heath and sand' whose commerce should not be loaded 'with the same indiscriminate burdens of England's ruinous wars in which they have no concern and from which they can derive no advantage.'

But Leith impressed Thomas Tucker. He described it as 'a pretty small town and having a drying harbour into which the Firth ebbs and flows every tide and a convenient quay on the one side thereof of a good length for the landing of goods by the merchants of Edinburgh this being the port thereof and did not that city (jealous of her own safety) obstruct and impede the growing of this place it would, from her wealth, in a few years become her rival. For as certain as the Castle of Edinburgh did first give rise to the growth of that city by offering shelter, strength and security in times of intestinal trouble, so now in times of peace the situation of Leith renders it fit to prove the most eminent mercantile place of the whole nation and would soon invite all the inhabitants of Edinburgh to descend from their proud hill into the more fruitful plain to be filled with the fullness and fatness thereof.' Oddly he does not mention Newhaven, possibly regarding it as part of North Leith. All he says is 'as for the tract of ground beyond Leith and yet in the district thereof, there are only a few fishermen with some two or three empty houses, the ruins of some salt works and the little country village of Cramond, not worth the placing of an officer there and for that cause left to the care of all the officers in general who may easily in the day time from the town of Leith discover any vessel coming to the shore.' If anything did slip ashore at night it still had to get past the walls of Edinburgh or Leith and would there be seized upon. It was in Edinburgh's interest to see that this was done for all goods entering the city paid a duty to the Corporation. Constant precautions were taken to build up the walls. Captain Forrester who had built a new tenement looking out to Leith Wynd in 1684 was ordered to grate up his windows so that no sack or brandy might be passed through. The Corporation was continually concerned to keep up the level of the North Loch, to keep out the smugglers. In the Great Frost of 1682 the Loch was frozen over for four months and the City was greatly exercised to chase smugglers over the ice.

Having set all to rights, Tucker now took his leave of Scotland. The country yawned and stretched and resumed her antique ways.

Until the Union of Parliaments! On May Day 1707 the border ceased to exist and that part of North Britain lately called Scotland was brought under the same customs and excise laws as England. The monstrous increases now imposed, insupportable to the rickety Scottish economy, brought apathy and decay to the fishing industry with salt being taxed out of reach, and threatened ruin to those traders who would stay inside the law while vastly increasing the profits of those who didn't. It was now seven times more difficult to resist the temptation to run in brandy while the tax on tea shot up to 119 per cent of its value. Scottish merchants made the happy find that patriotism and profit both pointed in the same direction. The result was an explosion of the contraband trade: smuggling became a national institution.

But before that they made one last nod in the direction of legal observance. In preparation for the Union they imported into Scotland vast quantities of high-duty goods from the continent, paying the old rates for the last time (or in some cases, the first!). After the first of May a fleet of 40 ships sailed out of the

Forth for London loaded to the gunwales with luxuries and free of all further taxes. Among that lot were 12000 hogsheads of Virginia tobacco on which Glasgow merchants had saved themselves £75,000.This was going to be quite a killing. But London merchants reacted with outrage and the Customs men seized the lot. The House of Commons discussed how to make the seizure legal but the House of Lords kept its sense of humour and suggested that as there was only one shot in that locker the Scots might be permitted to fire it.

Robert Watson of Edinburgh was a little late. His ship, the *Hope of Hustan*, didn't get into Leith from Hamburg with its £1500-load of brandy and claret until the 10th of May. He said he had been delayed by storms and violent winds but the Customs refused to admit the goods and made application 'to carry away the ship out of the Kingdom lately called Scotland.' He asked to be allowed to sail again on the promise that none of the goods would be landed in Britain but despite this he was found to have run the lot. He was ordered to appear before the Commissioners to explain this remarkable disappearance but the Clerk Messenger found him conveniently out so after six sharp knocks, nailed 'an authentick double of the libelled summons' to his door.

Others found the new regime biting harder. The *Marion of Prestonpans*, John Hogg master, arrived off Leith, her cargo comprising a cask of coffee berries, a bale of shoemakings, ankers of wine, vinegar and brandy, a firkin of currants, a barrel of prunes, a hogshead of sack, some olive oil, escatchonel, loaves of sugar and two pieces of muslin. The Customs confiscated the lot, including the ship and all her furniture and tackle. Maybe she had come from France, trading with which was forbidden on pain of confiscation because England was at war with her.

Shortly afterwards, the new authorities instituted a big clamp-down which resulted in 168 merchants, skippers, prominent men, bailies, and a Provost or two, from Edinburgh up to Elgin, being charged with smuggling or at the least with being accessories to such embezzlement. Among them were 13 skippers from Leith and Newhaven.

If the Customs men drew a blank as they usually did, there were always the Customs Riding Officers, often ex-Cavalrymen, who patrolled the countryside, colourful figures armed with swords and pistols to ambush the pack-horse teams around Newhaven, Prestonpans and Musselburgh. There were also the Excisemen concerned with the duty on manufactured goods. One of this breed, John Maitland, a general surveyor reported having discovered a work belonging to Mr Russell for the purpose of making a hundredweight of soap into four or five hundredweights by the addition of urine and other materials, 'without any duty which is hurtful to the revenue and injurious to the fair trader' (not to mention the 'consumer'!). He had seized a quantity of this soap and wanted to know what to do with it.

A Dangerous Life

If the smugglers had their intelligence network so too did the Customs men and they would have spies in foreign ports to pass the word home of what was being loaded and for where. There was big money to be made too, by informers, but it was a dangerous life. In 1775 David Christie a farmer at Newbigging was on his way home one night when his dog was fired at by two men with a musket and with their faces blacked. When having asked them in a civil manner why, they had damned him and his dog both, called him an informer and then attacked him and struck him down with sticks and having beaten him violently on many parts of his body by which his head was terribly cut in three places, they fired a shot at him which was composed of lead shot the size of peas and which had lodged in the back part of his left thigh. He remained lying on the ground for some time quite stupefied and senseless and having recovered himself came home with difficulty and spent a fortnight in bed. He knew who had attacked him he told the Court, because he had heard the defendant's daughter telling her classmates her father had shot him.

The collective memory has retained little of those days; among Newhaven folk there is very little lore on the subject. But among the archives of the Scottish Records Office are preserved dusty depositions telling of those far-off adventures, enough to fill a book on the Firth of Forth alone with stories from Anstruther around to Eyemouth. Even the Isle of May, spat out of the mouth of the Forth into the North Sea like a grape pip, is chronicled for it made a splendid place from which to run contraband and a tiny village of fisher-smugglers flourished there through the 18th century. One day in 1763 Thomas Wishart, Robert Norris and William Davidson from that village were sailing their boat towards the Lothian coast with 42 ankers of brandy (about 300 gallons) aboard. They were making for Gullane Bay when they spied the Revenue yacht *Royal Charlotte* making chase and gaining on them. Their lugsail bellying in the stiff breeze, they fell to the oars until their skiff fairly flew over the waves but still the yacht gained. Then a shot whistled over their heads and in panic they made for Fidra where they beached their boat and fled. The *Royal Charlotte* hove to, sent a boat ashore and picked up the booty at leisure and took it to North Berwick. Wishart was furious: They could have made it to Gullane and saved the brandy he claimed afterwards from the dock.

Few catches were as easy for the Customs men, who found the world against them and their very lives in continual jeopardy. John Home, excise officer at Duns got a whisper of landings at St Abbs Head. He called five of his assistants and set off for the spot, having left word for a party of soldiers to follow as fast as they could. Arriving at the beach they found 400 hogsheads of French brandy with their ends beat out and each about one third full. A crowd of between 50 and 60 local fishermen and women were emptying the hogsheads into casks, cogs and stoups and on his declaring to seize the brandy in the King's name, they threatened death if he tried. When the soldiers arrived the mob withdrew a distance but when the Customs men found three barrels of brandy in a cave and tried to remove them there was a concerted rush. One customs man had his head cut into the skull with a barrel stave so that he fainted and lost a great deal of blood. Another was thrown into the sea and beaten about the head with fists. But with the help of the soldiers they managed to win back a good part of the brandy to a safe place.

Another Customs man at Kirkcaldy reported that he had 'foregathered with a woman between sex and sevin of the clock at night having on her back a great burden of small cloth which she was going to put on to a boat at low water in a quiet place on Kirkcaldy Sands.' He took the cloth from her and was carrying it away in his arms when three seamen offered to help carry it. They ran off with the bundle into the sea where they threw it aboard a small boat which was rowed out to the ship *Daniel* which lay in the roads. When the Customs man tried to follow in another boat 'the men put violent hands upon his person, pulled his cloak from him held him fast while they struck him most shamefully, knocked him on his back, snatched his sword 'and were likely to have stoppit him therewith and bereft him of his life' had he not been rescued by certain well-disposed persons. The same man was back for more punishment a month later when, having said good evening to someone coming off a newly-arrived ship, he noticed that under his oxter was a heavy bag of rich wares which looked like gold lace and permentis. He grabbed the bag but someone came up behind and grabbed him 'until Black Alec Law could untie the ship's boat and escape shouting insults.'

Even when they had got the contraband, the Customs men were not safe from counter-attack. Alex Huston and James Masters, both members of the crew of the Customs sloop *Princess Ann*, were aboard the newly-arrived *Betsy* at Leith Docks making a search. In the cabin they found 15 stone bottles and 2 1/2 ankers (about 20 gallons) of spirits which the captain swore were for his own use. They were in the process of handing these overboard to their mates when one of the crew of the *Betsy*, John Conquer finding the sight unbearable, rushed up and wrestled for a keg with such violence that the customs officer fell overboard and Conquer went off with the keg. Continuing their search they found another 12 gallons of brandy which they got away safely while Conquer was off discussing his prize but about midnight a great body of men of Leith, estimated between 70 and 80, some of them disguised and armed with bludgeons and other weapons, rushed on board and beat the Customs officers who were on watch, forced their way into the cabin and almost smothered one of the Customs men in his bedclothes so that he cried out 'Don't murder me'. The crowd carried off two half ankers and one case of spirits and four ankers of black beer, locking the officers below-decks. They heard the crowd taking a great quantity of goods out of the hold which in the morning they discovered to be empty.

Sea Chase

The master of this same Customs yacht was anchored near Ely on a morning in March 1765 when he saw the Excise sloop *Wharton* in chase of a schooner and firing off her guns. Anxious to see the outcome he went up to a headland with a spyglass. Later in court he was to learn the details of the chase.

The Exise boat *Wharton* had crowded on all sail but the schooner, which had been beating up towards Leith under reefs, when she saw she was being chased stood down the Forth right before the wind letting out the reefs. During this coming about the Customs boat got within half a mile and fired several shots but now the schooner began to show a clean pair of heels. Her crew afterwards claimed they could have sailed three knots faster having still a large jib and a topsail in hand and so much did they despise the sloop that one of them held out the end of a rope calling 'There, will you take the end of a tow?' The *Wharton* falling back, dropped her topsail and gave up the chase.

And that, if fate had played fair, should have been that. But in running pell-mell from the Excise they ran smack into the arms of the Navy. Captain John Mudge of the tender *Egmont* had heard at Dunbar the previous day of a smuggler and set off in pursuit. About nine the following morning he saw two sails to windward which appeared to be coming down as if bound out of the Firth. The schooner seemed to be drawing away from her pursuer and was approaching fast. When she was within canon-shot the *Egmont* hoisted her naval pennant and fired athwart the bow to bring her to but the schooner's crew answered with three cheers of derision and swept by. They said afterwards they thought they could have got off by the goodness of their heels. The *Egmont* pursued and when within hailing distance Captain Mudge ordered the smuggler to bring to. When she refused Mudge fired a third and fourth gun past her, keeping close enough to talk with the master and crew. This had no effect so the Navy turned their guns on the smuggler's rigging, carrying away part of her main masthead. They were now so close that the schooner's bowsprit became jammed in the Naval ship's larboard shrouds and was broken off. She tried to stand away but finding she could not get off she finally struck to the *Egmont* who discovered she had captured the notorious smuggler *Hope of Leith*, inward bound from Rotterdam with a cargo of tea.

They were by now off Anstruther with a freshening westerly and Mudge reckoning he would not be able to get his damaged capture back to Leith put into Elie, left a prize crew of six men aboard the *Hope* and fearing an attack by the locals on her valuable cargo he set off for Burntisland where he knew a Naval man-o'-war was lying to bring reinforcements.

Meantime, baulked of his prey, Captain Duncan of the Excise yacht *Wharton* which had first flushed the quarry, was in a furious mood. It took him until the following day to find the captured *Hope* at Elie and by this time Mudge had departed. He stormed aboard and bursting into the schooner's cabin, demanded to know what the *Egmont* men were doing there. He threatened to seize the vessel in the King's name and ordered the prize crew ashore. Dr Hamilton

Lythgoe who had been left in charge, replied primly that he wasn't accustomed to such language and he wouldn't move until his captain told him to. Duncan said he had written orders to take the *Hope* to Leith and Lythgoe asked to see them. Duncan produced a paper but he would not show its contents and put it back in his pocket. This impasse was finally resolved by the arrival of a pinnace bearing Captain Mudge and a naval platoon who took over the vessel.

All around the coast such skirmishes were commonplace. Portobello, the name given to a hostelry on the coast east of Edinburgh by an old seaman, Hunter, who had served with Admiral Vernon at the siege of Portobello on the Spanish Main, was a notorious haunt of footpads, pirates and smugglers and it was at the Figgate Whins there that in the Heart of Midlothian Scott made Effie Deans escape in a smuggling lugger. In real life Lord George Murray escaped from there after Culloden. After being hidden for some months in Leith he made his way to the smugglers' rendezvous at Portobello where towards evening the lugger made her appearance and no time was lost running the cargo. But just as the operation was nearly finished and Murray was preparing to embark the whole party was surrounded by soldiers. The smugglers had no choice but to fight. But the soldiers were brought to a halt by a volley from the lugger and soon after a round shot from the same quarter put them to flight. Lord Murray proceeded aboard and reached Holland safely.

The Ayrshire Coast, adjacent to the duty-free Isle of Man was the scene of a full-scale enterprise with the owners of the smuggling luggers so powerful and with so much local support that often the excisemen even supported by soldiers were powerless to control the huge and ruthless gangs guarding convoys of as many as two hundred horses. The traffic was exceedingly well-organised and was in operation all down the south-west coast.

How could this state of affairs go on? Burns, Scott and Stevenson have portrayed the smuggler in a romantic light but the effect of so much organised lawlessness was to rot away the social fabric. Dark social changes were taking place, drunkenness, debauchery and dissolution becoming the norms with farming and fishing falling into neglect. In Edinburgh in what became known as the Porteous Riots the Captain of the Town Guard was hanged from a dyer's pole in the Grassmarket by an outraged citizenry albeit perhaps deservedly, following the arrest of two Fife smugglers.

No nation with pretensions to principles could long countenance this free-for-all, romantic or not. Something had to be done. A beginning was made by building up a fleet of fast, well-armed cutters to catch the smuggler at his most vulnerable - at sea. The coast was ringed with coastguards, one man every four miles, armed with musket and spyglass and sitting on his one-legged donkey stool that would tip him over if he fell asleep. Stiffer sentences - death for carrying arms against a Customs man, transportation to the colonies or five years in the Navy for lesser offences, had their effect but what, at a stroke made the smuggler almost redundant, was the drastic reduction of tariffs. The game was no longer worth the candle. And with the age of reform the smuggler became for the first time in British history a discredited character who was seen to be robbing the community as much as the coiner of counterfeit money. The growth of a social and religious conscience had begun.

CHAPTER 12

The Church

It is a remarkable fact that in a village where religion played so large a part, no church existed for most of its history.

The earliest reference to their religious life occurs in a charter of 1143 where the fisherfolk of the area of North Leith are referred to as serfs of the Church of St Cuthbert - at that time ownership of the fishing and the boats lay with the Church. By that Charter David I gave the fishing to the Abbey of Holyrood and the parishoners were required to attend the Holyrood church, crossing the river by ferry at the head of Sandport Street or at Bonnington ford. In 1486 Abbot Ballantyne replaced the ferry with a bridge and erected the Church of St Ninian on the North side to be known in all time coming as the paroch kirk of Leith benorth the bridge. The Church was damaged during Hertford's raids and at the Reformation fell into decay.

Later the chapel along with the Chaplain's house and the tithes of the fish brought into Newhaven and Leith were sold to the inhabitants of North Leith to support their Parish Church. The church and chaplain's house were rebuilt, work beginning in 1595 and being completed in 1600 and this became in 1606 the parish church and manse of North Leith and in 1631 of Newhaven also.

In the years around the '45 it was used as a storehouse for munitions because of the suspected sympathies of the locals. In 1814 it was replaced by the splendid parish church in Madeira Street built by the fashionable William Burn and modelled on a Greek temple. But the old church still stands, the Latin inscription and the date 1600 clearly visible, and to find it, built into the warren of mill buildings at the foot of Coburg Street, its latticed wooden tower struggling to rise above the industrial clutter, its cobwebbed windows lighted by naked bulbs, the whir of machinery behind its antique portals, is like coming on an old friend in reduced circumstances. One can picture the congregations of those days taking their ease, between the three Sabbath services, on the sunlit slopes of the graveyard that ran down to the river. Part of this graveyard was excavated recently to make a riverside walk and of the several skulls unearthed all were remarkable for their perfect sets of teeth. The riverside walk is part of a splendid programme to rescue historic Leith from the decay of centuries and it is heartening news that Barratt the builders who are already restoring the historic buildings on the Shore and the Timber Bush, have found the old church and have plans to restore it too.

But there was another Chapel in North Leith in the early times about whose history practically nothing is known except that it was erected long before St Ninians and in old charters is referred to as marking the Eastern boundary of Newhaven. It was the chapel of a hospice for the poor with burial ground

179

Remains of the Chapel of Our Lady and St James, built by James IV in 1506 for the shipwrights and fisherfolk of Newhaven.

attached and was known as St Nicholas after the patron saint of mariners:

> St Nicholas keepes the Mariners from danger and disease
> That beaten are by boistrous waves and tost in dreadful seas

James IV used it regularly before he built the village of Newhaven. It too was damaged by Hertford and fell ruinous and all records were lost. The ruins were used by General Monk when he built the Great Citadel by which Cromwell planned to put a bridle on Scotland. The burial ground had still been in use but Monk set aside a piece of ground in Coburg Street in its place and this served until the 19th century as the only burial ground for North Leith. This was a favourite haunt of grave robbers who could slip up the river under shadow of night. Dr Johnston and Dr Ireland, ministers of North Leith church were buried here last century as was Thomas Gladstone, a Leith merchant and grandfather of the Prime Minister, William Ewart Gladstone, and their headstones are still to be seen among many commemorating the mariners of Leith.

Another early hospice with Newhaven associations was the Hospital of St Anthony, near the Kirkgate, founded in 1430 by the first of the Logans to own the lands of Restalrig. One of the few things to survive is a fragment of the records entitled Rentale Buke of Sanct Anthoni's and Newhavin. The Rental Book tells of its foundation by Sir Robert Logan and of the names of its

Another view of the remains of St James' Chapel beyond which rises the steeple of St Andrews Church.

benefactors. It was a religious house catering for the poor and needy and a home for the old and infirm. The Order was the Augustinians as was that of Holyrood Abbey. The Churchyard was the burial ground. In 1475 Leith was sorely stricken by plague and the people fled from the town and a hospital was established on Inchkeith. All the Friars died save two and St Anthony's lay empty for a time. Revenue from gifts and from lands and rents and one quart of wine out of every cask imported were its source of upkeep. The hospital was greatly damaged by Hertford's invasions of 1544 and 1547 and by the cannon of the English at the seige of Leith in 1560 when the tower was destroyed. The hospital was suppressed at the Reformation in the same year and its rents and other properties including the lands, and gardens and windmill in Leith and Newhaven were eventually bestowed by James VI by the Golden Charter on the Kirk Session of South Leith. Those lands bestowed on South Leith were erected into a barony and managed by a member of the session known as the Baron Bailie of St Anthony. One of the ministers in 1635, caused the keeper of the Kirk kist in which the writs were kept to open it under pretence of obtaining a real confirmation of them and surreptitiously purchased the grant 'and sold the grant thereof of the said presbytery and chapels of St Anthony's and Newhaven to himself and by selling the same utterly ruined the said charge and poor thereof'.

In 1506 Newhaven was given its own chapel by a charter of James IV to George, Abbot of Holyrood who was ordained to offer the Holy Sacrifice at the

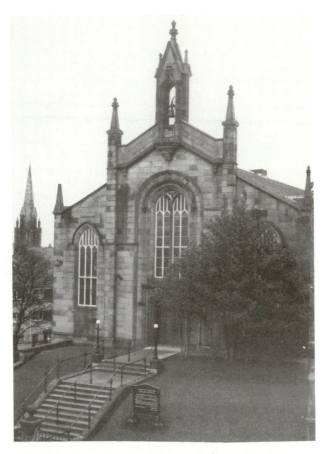

Newhaven-on-Forth Parish Church, Craighall Road, with which St Andrews Church (seen in the background) was amalgamated ten years ago.

altar of St Peter Apostle in the new Church of the Blessed Virgin Mary and St James in Newhaven. (It appears that James intended to have eventually not only a chapel but a church in Newhaven but this never happened and the chapel remained during its 50-year existence a dependency of St Anthony's, Leith). In ancient maps it is shown as having boasted a steeple but whether this was artistic licence on the part of the mapmakers, who tended to indicate a church by a steeple, is unknown. Sir James Cowie was appointed Chaplain ('Sir' being a substitute for Dominus with priests). Two years later James gave a warrant to his Bailie in Newhaven to pay over the whole annuals received from his land there for the maintenance of the Chaplain. Sir James remained at Newhaven for 12 years as chaplain being succeeded on his promotion to another incumbency by Sir David Wilson. Wilson was the last regular priest, which might indicate that he was there until the Reformation when the chapel

The Free Church (later St Andrews Church) before the addition of the spire in 1882.

Part of the elaborate stone carvings with a fishing motif which are a feature of St Andrews Church.

was suppressed, having first been ruined whether by Hertford or by Knox's mobs (to whom he gave the message 'Ding doon the nests and the craws will flee awa') is not clear.

After that Mr John Balfour, a Leith merchant, held the chaplaincy but this did not involve any religious duties. There is evidence of a graveyard attached to the chapel at this time. He was followed by James Balfour in 1595. He too had no spiritual duties but simply drew the income from the surrounding land. In 1611 he resigned the place where the chapel had stood, now ruinous, with the chapel yard and six acres of land in favour of the Kirk Session of South Leith on behalf of the poor of Leith. The Kirk Session thus became the superiors and for many centuries their representatives used to visit St James' Chapel once a year to collect feus. They also were responsible for the upkeep of the burial ground and as the sea encroached, made further grants of land towards it. The present Anchorfield east of Newhaven was called in those days Holybloodacre. In the ancient chapel there was an altar of the Holy Blood supported by revenues from Anchorfield.

The rude but massive western rubble wall of the little chapel still stands, down a winding close from Main Street, guarding the greensward remains of the burial ground. Some years ago an excavation of the site was carried out by Mr Basil Skinner, senior lecturer at Edinburgh University which established that the original chapel had been built on a foundation of oyster shells and was associated with the building of the Great Michael. The earliest human remains were stone coffins, lead-lined, in which the the bodies had been wrapped in winding sheets. Above them they found inexplicably a great jumble of bones, a subject for irreverent comment from the locals who linked it with the butcher's shop next door.

In 1631 Newhaven was taken out of the Parish of St Cuthberts and linked to North Leith and for the next 200 years its spiritual needs were administered to by the Church of St Ninian. These were days of strict religious discipline especially in the matter of attendance and Sabbath observance, but the church was, in addition to being the spiritual centre, the business and social centre as well. There were officers appointed to take note of any who might be idling about or otherwise breaking decent rules. There was also a legislator, the Baron Bailie, expressly appointed for trying such misdemeanour and steeples were sometimes used as lockups, just as the kirk itself was used as a place for transacting business and the kirkyard was regarded as a common meeting place for sports and dancing, pasture, and a common dumping ground and sanitary convenience. A person would be told to go and shut himself up in the Tolbooth or the steeple, but the 'netherhole incontinent' was a very different affair reserved for the worst offences.

No other parish in Scotland had more church bailies than North Leith. The bailie held regular court in Newhaven for trying those who deflected from proper behaviour in legal as well as moral conduct. Alexander Brown was fined £5 for letting a house to a man who had no testimonials. Keepers of lodging houses were interdicted from letting beds to strangers until their testimonials

Interior of St Andrews Church showing the altar, pulpit, choir stalls and organ. (Courtesy of Sandy Noble).

had been proved by some elder of their former district. A Kirk Session minute of 1605 records that Janet Merlin and Margaret Cook her mother made public repentance for keeping a bairn unbaptised in their house about 20 weeks and for calling it Janet. Another runs: Compeared Marion Anderson for craving curses and maledictions on the pastor and his family without any offence done by him and the session understanding that she had been banished before for being in the Lodge on the Links at the time of the plague with another woman's husband in a most scandalous manner she was ordered to go to her place of offence and crave mercy of God and further the Session ordered her never to appear again within their bounds under pain of being 'toties quoties in the jogis' (jongs or iron collar). The stocks and the branks are of the same date. David King 'pokman, actit with his awin consent never to be found drunken at na time hereafter under the pains of sotting in the stocks 24 hours upon bread and water.'

In 1605 a woman who missed kirk was fined £5 and a man was found guilty of irreverent speech by saying 'The devil take the poor's silver'. If he did it again he was to be deprived of the office of bellringer. Janet Thompson who was absent from Kirk with company in her house was made to go on her knees and confess her sins and fined £5. She was heard to say 'The fiend let the penaltie never do thame guid that recavis it' and had to go through the whole process again. In 1601 a man was tried at Leith for stealing grain from a store he had broken into by means of false keys. He was sentenced to have his hands tied behind his back and to be left on the sands to drown.

The Reverend Dr James Fairbairn, much-loved Moderator of the Free Church, with members of his flock (Photograph by Hill and Adamson, Courtesy of the Scottish National Portrait Gallery).

It was a rough tough time with brawls and murders commonplace. Edinburgh was a place of butchery, revenge and daily fights, 'the parish churches and churchyards being more frequented upon the Sunday for advantages of neighbourly malice and mischief than for God's service.' Merchants of Edinburgh were waited on in their passage to Leith to be made prisoners and ransomed. But there was no record of this riotous behaviour infecting Newhaven, perhaps because there were no idle hands for which the Devil could find mischief.

The spirit of the Reformation was in Scotland long before it broke up the papal power in 1560. It was only the power of the Regent Mary that stayed the onward march. But Presbyterianism didn't come all at once. The Roman Catholic Church had been wealthy and after 1560 there was a great scramble for the revenues of the old system. The nobles introduced a bastard form of episcopacy and got the bishops and priors to transfer the Church's property to them. These bishops were known as Tulchan bishops, a tulchan being a straw-stuffed hide which induces the reluctant cow to part with her milk. Only with great difficulty was the Reformed Church able to get rid of these bishops. Newhaven became very early a thoroughly Protestant place.

Dr and Mrs Fairbairn pose for a calotype by Hill and Adamson (Courtesy of the Scottish National Portrait Gallery).

Great Pastors

Newhaven has through the centuries been fortunate in its ministers and a great benefactor was Dr David Johnston, of North Leith.

Born in 1734 into a clerical family, he was ordained at Langton Berwickshire in 1759 and called to North Leith in 1765. He and the session managed to make this one of the most valuable livings in Scotland by feuing nearly the whole of the glebe for building purposes. He married a Leith woman and had a large family, though several died young and a son died in Bombay aged 25 and two daughters married early and settled in Glasgow leaving him a lonely man. Shortly after his arrival he asked for a rise of 400 marks to help support his growing family and received 300.

Coming into the parish when it was still thinly populated he became personally acquainted with all its members and identified himself with their interests ad helped them in time of trouble. In a maritime district such as North Leith where a large portion of the inhabitants were engaged in the precarious and dangerous occupation of the sea, casualties were frequent occurrences. The moment he heard of a case of distress he did something to assist. It was no ordinary sight to see the stern weatherbeaten faces of these hardy seamen subdued by an expression of deep reverence and humility before their minister.

In 1779 the notorious pirate John Paul Jones whose grandfather had kept a public garden near Newhaven and who had become acquainted with Leith in his youth formed a design to come upon Leith and hold it to ransom. But when his squadron was off Kirkcaldy the Rev Mr Shirra repaired to the beach and there surrounded by a larger congregation than he might have found in his kirk, prayed fervently that 'this wicked enterprise be frustrated'. He must have been in good voice for scarcely had he ended before a strong westerly gale rose which blew Jones's squadron out to sea and saved both Kirkcaldy and Leith.

In the meantime, Dr Johnston had summoned his congregation to resist to the death this notorious pirate, offering to lead them in the enterprise. The City Fathers brought out some old rusty canon, the carriages of which had been rotting for years in the Timber Bush and by almost superhuman exertion they were dragged across the old inner bridge to the Coalhill and mounted on the ruins of the Citadel. By great good fortune the defenders were not called upon to use them for they would surely have presented a greater danger to their crews than to those against whom it was proposed to direct them. A lesson learned, however, was just how completely naked Leith and Edinburgh were to seaborne threats. The building of Leith Fort was immediately put in hand.

Dangers continued to threaten for in 1803 when Bonaparte's invasion was anticipated, Dr Johnston earnestly exhorted his people not only to pray but to become volunteers for national defence. Now 69 years of age, he proposed to be himself one of their number.

If a widow's son was taken prisoner by the French on the high seas or was seized by the press gang she went straight to the manse and the minister set about securing the release. His writing was well known in Government offices in London and his requests always complied with. He succeeded when dukes and lords tried in vain for their dependents. In 1793 he received the appointment of Chaplain in Ordinary to George III with a salary of £50. In 1808 he was responsible for getting the road through Newhaven built. The road was laid and finished that summer. He founded the Blind Asylum of Edinburgh and published his sermons, raising £300 which he donated to the Asylum. At the age of 82 he walked to Glasgow and back. Handsome in dress and manner 'the bonny Dr Johnston' died at Leith in 1824 at the age of 90.

For the 59 years of his incumbency there always was a numerous attendance of Newhaven people at his kirk among whom very tender grateful memories of the great man continued after his death. His colleague and successor Dr Ireland died 4 years later.

A letter to the boxmaster of the time, John Johnston, regarding a successor cleared up a question the Newhaven folk had asked. The session clerk replied that the whole parish had the right to vote who were of the age of 12 if female and 14 if male. But he subsequently amended this by saying that only the heads of families, as formerly, should be allowed to vote and not young people and servants who cared for none of the spiritual things of the parish.

The Rev Jas Buchanan who came to North Leith in 1828 was in the habit of conducting mid-week services in Newhaven school for the benefit of the aged and infirm but these services became so popular among young folk that it was obvious a church was needed in Newhaven. He contributed a large amount of his own money to the project and a site was found just up the hill in the newly-opened Cut (Craighall Road) and a plain perpendicular building was erected in 1836 as a chapel or mission of North Leith Parish Church with a seating capacity of about 400, preference being given in the letting to Newhaven folk. The ministers of North Leith continued to dispense the sacrament until, in 1838, the Rev Jas Fairbairn was appointed the first minister. Elders were appointed and the Sunday school handed over to their care.

Three hundred years had elapsed since the community had last had a church of their own in the village but barely had the new minister settled to his charge, than the Disruption split the Church of Scotland, the issue being largely one of patronage as against the right of a congregation to choose its own minister. The Session met in May 1843 and unanimously resolved to go out into the wilderness and 'cast in their lot with the Brethren who had given up the privileges and adornments of the national establishment in order that they might maintain their allegiance to Christ as their sole King and Head of His Church.' They constituted themselves a court of the Free Protesting Church of Scotland and appointed James Flucker, fisherman, to represent them in the General Assembly of that Church, which was holding its sittings in Tanfield Hall, Canonmills. The minute was signed by the Rev. James Fairbairn as Moderator and the subscribing elders were James Flucker, John Flucker, James Carnie, James Mathew, William Finlay, Thomas Flucker, James Carnie, Martin Ramsay, Thomas Noble and John Marshall. The majority of the congregation followed them out.

The session quickly got down to the business of supervising the spiritual welfare of its flock, all members who walked disorderly to be dealt with by the elders of the church in private. The Communion Roll was read over, discussed and purged and certain individuals suspected of drunkenness and other sins were dealt with privately by the Moderator, a deacon was suspended for drunkenness and a committee set up to look into temperance. Several members of the congregation who had opened their shops on the Sabbath were spoken to, as was the Edinburgh and Glasgow Railway which was presuming to run Sunday trains. A young woman who had borne a child out of wedlock was admonished and absolved as were several married couples, 'guilty of ante-nuptial fornication'. (This last sin occupied a good deal of the attention of the Session during the next half century but they were pushing against a deeply-ingrained habit among the Scottish peasantry.)

The Church of Scotland wrote suggesting a joint collection be made for the poor to supply them with coal, but the Session wrote back saying that they themselves would look after the poor of Newhaven.

The strain of the Disruption had told on the health, never robust, of James Fairbairn, and he spent the winter of 1846-7 in Malta, in constant correspondence with his Session.

Services had continued to be held in the church building for several years but legal action by the Established Church to regain possession was successful and they had had to hand over the keys. Now they were without a place of worship.

At first they worshipped in the Park then they erected a wooden hut in Maitland Place at the West end of Main Street. Here the evicted congregation were comforted by their Pastor who congratulated them on the firmness and quiet determination with which they had 'clung together in the face of the solicitations of parties opposed to us. These have only prompted the members to increase the consolidation which has been going on in the congregation during the last 12 months.' He thought it 'expedient to meet the misrepresentations that had been industriously circulated, by a statement as to the real position occupied by this congregation of the Free Church which have recently been ejected in contrast to the position of the congregations which have now taken possession of these buildings.' (There followed a long argument in support of their theological position).

They thanked God for His goodness to them in their time of difficulty and decided to build a church.

The congregation was assembled in Victoria School by their Pastor. A building committee was set up, sites and designs were considered and John Flucker and James Mather appointed treasurers and the letting of seats proceeded with. Circulars were distributed and door to door collections begun. They seemed to have been no whit abashed by the enormity of the sum they proposed to raise. Such a church today would cost over a million pounds.

A year later, in 1850, the Deacon's Court was able to express its satisfaction at the financial prosperity of the congregation. Altogether the sums placed at their disposal during the year had amounted to approximately £220,000 in modern terms. There had been difficulties over the site chosen at Maitland Street and another and more suitable site finally obtained between the head of the stone pier and the west end of the village belonging to the Society of Free Fishermen. Work would be commenced with some progress made during the current season. Immediate erection of a manse was however postponed. Early in 1852 they agreed to borrow £600 from the National Bank of Scotland to finish off the work and on 2nd Nov 1852 the Committee met for first time in their new church, a handsome gothic pile with vestry and hall with seating for 600 and a further 200 in the gallery, half as large again as the church they had left.

'The church is closed up now but if you can get in you will see two stone tablets on the wall commemorating two ministers, both Doctors of Divinity, and if you take the dates of these tablets there is over a hundred years of service between them.

'It puzzles me often today,' continued the old fish salesman James Watson, 'how a little hamlet, uneducated, narrow minded, and you can have all the things that you can think of about them, they were that way, you know what I mean? Couldnae see past their own selves and they would have nothing to do

The manse which his grateful parishioners provided for Dr Fairbairn is in use today to serve the combined churches.

with any other community outside it, yet they could keep these two Doctors of Divinity that could have been at St George's West or some other big fashionable church, they stayed in the village beside these people and were content to stay there.

'Because they took their church seriously. There is a steeple at St Andrews Church and these fishermen used their boats to bring the stones across from Fife to build that steeple. That is how close they felt to it. They had to have something to do with it, not just go there on a Sunday.

'I've seen architectural students doon there looking at the stonework outside and there is a design over each window as if it was a rope and instead of the rope ending in a knot or a tassel there are shellfish and mussels and crabs, all kinds of shell fish carved out of stone to finish off the design. There are few churches throughout Scotland that can have been so close to their congregation. It was a fishermen's church.'

Dr James Fairbairn

What manner of man was this that had led them to their spiritual haven? James Fairbairn was born at Huntington in Lauderdale in 1804, son of a local farmer.

His distinguished relatives included Sir William and Sir Peter Fairbairn, celebrated engineers, Principal Fairbairn of the Free Church College, Glasgow and other divines. He was educated at Lauder School and Edinburgh University. Laid up with ill health for some years he was later tutor to the Dundas family of Arniston and assistant in Dalkeith Church of Scotland before coming to Newhaven where it was said of him 'No minister could have suited them better. His fine open generous nature, his genial spirit his tender loving heart and the broad humanity of the man enabled him to enter into the thoughts and feelings of every member of his church. As a matter of course he had much influence over his people and they had implicit trust in him as their best and firmest friend and they found by following his counsels that they were much advantaged.'

The Free Church congregation at Newhaven consisted of two well-defined classes. Besides the fishermen and their families there were the residents of the numerous villas of Trinity and the surrounding district many of whom were of considerable wealth and of some refinement and culture. So their minister had to make his preaching suitable and profitable to both. He managed to accomplish this for although a highly cultured man, in the pulpit he could accommodate his discourse admirably to his auditors. He was decidedly evangelical and looked with a considerable amount of disapprobation on all attempts to deviate from the standard of truth. In ecclesiastical politics he was a conservative.

Perhaps the most redeeming feature of that rather unequal novel, *Christie Johnstone*, was this fine description of him comforting his people following a drowning:

> 'All further debate was cut short by the entrance of one who came expressly to discharge the sad duty all had found so difficult. It was the Presbyterian clergyman of the place; he waved them back. 'I know, I know,' said he solemnly. 'Where is the wife?'
> She came out of her house at this moment, as it happened, to purchase something at Drysdale's shop, which was opposite.
> 'Beeny,' said the clergyman, 'I have sorrowful tidings.'
> 'Tell me them, sir,' said she unmoved. 'Is it a deeth?' added she quietly.
> 'It is! - death, sudden and terrible; in your own house I must tell it you, - (and may God show me how to break it to her).' He entered her house.
> 'Aweel,' said the woman to the others, 'it maun be some far awa cousin, or the like, for Liston an' me hae nae near freends. Meg, ye idle hizzy,' screamed she to her servant, who was one of the spectators, 'your pat is no' on yet; div ye think the men will no' be hungry when they come in fra the sea?'
> 'They will never hunger nor thirst ony mair,' said Jean solemnly, as the bereaved woman entered her own door.
> There ensued a listless and fearful silence.
> Every moment some sign of bitter sorrow was expected to break forth from the house, but none came; and amidst the expectation and silence the waves dashed louder and louder, as it seemed, against the dyke, conscious of what they had done.

At last, in a moment, a cry of agony arose, so terrible that all who heard
it trembled, and more than one woman shrieked in return, and fled from
the door; at which the next moment, the clergyman stood alone, collected, but pale, and beckoned. Several women advanced.
'One woman,' said he.
Jean Carnie was admitted, and after a while returned.
'She is come to hersel,' whispered she; 'I am no weel mysel.' And she
passed into her own house. Then Flucker crept to the door to see.
'Oh, dinna spy on her,' cried Christie.
'Oh, yes, Flucker,' said many voices.
'He is kneelin,' said Flucker. 'He has her hand, to gar her kneel tae, - she
winna, - she does na see him, nor hear him; he will hae her. He has won
her to kneel, - he is prayin, and greetin aside her. I canna see noo, my
een's blinded.'

Under his ministry there was a remarkable spiritual revival as this minute of
1860 from the Session's records testifies:

'The session directed their attention to the remarkable state of religious
feeling which has existed in the congregation for the last two or three months.
It appears to the members of the Session that a great awakening with regard to
divine things has prevailed in the congregation generally and among many
members and adherents of the flock in particular during the period aforesaid
which the Session trust and believe to have been the work of the Holy Spirit of
God. They had also reason to believe that many sinners had been brought to
repentance and the acknowledgment of the truth while the poeple of God had
been rebuked and edified.

'The Session therefore decided to record their humble and fervent gratitude
to Almighty God for this manifestation of His Grace and their earnest prayer
that He may be pleased to carry on this great work through faith unto
salvation.

'The Session further acknowledge the events that have taken place as con-
stituting a loud call upon themselves to continue instantly in prayer for their
own souls, for each other, and for all the flock and to give themselves with
renewed diligence to the discharge of the personal and official work which the
great Head of the Church has given them to do.'

He was ever active in schemes for the benefit of the public. Every plan of
ameliorating the condition of his fisherfolk congregation he did his best to render sucessful. Perhaps the most useful was that of the recontruction of the
Newhaven fishing fleet. He saw that the boats in use were no longer suited to
the changed conditions which required the fishermen to go further to sea, and
some years before his death he made a plan for replacing them by bigger decked boats. Thirty large boats, each costing £250 with compartments for
accommodation and fishing gear were the results of his efforts.

He was the originator of a movement to establish a lectureship in connection
with the Free Church and had the gratification of seeing the Cunningham Lectureship instituted at Edinburgh in 1862. In 1876 the University conferrred on
him the degree of Doctor of Divinity. He died in 1879 at the age of 75. He was
buried among much public respect at Warriston. Relays of fishermen carried
him to the grave and hundreds stood around his grave weeping openly.

The Session recorded its deep sense of loss: 'It having pleased the Lord to take to himself their beloved Pastor the Rev Dr Fairbairn since the last meeting of the session they hereby record their deep sense of the unspeakable loss which they and the congregation have sustained by his removal. Their fond recollections of effective preaching and of manifold works of faith and labours of love and their full conviction of the blessed fruits of his Ministry will continue long to appear among the people of this place. The members of the session also resolve that endeavouring meekly to bow under this sore bereavement they will give themselves to prayer that the Lord may be pleased to send them a pastor who, walking in the footsteps of Dr Fairbairn, may feed them with the bread of life.'

His pulpit gown was requested by a Miss Bryden but she subsequently abandoned her claim and left it to the church.

It was said that from his abilities, scholarship and high culture he could have obtained a more conspicuous position in his church. But he never entertained the idea. He was too tenderly attached to his beloved people. The Rev Alex R Aitken who today ministers to the combined charge in Newhaven sums up the attitude that prevails even a century later: 'He was a minister in the very finest tradition of our Church. He had many saintly qualities.'

Not long afterwards, Dr Wm Finlay, St Colme, Trinity, senior elder of the congregation, died. He was the much-loved doctor in Newhaven and one of the first elders of the United Free Church, a great helper to Dr Fairbairn and largely responsible for the financing of the new church. It had been his wish to live to see the debt entirely wiped out. As a kind of memorial the elders hoped the congregation would ere long remove the balance still remaining. Dr Finlay's son, Robert Bannatyne Finlay, born in Newhaven in 1868, who as a boy often helped serve in the chemist shop in Main Street and worshipped in the United Free Church, took degrees in medicine and law at Edinburgh, subsequently becoming Solicitor General and then Lord Chancellor, passing to the Lords as Viscount Nairn.

Dr David Kilpatrick

In September 1879 Dr David Kilpatrick was appointed to the vacancy. He was by contrast a dynamic character whose great preoccupation was education and it was largely in this sphere that he gained a wide reputation. One of his first acts was the building of a fine 120-ft spire to the church, a refinement Dr Fairbairn had long desired but failed to live to see. Born at Glasgow in 1849, the son of a minister, he was educated at Glasgow Academy and Glasgow University and after serving at Garelochhead came to Newhaven where he was held in the deepest affection. He took an active part in the work of many charitable institutions but his keenest interest was education and this led to his election to a number of educational bodies. For over 30 years he was a member of Leith School Board. Because of his great administrative gifts and judicial

The Rev. Dr David Kilpatrick, who succeeded Dr Fairbairn, had a distinguished career as an educationist (Courtesy of C Aitken).

intellect, his dignity, tact and impartiality, he was soon appointed chairman. In 1908 on the completion of 25 years with the Board he received a public presentation of a silver plate, an illuminated address and a cheque which he invested to provide dux medals for Leith and Trinity Academys. His services gained further recognition in 1913 when the new school in North Junction Street was named after him. In 1914 Glasgow University conferred on him the degree of Doctor of Divinity. He retired in 1917 and died in 1927.

Dr William Graham

When the Church of Scotland regained possession of Newhaven Church in 1849 services were resumed as a mission of North Leith. The new treasurer was asked to make inquiries about the Communion cups, flagons, tokens and linens, minute books and feu charter which belonged to the church and had not been given up. By the end of the year about 150 seats had been taken up. In the following year, the congregation unanimously issued a call to the Rev Dr William Graham to become their missionary. In 1859 the church was erected to full parish status as a quoad sacra daughter church of North Leith.

Dr Graham, who had now embarked on a long and memorable ministry, was born in 1820 and educated at Lochmaben School and the Universities of Edinburgh and St Andrews. He was a man of untiring energy, inspired vision and broad sympathies with a deep spiritual insight and completely consecrated, who now set about rebuilding the church spiritually and physically. For 37 years he continued to be a familiar figure in Newhaven streets, streets which like those of many other Scottish towns of the time, offended more senses than one. Fresh air and pure water were articles of his creed and he sought to forward movements which some labelled secular and deplored his interest in. He threw his energies into the cleaning and relaying of the streets, the opening up of the terrace walk between the railway and the sea, the erection of new houses in Victoria Place. He was supportive of the fishermen's cause in their confrontation with Edinburgh over the oyster fishing rights. He served as interim secretary to the delegates' committee on behalf of the fishermen of the East Coast of Scotland in connection with the alleged grievance of trawling and he helped greatly to bring about the Royal Commission which banned trawling from inshore waters. For his efforts in their behalf the fisherfolk gave him acknowledgment in the form of a silver salver.

It was characteristic that when the cholera raged in the country in 1866 and the Queen sent down orders to the ministers of the Church of Scotland that prayers should be offered in the public services that he should stand up and say in his place in the Edinburgh Presbytery: 'We are all at one on the necessity to persevere in prayer but I hold that the care of the body is a religious duty as well as the care of the soul. We should point out to our parishioners the necessity to remedy defects in ventilation and in the internal and external cleanliness of our houses and common stairs. I am glad to see that the authorities of Edinburgh are earnestly at work in this matter and I am sure that the missionaries, school teachers and others will assist them in their work. I am happy to think that under Provost Lindsay (of Leith) great good has been done in this respect in Leith and Newhaven. Let us urge on landlords the duty of seeing that their houses are fit for human habitation for I know places in the country where the farm animals are better housed than the work people.'

He worked continually for the improvement of the village and he left it an endowed parish, a church with stained glass windows, modernised interior, generally free from debt with a manse in the same enviable position and the Madras School and Victoria School taking about 400 children annually, savings banks, soup kitchens, collections taken annually for the poor and bread, broth, sugar and coals without regard to denomination distributed among the needy.

In 1863 he originated a scheme whereby fishermen bought their own houses, the houses south of the Main Street being the result of that movement. He introduced the organ - one of the first in Scotland to do so for the men and women of Newhaven were notable for their singing, and was instrumental in 1872 in stopping gunpowder shipments from the port. He also brought about changes to the Mantrap on the way to Leith. He left 200 or more proprietors of

The war memorials in Newhaven Parish Church which were removed there on the closure of St Andrews Church (Courtesy of W L Wilson).

houses in the village, assisted Dr Fairbairn in providing larger decked boats, helped the Society in its efforts for an extension of the harbour. He also instituted penny readings, spoke up for women's rights and wrote a book about astronomy and helped found the Edinburgh Scottish Coast Mission to Seamen.

There was no scheme for the mutual benefit of the village and its moral and religious welfare into which Mr Graham did not throw all his characteristic zeal. He was held as a faithful and true friend.

His doctrine was evangelical and his oratory eloquent. He did much to improve the church and left a beautiful edifice.

In 1864 he originated Edinburgh Working Men's Club. He helped launch the Church of Scotland Magazine in 1853. As an Established Church minister he said that when the bulk of the nation demanded disestablishment he would then be ready for it but he hoped and believed that it would not come in the time of anyone present. He had a firm hope that in place of disestablishment they would rather have a restoration of the old Church of Scotland.

Yet between him and Dr Fairbairn there existed a cordial relationship. It was a tribute to both men that they were unaffected by the doctrinal self-righteousness that characterised other neighbouring Edinburgh churches depicted by R.L.Stevenson: 'There is but a street between them in space, but a shadow between them in principle, and yet there they sit enchained and in admonitory accents pray for each other's growth in grace.'.

He died in 1887 in the manse at Primrose Bank Road. Relays of fishermen carried his coffin to Warriston and he was followed to the grave by a large congregation and sincerely mourned by the village to which he gave a lifetime. At the head of the grave stands a fine granite obelisk raised by the people of Newhaven irrespective of Church or creed, a lasting tribute to gratitude and affection of his memory.

He was followed by the Rev Thos Pearson. Different from Graham in many ways, he was a cultured preacher who attracted many cultured people to his church though a certain remoteness led to misunderstandings. He introduced a paid quartet and this led to the choir going on strike. Other innovations were Communion cards instead of tokens, sewing meetings, flowers in church, all of which led to the congregation growing. Another fine piece of work was the maintaining of a soup kitchen throughout the winter months for all poor persons, none being denied a periodic supply of soup meat and bread on account of their church connections. He carried out extensive alterations to the church and manse. Another improvement in 1900 was the installation of a hydraulic engine for driving the organ. Up till then the organ had always required the service of a blower as well as that of the organist and from time to time the minutes record friction between these two co-workers. The introduction left the organist in sole command of the field though not apparently without mechanical problems. Mr Pearson resigned in 1916 owing to ill health and died in 1920, lost in a changing world.

The Rev Munro Somerville came in 1916. Mr Somerville volunteered for the Army but poor health kept him out. However he raised money for troops with notable lectures. Over 200 men from the church enlisted during the war, many in minesweepers. Peter Thomson an elder on service was awarded the Gold Albert Medal for bravery. His vessel had been torpedoed and was sinking rapidly. Her crew got into the starboard lifeboat and cut the painter. The lifeline was however found to be curled round Peter Thomson's leg and realising the danger to all his comrades involved in delay he jumped overboard and so deliberately offered the sacrifice of his own life. Under water he managed to get the line clear and was picked up. It was such men that Newhaven gave to the defence of her country.

In 1919 a war memorial was placed in the vestibule of the church to the 24 men of the church who fell and the 184 men who served.

The Rev David Silver Johnston served the church from 1923 until 1931 and it was during his incumbency, in 1929 that the union of the Church of Scotland and Free Church occurred. Later the original parish was divided between St Andrews, the name now assumed by the old United Free Church, and Newhaven Parish Church. Mr Johnston was followed by a succession of five ministers.

At St Andrews the Rev Jas Irwin, the Rev D.H. Neilson and the Rev. William Birrell followed Dr Kilpatrick. With the decline of the village congregations also declined. When Mr Birrell came to Newhaven he said, he had had 15 trawler skippers among the membership. Ten years later there were just four. Where fully 300 fishermen had been based on the harbour at one time the number by the mid sixties had dropped to perhaps a dozen.

When Mr Birrell retired it became clear that Newhaven could no longer support two churches. There was much heart-searching as to which should be retained and the matter went to arbitration. Both the kirks 'up the Cut' and 'doon the pier' needed extensive repairs. Neither the relative size of the congregations nor their financial state was a significant factor and what probably influenced the decision was the much superior hall accommodation up the Cut. There was much unhappiness at the decision and great efforts were made to keep the pier church going, but without a minister or an adequate congregation there was little could be done and St Andrews was closed and the two congregations joined.

The joining of the two churches took place in 1974 and the Rev Alex R Aitken came as the first minister of the United Church in January 1975. About 50 or 60 Newhaven families from St Andrews are now happily members of the church, a tribute to his ministry. Mementos of St Andrews Church gracing the combined church include the pewter Communion plate used when the congregation held their open-air meetings in Starbank Park, a fine portrait of Dr Fairbairn, several photographs by D.O.Hill, and the wood-carved war memorials to the dead of both World Wars. The congregation is involved at present in plans for the celebration of the 150th anniversary of the church in 1986.

Revival Movement

The Revival movement which took root in Scotland, having reached this country from America via Northern Ireland, had less effect in Newhaven than in the other fishing villages, possibly because of the close ties to the church. The leader of the religious movement in the North East was a Peterhead cooper James Turner who kept on preaching and praying half the night until everybody had 'gone forrit' amid a sea of eager faces and shouts of 'Hallelujah'. In many places the newly-converted, finding conventional religion cold and unemotional, formed themselves into groups of Brethren and dissociated themselves from other Protestant bodies. There was no organised ministry, every male member having a right to preach. The movement, anti-clerical, separation from the world and its pleasures being insisted upon, has as its central tenet the infallibility of the Bible.

'The Brethren was a thing apart in Newhaven' said Rena Barnes. 'There was only a few people went to the Brethren. There was my father and Jimmy Wilson and Willie Ramsay - that was the man that used to say 'Now, bairns, it's a blessing, shut your eyes.' I would think there was only a dozen families went to the meeting.'

Hardly had this had time to cool down than the Salvation Army appeared with all the panoply of banners and brass bands and the waving of tambourines and this appealed even more than the open and closed Brethren.

Other religious bodies were also active. There was a good deal of missionary work aimed at the fisherfolk including the People's Mission, the Royal

National Mission to Deep Sea Fishermen, and the Church of Scotland's Mission to Workers in the Herring Industry. There was also a Mr Hall who ran the Scottish Coast Mission and he was based in Newhaven. It was non-denominational and he was highly spoken of. Folk flocked to his open-air meetings. 'I never hear the old hymns but what I think of Mr Hall holding those meetings down on the beach on a Summer's night.'

CHAPTER 13

The Society

The antecedents of the Society of Free Fishermen of Newhaven are lost beyond the horizons of the past and the motto on its flag -'Immemorial' - is the Society's own estimate of that antiquity.

The oldest document extant is an instrument of sasine dated 1572 but tradition at least carries the Society back more than 500 years and some have said it is the oldest trade association in Scotland. James VI gave it a charter in 1573 confirming its incorporation. The body is very exclusive, no one being admitted to membership unless he is the lawful son of a fisherman whose name is clear on the books.

This was not always the rule for previous to 1817 any fisherman could become a member on paying the dues. Since membership conveyed the right to dredge for oysters, numbers became so great that the Society to protect the villagers' rights adopted the exclusive rule. But with competition from outsiders removed, there developed a reluctance to pay the dues though the village was enjoying prosperity at the time. This brought the Society to a standstill in 1849. After a dormant three years, a dedicated Boxmaster, James Wilson, revived its fortunes and by 1867 it had achieved its highest membership of 400 and its greatest fame, the Sheriff Substitute of Orkney writing for a copy of the rules so that a similar society might be formed there.

This exclusive brotherhood of the sea is described in *The Free Fishers* which John Buchan modelled on the Newhaven Society, though in the novel he transfers the locale to Fife:

'To be a member was to have behind one, so long as one obeyed the rules, a posse of stalwart allies. It had been founded long ago - no man knew when, though there were many legends. Often it had fallen foul of the law, as in the Jacobite troubles, when it had ferried more than one much-sought gentleman between France and Scotland. Its ostensible purpose was the protection of fisher rights and a kind of co-operative insurance against the perils of the sea, but these rights were generously interpreted and there had been times when free trade was its main concern and the east-coast gaugers led a weary life.'

The Society is governed by a Preses and Boxmaster and committee who are changed annually. The election gave Newhaven its annual gala night when a great torchlight procession was formed for the 'lifting of the box' and its conveyance to the house of the new boxmaster for the year. This event was followed by a supper noted for its flowing bowl. It was in this annual change-over that many of the ancient records were lost.

There is one respect in which the Society was different from the other trade associations - it was the only one, in the Lothians at least, to become what amounted to a town council.

This came about for several reasons: the Church and the Civic fathers were too remote to exercise much direct control and the village in its self-imposed solitude made no attempt to narrow the gap. Local government as we know it virtually did not exist at that time. The church looked after the poor and appointed a baron bailie to collect tithes and punish offenders and a town drummer to announce such proclamations as Royal birthdays, markets, wars and flittings. (One such proclamation in Newhaven in 1743 announced by tuck of drum that George II's birthday would be celebrated by all the boats in the harbour putting out all flags and all masters and mistresses of families put lighted candles in their windows but not to throw squibs or stones at windows).

In 1631, when Newhaven was taken out of the Parish of St Cuthberts for religious purposes and added to North Leith, it was not surprising that their new spiritual mentors should have shied away from the awesome burden of looking after the physical welfare of a village with such a dangerous way of life. So the Society gave a bond absolving the Kirk of its legal obligation and under-took itself to look after the poor, decayed and destitute within the little township. This bond they renewed through the centuries on each change of minister. (The bond of 1706 which is still preserved was subscribed to by 72 fishermen, some of whom could write, the majority making their mark with their initials or a cross). So what had begun as a voluntary association, founded to help its members in time of trouble, became formalised into a body with legal obligations.

The story of the Society's development from these early beginnings is admirably told by Robin M. Black in a short history compiled from the records of James Wilson, former Boxmaster, and from the Society's papers now held in the Scottish Records Office, which give an invaluable glimpse into the past.

Giving out funeral grants led the Society to acquire a burial ground and other property and this brought so many additional public duties that it became responsible for the conduct of the affairs of the whole community and became recognised by other authorities in this role. It took care of the cleaning and paving of the streets, the upkeep of the harbour, the school, the building and renting of houses, the protection of the oyster beds, the resisting of pressures from the Town Council and the Church and the Navy and other regulating bodies where these bore too heavily upon its people, wrestling to keep its funds out of the hands of the lawyers, and a multitude of other tasks involving the welfare of its community.

Unpaid, often unthanked and alas sometimes unloved, it persevered against external pressures to preserve for its people the immemorial privileges which without it would have been swallowed up by the clamouring greed of neighbours.

Periodically the Lord Provost and magistrates would visit Newhaven and hold court and make appreciative speeches about the fine work of the fishermen. In 1827, after a thirty-year absence, one such visit was held in the centre of the village and on departure the Civic leaders left five guineas for the poor and another guinea to the Society to drink the health of the Council 'which they did three times three and His Majesty's health four times four with grat glee'.

To Succour the Poor

But the Society's primary function was to succour the poor, irrespective of moral judgment - there were none such as the Victorians would call the undeserving poor.

To this end it had a round strong and 'sufficient secure box' with two locks and keys and a hole in the lid to let the money in. From its very beginnings, every fisherman in Newhaven had to take his turn and stand at the foot of the Whale Brae with a large pewter plate before him and a notice beside the plate saying 'Please remember the poor of Newhaven' and the takings were solemnly posted away in the Box which was opened by the Boxmaster, in the presence of the Kirk Session who held the other key, before the proceeds were distributed to the poor. To augment these contributions a scale of charges for membership was laid down: sixteen shillings Scots for every man that draws an deal (oar) within a boat (the Scots shilling was worth only a penny sterling); every master that takes an apprentice, the same; every apprentice at his entry fourty shillings, every new entrant to the Society four pounds Scots and every boat going to the Lammas herring drave (drive) at Dunbar twenty-six shillings and eightpence Scots. But any stranger that marries not a woman that belongs to the Incorporation shall pay into the Box at his entry the sum of eight pounds.

James Wilson makes this comment: 'The particular year in which the plate was done away with and the poor handed over to the parish of North Leith I cannot state, but it is well known that the poor of Newhaven were far better looked to and more given to them by means of the plate than since they were handed over to the parish.'

When the Society first acquired the burial ground adjoining St James' Chapel is not recorded but it was probably sometime in the 16th century not long after the Reformation and at that time the little graveyard crowded the shore as though the departed must still be within sound of the sea. A funeral was as much a social event as a wedding and a great procession would form, the body wrapped in the mort-cloth hired from the Society would be borne along on poles held by the chief mourners and as it passed within the burial ground each follower would drop into the plate beside the entrance his contribution to provide for the subsequent jollification of the lykewake, for death was looked on then as very much a fact of life, an attitude that might now be regarded as callous.

In the churchyard was the 'dead house', a small cellar-like building where the relatives of the dead would keep watch for six weeks afterwards to ward off

the attentions of the 'Dummy Doctors' and many a strange story of eerie spec-
tral incidents emanated from this cold vigil. So persistent were the attentions
of the body-snatchers at the beginning of the 19th century that the Society
decided to rebuild the watch house above the old one with a door to the south
and a window to the north and to put in two muskets with powder and ball
together with other weapons for the use of the occupants, 'the watch to continue while health and life endures and likewise no strangers to be allowed
burial.'

Some of the younger element took an irreverent view of the arrangements
and crept into the graveyard under cloud of night, attired in sheets and utter-
ing weird shreiks in a riotous manner. They took to their heels however under
musket-fire and were subsequently fined and cautioned by the Society.

But the threat was real enough and not only to the dead. Mrs Colley, who
was secretary to the Society for a record 34 years, tells of an old retired seaman
who lived in New Lane with his daughter about this period and had the job of
going round the houses in the early hours, wakening the fishermen so that they
could catch the tide. One morning he got up as usual just as dawn was breaking
but he didn't go round the houses and he didn't come back home. He had simply disappeared. Could the Dummy Doctors have got him? Not long afterwards a fisherman called 'Banniky' rose early and strolled down New Lane to
the shore to admire the sun coming up over the South Bay. He saw a cab
approaching from Leith with two men in tile hats up front. But it wasn't making
any noise - there must be something on the horses' hooves. He took to his heels
and the men in tile hats ran after him up New Lane and up the outside stair to
his house where he slammed and bolted the door and they hammered on it
while he and his family crouched inside until the racket ceased.

A later mystery occurred when James Liston left home one midnight in 1875
to call his crew to make ready for the herring fishing as was the custom on Monday mornings. He never was heard to call his crew nor was it ever known where
he went or what happened to him. It was bright moonlight that night until
daybreak but no clue was ever found.

The graveyard became so full that it was impossible to bury the corpse
without disinterring the bones of the past dead and in 1842 the Society closed
it and funerals were transferred to the newly-opened Rosebank Cemetery
at Bonnington.

In their efforts to preserve the village's ancient fishing rights on the oyster
beds, the Society had frequent recourse to the law, Mr James Wilson ruefully
remarking that from 1839 to 1889 the Society had paid to lawyers the sum of
£2481 19s 11 1/2d - a great sum indeed. Reading through the old papers it is
difficult to resist the suspicion that many of the hares chased by the legal
fraternity through the courts were of their own starting as for example when a
lawyer tried to get them to take out an injunction against Edinburgh Corporation or again to resist the building of the new harbour and the new
fishmarket.

There was an anonymous letter to the Edinburgh Town Council alleging

Mr James Wilson, Secretary, Boxmaster and chronicler of the Society of Free Fishermen of Newhaven, who gave devoted service to the Society in a variety of ways over many years. (Courtesy of J Aitken).

that the fishermen were taking undersized oysters. This was investigated by a law agent who was able at no small cost to the Society to give the most unqualified refutation. 'Not being satisfied with the explanation of the men,' he told the Town Clerk, 'I went to the pier and caused one of the casks that had been filled the day before you received the anonymous communication and nailed up ready for export to be broken open and with my own hands I dug down to the centre of the cask and took out 50 oysters (which I have now the pleasure to send you herewith as a gift from Newhaven) and among these there will not be found a single brood oyster.'

Finally they got fed up with this particular lawyer and got the Rev Dr Graham to act for them. They gave the legal gentleman a dose of his own medicine by taking him to law and found that he had overcharged them by a substantial amount but he wouldn't pay up, writing instead asking for more money: 'One of my clerks has run away and robbed me of a large sum of money. I would be obliged if you could favour me with a further payment.'

The Fish Tythes

A medieval survival against which the Society fought successfully was the minister's tiends - a right of the parish minister to a share in all fish brought into Leith and Newhaven. These tythes or taxes were detested by the fishermen who from earliest times fought against paying them. Land tythes were of ancient origin but sea-tythes were a comparatively unknown imposition. The first recorded quarrel in the matter occurs in 1630 when James Drummond, the tacksman for Lord Holyroodhouse pursued spulzie (took them to court) for non-payment, alleging that they had been paying up in the past. The Courts tended to favour the fishermen and reduced the amount to be paid. In any event in the following year Newhaven was taken out of the jurisdiction o: Holyrood and became part of North Leith parish. Here by ancient right re affirmed by the House of Lords in 1781 the tythes on fish landed at Leitl belonged to the Kirk Session who used them for the support of the ministei reader and schoolmaster. The tythes were let out to a tacksman who paid s much to the church and did his utmost to squeeze every penny he could froi the fishers. Since Newhaven had pledged to look after its own affairs it may have felt some moral justification in again refusing payment. In any case an annual payment, in lieu of the Newhaven tax, was being made by the Magistrates of Edinburgh to the minister to encourage the fishermen to supply Edinburgh market with fresh fish.

In 1820 a tacksman James Comb tried to collect ls for every boat coming into Newhaven. The fishermen would not pay. He summoned one of them, John Young, to appear before the Lord Provost. Young failed to appear and as a result was committed to prison. Then Comb summoned another, William Wilson. The Society decided this game had gone far enough. They fought the case before the Magistrates and won.

In 1828 when a new minister came to North Leith it seems a new tacksman a Mr Giffen was appointed who decided to get tough again with the fishermen. 'In my view,' he said, 'the minister has a right to a tenth part of all fresh fish brought into Newhaven and if it were strictly exacted I think I may say without mistake that the sum exigible from each of the fishermen would be nearer three pounds than three shillings.' As a concession, he was willing to let the fishermen do the collection themselves and hand it over to him in bulk. 'This is the furthest I can go.' He was much surprised by their refusal and threatened that the minister would let the tythes by public roup which would subject the fishermen to a demand for very much more than he was asking. He appears to have met with as much success as previous tacksmen and to have given up in despair for two years later another appears on the scene, a Mr Spence. He demanded considerably more, asking for 11s 8d each from 55 boats. In the face of a stoic disinterest he greatly moderated his demands to an outright annual payment of £18 from the village.

It appears that at this point the Parish minister Dr Buchanan, heard what was being done in his name and all demands for tythes from Newhaven were

The Free Fishermen's Society Hall in Main Street which for close to 100 years served as their meeting place and as a hall for other organisations in the village.

dropped. James Wilson records in 1855 that he never found any receipts among the Society's papers for the payment of tythes and from his inquiries he believed that for 40 years before his own time not a penny had been paid. And so passive resistance carried the day.

An odd footnote occurred nearly half a century later when a lighthousekeeper in the employment of Leith Dock Commission is said to have tried to revive the tax. The Dock Commission issued a public denial that it had any intentions of reintroducing the odious impost and that was the last ever heard on the subject.

Another tax which was strongly resented was exacted by Leith and by Edinburgh. In both places every fisherlass going to the town with a burden of fish or oysters was not allowed out again without paying tuppence. The Society frequently protested against these charges and James Wilson reports that he attended a meeting where the Preses James Flucker, better known as 'Long Sam' urged the members to make another strong protest. This appears to have been done and Edinburgh abolished the practice, evidently in 1828, and some time later Leith was forced to do the same.

For nearly a quarter of a century Newhaven harbour was used for shipping large quantities of gunpowder. This was brought in convoys of farm carts and the barrels were taken out in the fishing boats to schooners lying in the roads. The whole operation was recklessly casual, the barrels being thrown from the carts on to the crowded pier where they sometimes split open and spilt their contents and all the while fishing boats arrived and departed with their cooking fires alight and the stevedores puffed at their clay pipes and the fishermen did their primitive joinery, boring holes with red-hot pokers. When the carts arrived too late at night to unload they would be parked under the windows of the houses. Defoe was appalled by the practice and noted that at Rosslyn a whole street had been blown up. The Society, led by Dr Graham, forced a public inquiry. 'We must have that black enemy away from amongst us.' As a result the shipments were transferred to Leith Docks.

Cleaning the Streets

Royal Edinburgh, said Defoe, was the finest city in Europe. It was also to his mind one of the dirtiest. The gutters were nothing but open sewers. People tried to keep to the crown of the street for middens were piled high on either side and were added to from on high following a cry of 'gardyloo!'. And this was true too of Leith and of Newhaven. When the folk of Leith objected to Edinburgh's sewage floating down the river, they were assured it was quite wholesome so long as it was kept in motion!

Each household accumulated its rubbish outside its own front door. Bertram in *The Harvest of the Sea* wrote of 'all that wonderful filth scattered about which is a sanitary peculiarity' of the fishing village where in the days of white fishing every house had its ain midden heap, for the shells of mussels that were so necessary to this particular industry were thrown out on the street daily.

The cleaning of the streets was looked on as a source of funds to the Society for the farmers were willing to pay well for the dung or fulzie and they provided the scavengers who worked through the night to carry it off. Newhaven had an additional source of revenue: the gutting that followed the herring fleets produced large quantities of saleable offal.

When the Society decided to do something about the insanitary state, the fisherfolk asked 'Why do you want to clean up the village? You say it's not good for folk's health. Look and ye'll see that the scavengers in Edinburgh and Leith are the healthiest people.'

But sometimes the Society took a less enlightened view. On another occasion a deputation consisting of the Preces and the Boxmaster waited upon one of the cleaning committees of Leith Town Council to represent that if they persisted in introducing gas lamps into Newhaven the effect would be to 'blear oor een and when we come to the pierheid to step into the boat oor een will be sae bleared that we will mistake the wave for the boat and ye'll droon us.'

The barometer and weather board provided and maintained by the Society at the pierhead from 1775.

The village was supplied by four wells, the principal one being in St Andrew's Square (now Fishermen's Square) and others in Westmost Close and in New Lane. There was no burn, though one flowed along the top of the village, emerging at Anchorfield. It was later piped in and its bed was followed by the railway line. The Society received a letter in 1828 from an enterprising plumber who offered to lay on a pipe to the Society's property and to build them a house, all for the sum of £9.

After Leith received its independence from Edinburgh in 1833 and set up its own town council, many of these municipal responsibilities passed out of the hands of the Society.

The School

Romantic concepts of an educated peasantry take no account of the harsh facts of pre-industrial society. The tremendous bustle and energy that characterised Newhaven was directed to one purpose only - winning a living from the sea. Beyond that and the Kirk there was time for little. Children helped their mother bait the lines until at ten the boys were old enough to go to sea with their fathers and the girls to help carry the creel.

Yet from the time when the Society assumed responsibility for its own poor, it also took on the other secular duty that fell normally to the Church, that of providing a school.

The first Newhaven school stood for more than 200 years in School Close, now known as Lamb's Close. The Society paid the schoolmaster six pounds a year and he got what he could for tuition. He taught reading, writing and arithmetic, pupils to furnish their own paper, quills and ink. Any children bringing a certificate from the Boxmaster that their parents were unable to pay would be taught free.

'Out of that same school,' said James Wilson, 'there were some very good and honourable men who in their day were an honour to themselves and to the town they belonged to, and best of all an honour and pillars in the church of Christ, and some of them well qualified even at the pen.'

Early in the 19th century the school had become so decrepit that a new one was built on the West Links at the spot now occupied by the Free Fishermen's Hall. The Society was instrumental in securing the ground from Edinburgh Town Council, 'the Fishermen and the City Magistrates being very gracious towards each other at this time,' said Mr Wilson. The Society raised the necessary £140 from its own funds and by subscription, the Duke of Buccleuch and Lord Melville giving £5 each and the City of Edinburgh £10, and 20 cartloads of best rubble were donated by the owners of Craigleith Quarry. To mark the laying of the foundation stone the fishermen walked through the town with their banners flying, followed by the women and bairns to the site of the new school. Here an immense ring was formed in the centre of which the Society's office-bearers and some of the leading citizens of Edinburgh took their places. A Mr Moss was appointed schoolmaster on the promise that he would bring up the children in the fear and admiration of the Lord and his wife would teach the girls sewing.

His performance appears to have been less than promised because a Sunday school society to promote religious instruction, founded by the Rev Dr Ireland of North Leith Church, found their efforts hampered by the standard of literacy of the children. 'Shall we only help if asked?' they said. 'It would be like going down the pier and seeing a man drowning and saying to him: Shall I take you out? And the man being past speaking you reply: If you do not choose to ask my assistance you shall not have it.' So they offered to take over the Newhaven school. The Society accepted but continued to upkeep the building and even on occasions refused to take a rent. The new school board quickly extended the school to include girls and infants, taking over the house above the school for this purpose. (In 1852 this top flat reverted to the Society for use as an office).

Very soon the building proved too small and Dr Ireland's successor, the Rev Dr Buchanan, secured the feu of the ground on which Victoria School was built. A third school, the Madras School, was built immediately behind the

The 1985 office-bearers and committee of the Society of Free Fishermen of Newhaven photographed in their clubroom at Wester Close Newhaven.

Back row (l to r): J.R. Wilson, J. Carnie, J.C. Wilson, W. Liston, A. Noble, W. Noble, I. Rutherford, J. Lyle, T. Wilson, W. Wilson.

Front Row; J. Liston, Trustee, G. Liston, Trustee, W. Logan Wilson, Boxmaster, J. Kitchener Liston, President, J. Carnie, Trustee, A. Linton. The President holds the Texel Cup and he and the Boxmaster wear the historic silver medals.

Newhaven Church. (It is now the church hall). At one time there were five schools in the village but as Victoria School was extended and parish schools were centralised under local school boards the others were closed down and amalgamated in Victoria School. Generations of Newhaven children have been educated within its walls and have scattered to all parts of the world. The present Headmaster, Mr Ball, says that when the school celebrated its centenary in 1944 with a pageant of the village in the Usher Hall, former pupils from many distant lands sent a stream of contributions to help swell the funds which were devoted by the school to the endowment of a three-cot children's ward at Leith Hospital.

When the school at the west end of Main Street was closed down the Society decided to try to get the site to build a new hall, since they could not accommodate their numbers for meetings in Victoria School. Although the Corporation had given the site gratis to the village it had been for public use and the building of a hall for the fishermen could not be regarded as public use. So the Corporation got around it by putting the ground up for public auction with the stipulation that whoever got the ground must build a hall for the fishermen. There being no other takers, the Society got the feu. The hall was soon built along with two shops in Main Street and three houses at the back in Pier Place. In 1878 the new hall was opened with a grand soiree. Dr Fairbairn was in the chair, supported by Dr Graham, and in his remarks congratulated the fisher-folk on their new hall and new harbour. He referred to the kindly way H.M. The Queen had recently alluded to the Newhaven folk in her book. Mr Wilson remarks 'That night was a very lively one in Newhaven'.

The hall was an immediate success and was in constant demand from a variety of religious and secular bodies. But the cost had been unexpectedly high, partly through mistakes on the mason's part, and totalled £1578 when the average weekly wage was less than £1. A sum of £1400 had been borrowed from Leith Property Investment Company and this weighed heavily on the Society. For ten years they struggled on, reducing the debt by some £600, then they hit on the idea of a grand two-day bazaar in the Music Hall, Edinburgh. In 1888 an appeal was printed and widely distributed which briefly told the history of the Society and appealed for public support. So successful was this effort and a subsequent concert that the Society was able to clear off all its debts and at a public meeting the Boxmaster, Robert Wilson, was presented by the Investment Company with the titles of the hall shops and houses. To commemorate the event the Bazaar Committee presented the Preses, Alexander Linton, with a silver medal similar to the one worn by the Boxmaster and a brooch to his wife, similar to the one worn by the Boxmaster's wife. A balance of cash in hand of £7 was solemnly handed over to the Boxmaster.

Men of Property

As property-owners the Society had varied fortunes. The ground on which St Andrews Church was built and which was feued to it at £10 a year, was bought in 1766 at a bargain price of £55. It had formed part of St James Chapel garden and there were four houses on it. These were taken down and part of the ground given over to the cemetery. But, said James Wilson, 'although it was gotten at the time cheap enough still in after time it has been very dear ground.'. The original transaction was done by the then Boxmaster, William Durham. Fifty years later in an unexplained transaction, David Durham sold it to a Mr Butler. To try to regain possession the Society embarked on a long lawsuit which cost £600 in legal fees. They were short by £350 of this total but went around the doors seeking contributions until they had raised it.

An unexpected result was that the Society found themselves owners of property in East Wemyss seized from Butler's heirs. This was administered for them by a Kirkcaldy lawyer but despite repeated trips to Kirkcaldy to try and collect the money due 'they always got very little' and on his being asked to make a final reckoning, the Society found itself in his debt. Finally the Society did the houses up and sold them with much relief.

The latter part of the 18th century seems to have been a time of acquisition for the records show the Society buying six houses in 1766 and a piece of waste ground in 1772 which they added to the burial ground. In 1806 they bought two more houses and demolished them to the same end. They also had a number of houses in Westmost Close.

They had extensive property at the pier, having bought this in 1794. In 1867 they knocked down the old property and built a three-storey house on the site at a cost of £900. In the old property had been a barber's shop which had lost its trade when the ferries moved to Granton. They decided not to have a shop in the new premises though they would put up a clock tower facing out to sea. The clock was by Jas Ritchie and Sons, Edinburgh with wheelwork of heavy yellow brass, hand hammered and fully polished and would go for eight days at a winding. It cost £30 and was paid for by public subscription and the gas for lighting was supplied free by the Edinburgh and Leith Gas Company. The adjacent old Watch House, not now required since the burial ground had been closed, was knocked down and an office and cellar added to the new building. On the front of the new building at the pierhead was placed the Society's barometer and the weather report box with tidal information. The Society continued to build houses from time to time and in 1876 completed two blocks in Lamb's Court and two flats of a tenement in Westmost Close.

The old town of Newhaven had long lacked a suitable place for drying and tanning its nets. The new town area around Annfield was happier in this respect, having a fine beach and a small park but in the old town the nets were dried on masts resting across boats or on the harbour walls. But there was a large area of cultivated ground to the east of Whale Brae which belonged to the Admiralty. After some negotiation the Society got the renting of it for £20 a year and the money was collected from boat crews as they came home from the Lammas herring fishing. In 1870 the Admiralty intimated they were selling off all their local lands. The Society, alarmed, sent a deputation to the Secretary of the Board of Fisheries. He proved a good friend and after he had informed the Admiralty of the Newhaven men's long history of patriotic service in the Navy, they granted the Society a 999-year lease. The park, apart from housing the net-boiling vats, a boatbuilding yard, a stand for wintering the yawls, a sailmaker's loft, a kippering shed and a blacksmith's forge, served as a village green.

Eventually with the development of local government, the Society found itself relieved of many of its earlier responsibilities. After relief of the poor and street cleaning were by statute thrown on the ratepayers and education became the reponsibility of the School Boards, and the growth of local authorities and the decline of the fishing robbed it of much of its role, it concentrated more on providing aliment in sickness and death. In 1845 a revised set of printed rules received official approval in terms of the Friendly Society Acts (though there was some difficulty in registration due to the many other facets of the Society's activities).

The Society has had a long line of devoted office-bearers outstanding among whom have been James Wilson who served for more than two decades as secretary, and Mrs Minnie Colley, brought in during the last war to fill a temporary gap and who stayed on for a record 32 years. Under the present Boxmaster, William L. Wilson, the Society's finances have been streamlined, benefits increased, and the membership role brought to over 100 including, says Mr Wilson, doctors, lawyers, architects, pilots, captains, professional men of every kind and in every part of the world though entry is still restricted to descendants of the male line. The Society has social occasions twice a year, a Christmas dinner at the Peacock Inn and a bus outing in the summer.

With no further use for the large hall, the Society sold it some years ago and it is now the headquarters of Leith Motor Boat Club which uses Newhaven harbour for its boats. The money realised was invested to provide increased benefits for the members. In a recent report Mr Wilson writes: 'The Society is in good heart with new members joining, a mixture of proffessional and artisan, each grasping the invitation to align themselves with a kinship who have jealously protected the unique society lineage down the ages, entry to which neither rank, class or position is a basis - all are quite rare and unknown in other brotherhoods. Today our funds have developed so that no longer are we limited to sickness and death benefits but are able to provide increased pensions and other subsidiary benefits and to divert funds for management, propaganda and social functions so that a closer kinship in the Society may be ours. In May we presented the local community, through Edinburgh District Council, with a commemorative bench, placed in a special and popular position at the entrance of the Fishmarket.' The Society, which, from time immemorial has an unsupassed record of service, continues that fine tradition in today's altered circumstances.

CHAPTER 14

Personally Speaking

Perhaps because of its self-imposed isolation Newhaven seems to have had more than its share of characters. To me one of these was my grandmother Maggie Noble who was widowed at 33 with four children under ten. Her man, David Paterson, had been ill for months, unable to get to the fishing. Malaria, they thought, picked up in South Africa. She bought a Siedlitz powder for him but when she went in the morning he was dead. So she took it herself and went out and got a job.

In fact she took on three jobs, her daughter Rena Barnes recalls. 'She went to the fishmarket at about 6 o'clock and then sold the fish around Trinity and then in the afternoon she would go back to Trinity and do the washing for the gentry or some housework. And in the evening she went and washed up after their parties at night and she would bring stuff home. We were fed from the best of the land. Who looked after us? We were just ourselves. At first Jenny used to take me to school with her - I was just two at the time. They were allowed to do that. Then there was a woman in Main Street had a paraffin oil shop, a Mrs Gow, she looked after me. I remember Rita used to climb on Davie's back to get at the lock when they came home from school.

'When my father died the Church put a bag of coal at her door. And she says: Whaes are they coals? I never ordered they coals. He says: They're for you Maggie. She says: When I want coal I will tell you, but, she says, I am not needing your coal just now.

'For nine months everything was black. Jenny (the eldest) was her right hand, then Jenny fell ill. Mr Hall the missionary came on the Friday afternoon and said: I think we will put up a prayer for Jenny. Oh Lord, if it be Thy will, make Jenny better. She was staggered. 'If it be Thy will'? Jenny's bound to get better. It's not possible that Jenny would die. And Jenny died just almost after that. (Sadly) It was her heart. However, after that she had this vision that she talked about. She dreamed she was in the cemetery at Rosebank and she was just coming out of the gate when the Heavens opened and Jenny says: You are not to worry, I am all right. And this was the new vision she had and from that on she went from strength to strength.

'She would be at the fishmarket about six in the morning and all you would hear were the auctioneers selling the fish like what any auctioneer sounds: Nananana...When I was maybe about eight or nine I would go along and see if I could see her and there she would be standing in a group and there would maybe be about six of them. And they would buy a box of fish between the six of them and they would divide the fish into six piles. If there was anybody passing they would each give that person a something to put on each bundle. If he put your wee pocket knife or pencil on a pile it was yours. There were quite a few groups of five or six in a group. They used to call it 'kyling' the fish.

'So,' continued Rena Barnes, 'she had these three jobs and she saved all the half crowns she got for her work. She got half a crown at night and half a crown in the afternoon and she had these biscuit barrels. And I remember asking for a ha'penny and she says: Where would I have a ha'penny? I says: You have got it in these two barrels there, they're fair bursting. And then she bought a piano with all these half crowns. Nobody else had a piano but my mother. She sent us to piano lessons. I remember the tutor. He had a grocer's shop at the harbour and you got a store book and you ordered your coal there and my mother used to order two half loaves and a bag of coal. Nono, that's not a funny order. As long as you had a fire and a bit of bread you were all right. 'Gather up the fragments, let nothing be lost,' she would say. And: 'Guid meat doesnae need sauce, and bad meat doesnae deserve it.'

'Well things got better. There was this Miss Combe that lived in Anchorfield and she had two nieces that were school teachers. She had this fish run in Juniper Green and she came to my mother one night. I was about nine or ten at the time. She was a great one in the Suffragette movement and we all had badges through her and I remember her knocking at the door in New Lane and she says: Maggie, the two girls want me to look after them, keep house for them. I was wondering if you would take my round. It is really worth while. This Miss Combe was a teacher herself at one time and she took her glove and slapped a lassie's face with her leather glove and she was sacked so she took up the fish round. Her brother was a headmaster in Leith. I remember that woman coming very often at night and she would be sitting and the clock would strike midnight and she would sing: Twelve o'clock, twelve o'clock. This was us sitting round the fire with my mother at twelve o'clock at night. No early bedders. We waited for her coming back from the parties.

'The round was Juniper Green. It was every day to Babberton Golf Course and Dr Bramwell's house away down the avenue from the golf course. A few people in Lanark Road, a few in Babberton Avenue and a few in Currie. That was a fair walk (something like 16 miles?) - no wonder she had corns and bunions. She used to wear boys' shoes. During the first world war she started taking the train at Newhaven to Dalry Road and another to Juniper Green. But sometimes she would take the train just to Slateford and walk the rest. There was a special window at Newhaven Station just for the fishwives and her creel was so heavy it used to take three porters to lift it on her back - that was Wee Maggie Noble. I was 15 at the time and I used to make up her books. It was accounts she used to give these people. And then Dr Bramwell asked her to come to some professors in the West End so she served these gentry at Randolph Crescent and Chester Street and Manor Place in the West End. Sometimes she got the chance of bottles of brandy from seamen at Leith docks and she would sell them at Babberton Golf Club. She made a lot of money and bought a house in Prince Regent Street, Leith and she had a bigger house in Annfield (where the pilots lived) - five rooms. She used to leave her basket and fishwife's clothes in Auntie Meg's and change there. She was very ambitious, wanted everything right. She gave us both watches and fur coats when nobody

Maggie Noble (Courtesy of Mrs Greta Dyer).

else had fur coats. Her family had fallen out with her for marrying 'beneath her' and into the Brethren for Granny Carnie was Kirk and very proud. Grannie Carnie, it was said, was that angry she threw the Bible at her.

'Then they all went to Canada and made a lot of money and when they died Uncle Alec wrote to my mother and said if she wanted any of the money she would have to see to it herself. She wrote back to say: I am managing quite well without it so I will not bother. She didn't only fillet fish on the spot she used to do them all with the tail through the eyes and all sorts of things. It was a fish business she had, she wasn't just a fishwife.'

One of the great characters of Newhaven was fishwife Meggie Ramsay, relates Ian Nimmo in his *Portrait of Edinburgh*. Meggie was an acknowledged beauty in her day but the bite of her tongue was even more famous than her looks. Once one of Edinburgh's gay young men about town decided to hold a fish supper in the village and during the evening took the chance to deliver a stinging attack on the fishy smell of Newhaven. It was too much for Meg. Up she jumped shaking her fist. There was not a man there dare stop her. 'De'il scrape the parlin face o' ye,' she cried. 'The last I saw ye ye were in the auld To'buith for debt. Forby ye are owing me 6d for the brood o' oysters ye got the water caddie tae wile oot o' me. I'll be obliged tae ye for it this verra meenit. Smell! Ye'll dowm a guid honest stink where there's nane. In fact the To'buith's whiles like tae gar me faint.'

Another character was an old Newhaven pilot by the name of Noble who had been married four times and had had four families. There were six in the last family. This is how I heard the story: 'There was one time two pilots were introduced to each other of the same name and after a wee bit conversation they shook hands as stepbrothers! If there was no will the lawyers must have had a great time - you know what I mean? Have you got me? Now that's not the end of my story. After his first wife was buried and he married his second wife he brought her up and showed her where Maggie was: 'That's where you'll lie.' And similarly with the third one, he showed her where the first two were. And the fourth wife he did the same. But she outlived him. There was supposed to be a text at the bottom which read: 'Be ye also ready' and there was also 'Blessed are they that die in the Lord for they rest from their labours and their works do follow them.' When he died he was 79 and the oldest pilot in Leith.'

Sandy Noble, another Newhaven notable, probably knows all there is to know about the village. He is a marvellous raconteur and it is difficult to believe that as a child he had a terrible stutter. 'At Trinity school poetry was murder for me, I never knew what was going to come out. But I remember my brother Peter getting *The Execution of Montrose*. He was to learn it: 'Come hither Cameron, Come stand beside my knee..'etc. Well the teacher called me and the class looked around and sniggered, 'What kind of a show are we going to get this time?' But I stood up and tried to put myself in the person who was saying the words and it came out perfectly. Their silence was deafening. They were stupefied. It was magnificent but they never got the shock of their lives that I did. It was a thrill and the teacher said: 'Why can't you do that always?' The ability was there, what kept it? But I wasn't finished with it yet. For ten years it was agony and I got a job and saved up pennies and tuppences and went to a great elocution teacher, Robert C. Bell of Princes Street. He gave me a philosophy that was really marvellous. I got an invitation to speak at a meeting and he said: 'You must, and you must speak for ten minutes.' Well I didn't realise until afterwards that I had spoken for eighteen and a half minutes. I loved to sing and I was all right when I was singing. The salvation of the whole thing is - singing. I was 52 years in the Royal Choral Union.' Sandy had been three when his mother died. 'There were six of us in a but and ben and father was at sea so my eldest sister was kept from school to look after us. I went to Newhaven School and after that I got a bursary to Trinity Academy. It was not academic results they looked for but: Attendance, perfect; Health, excellent; Deportment, correct. When I got my bursary of £11 for three years it paid for all the books as well but in those days the same book did for ten years so I could use my brother's. When I decided to leave the Rector sent for me: 'Why are you going?' I was not in a fit state to tell him but he understood. 'Open that door and look inside.' It was a press filled from floor to ceiling with books, books that would take you to the Prelim and to University. 'One set is for you if you will stay.' But he did not know that I had not a small room to study and if you haven't got that you can't do it, not among six others. I never told the family for 30 years.'

Mrs Esther Liston, Newhaven's last fishwife (Courtesy of George Liston).

Another Alexander Noble, my great grandfather, known as Auld Currish, seems to have been a bit of a card himself. He owned three boats, manned mainly by his sons (he had eight of a family) but when he saw the advance of the trawlers he recognised the end of his way of fishing and though he was over 60 took his family and their wives and husbands and fiances (except two daughters, and one son who became a doctor in Glasgow) off to British Columbia where they began to open up the Skeena River as a salmon fishery and prospered exceedingly. (In a farewell sermon Dr Kilpatrick paid tribute to a family 'Noble in name and in nature,' so says family lore). They bought land which they later sold to the Railway. At that time the area was so remote that when one of them died it took a week of waving a sheet to stop a train.

Auld Currish liked his dram as much as the rest. Rena Barnes recalls him in his Newhaven days: 'He worked awfie hard at the fishing. He would come in tired and he would have a big cod's heid and he used to sing 'The Lord's my Shepherd, I'll not want.' Eh? He was half drunk. What was he doing with the cod's head? He was eating all the flesh off it. Raw? Nono, it was biled. Did he drink a lot? Well they all did, it was so cheap.' Aunt Nell Wright elaborated: 'I've heard my mother say that he'd be away fishing for some time and when he came back he'd have a blow-out. That didnae please Granny. I've heard her say that they had a cat and that cat must ha' known when the boat was comin' in for it used to go down to the pier. Mebbe the cat had a drouth too.'

Aunt Nell at eighty is great fun. I asked her recently if she had the family bible from her father's side - a Borders man. 'It went back to 1700,' she said, 'but it wasnae nice readin'. I threw it out.' She tells of one of the Canadian aunts coming back on a visit: 'On the Sunday morning she had a long lie. She got up and came into the kitchen and got her breakfast and then she went back into the bedroom and brought in a jewel box, a beautiful jewel box, full of the most beautiful jewellery you ever saw which was her daughter's that died. She had been pretty well married this daughter. Nettie and I at that time would maybe have a string of beads out of Woolworth. She takes out lovely rings, oh, beautiful rings, you never saw anything like it and I'm waiting for her saying would you like something. She put them a' back in the box, shut the box and she said: 'That's a' for Harold.' That's her grandson. Well he never got it, for the pair of them died in a gassing accident. His father got everything and married again.'

There were ten in Auld Currish's family and they lived in two ends, a room and kitchen in James Street. 'Now the thing is this,' said Rena Barnes. 'Where did they all sleep? There was a bed that was full o' nets.' 'Nobody slept in the bed?' 'Oh, aye, they slept in the bed but they kept the nets in it too. The nets would be put at the bottom. They came in from the fishing and they had to dry their clothes and they did all that in these two ends. They flitted from there to Willowbank Row. They were still in two rooms but they were bigger rooms.'

Though they kept one room for best the kitchen served a dual purpose as living quarters and workshop. 'Oh, I used to hate it when it rained,' Esther Liston, who retired at 78 some years back as Newhaven's last fishwife told Sarah Dyer. 'My father used to mend the nets in the house putting them over the top of the mantelpiece - I mind o' the dust. And my mother used to bait the lines in the house if it rained. Oh we were thankful to see my Dad taking them away down to the boat.' And Kitty Banyards her friend added: 'Lizzie Gilbertson's mother used to go to Granton for the mussells - they were away in the early morning and brought back bags of them and let them lie in their lobby - nae fancy polishing nor nothin' they days.'

Esther Liston: 'When my father went to the mussels he'd maybe get two or three oysters in among them and he'd bring up maybe half a dozen for hissel' and he would open them and put pepper and salt in them and just put it straight over - it was very good for the stomach. When he was at the lines he would bring up maybe a sookit haddie or a sookit coodle, a codling - that's some other fish had taken a bite o't you see, and it took all the blood out o't and it was pure white -we didnae sell that, we maybe took it up for the cat, but it was good eating, it depended on where it was touched. I like fish. I'm no' awfie keen on herring or kippers 'cause they repeat. But I like a finnan.

'The fish is different altogether now than when I was selling and no sae nice that they were long ago - and you got a far better variety. Because there were

A bizarre connection - Richard Dadd, the mad painter of fairy scenes, committed to an asylum for murdering his father, painted this portrait of his doctor with a background of **Anchorfield House, Newhaven, though he had never been there.** (Scottish National Portrait Gallery).

girmits - and that's a thing that you never see. That was a fish very like a haddock but it was a very difficult fish to fillet because you got an awfy jags - you had to be very very careful wi' it. You bought maybe a box o' haddies, a box o' whitin', a box o' cod, and some flats and you dividit it - maybe there were six of you, six neighbours and then sometimes you had herrin' and kippers and finnans along wi' that, you see? And you didnae fillet them then, you filleted them at the houses.'

James Watson did his selling from a van - one of the first to do so. He had taken over his mother's fish run when the Leith shipyard he was working for closed down just after building the biggest sailing ship in the world for the Danish Government - the Kobenhavn. 'There was a terrible slump in the thirties and I could see no future in shipbuilding and it was a waste of time looking for a job. They could strike you off the dole for not genuinely seeking work. I had a pal who had gone round 300 firms in Edinburgh. He got a signature from every one and he took them to the Labour Exchange and showed them how he had been looking for a job. He was a pretty game man, you know one of those kind that is a bit of a rebel against authority. He showed he was not scared of them. He said to them: 'I could do what these clerks are doing. What about a job here? This is the only place I have seen where there is any likelihood of a job. You have a queue out there 200 yards long and in the last half hour you have only taken ten.'

James Watson recalls his own method of kyling (putting your mark on) fish. 'Before the market was built they used just to sell the fish on the pier. It was just laid out and as boys we would get a long bit of string and a hook. We would get a chance to slip the hook into a cod and just walk away. And there was a close they used to ca' Wester Close. We'd hide there and one would keep watch and then we'd pull the cod round the corner. Sort of dry-land fishing. Oh it was a great place in those days.'

Mrs Ellen McWalter, now 84, took a more detached view of Newhaven for she still regards herself as an incomer. 'They were a very clannish lot. You couldn't talk to them. If you mentioned somebody they'd say: 'That's my sister' or 'That's my cousin'. You see they were married through each other. Every door was kept open and it was a case of being in and out. They were all related. It was the fourteen-eighteen war that broke the barrier. The Australians and New Zealanders and Canadians came here to Newhaven because there were blood relations that had come from here. And they took the pick of the lassies away. But before that if you came to the brig our lads had a stick and they daurna pass that place or they walloped them. They were not getting in to steal our lassies.

'They were cannie wi' their money, quite prosperous but you never knew what they had - I knew a man that walked about Newhaven had his money in a tile hat. You would never get a poor Newhavener. They were all fat, fair and fresh and grand eaters. They would think nothing of eating a two-foot fish, a pint o' beer and twa pies. And they were very clean and very houseproud. It was all scrubbed tables and plain scrubbed chairs, the lino was scrubbed and the floor under the lino too; there were no carpets. Everything was scrubbed to death - if you stood still you would be scrubbed along with them. They were all wanting to be cleaner than the other. I've seen them even dust their coal. They had big shelves and at every corner a white jug tied with a blue ribbon and the bedspreads and vallance and curtains and posts were all tied with blue ribbons. The women a' had six or seven petticoats and a skirt on top of it, like wee whales. They were a peaceable crowd but they were wonderful patient wi' a grudge.

'Aye, they had long memories. Beeny Allen had a draper's shop in Main Street during the first world war and at 15 I had to stand on my own feet so I got a job there. After the war I left Newhaven and I've only been back a few years. Well, I was standing at the bus stop no' long back and this auld woman was standing there and taking me in from my feet to my head and I was just away to say: 'Is there something wrong wi me' when she pounces: 'I ken you.' 'I'm afraid I don't know you.' 'Oh, aye, you ken me. You're the wee limmer that worked in the Beehive. You mind that day when you wouldnae sell me the blue flannel for my man's drawers. And you had a' the Klondyke building wi the same curtains when their men's yawls were comin' in, they a' had fine windaes and fine curtains up. I would ken you in a hundert..' Well, I'm 84 now and I had been away from the village for nigh on 70 years! They were strange folk. There was Fish Meg that lost her man at sea. Till the day she died she wandered the seashore every night looking for his body.'

Newhaven folk recall the village in the days of their youth as a magical place with the shimmering Forth beyond the long stretch of beach where they could stand up to their armpits puffing and ducking or when the tide was out catching flatfish with their bare feet on the ribbed sands while out there the sailing craft nodded and ducked and the steamer trailed a smudge across the sky. Knots of bare-legged boys would haunt the boats about to depart for the throw on to the harbour way of the hard cabin biscuits that time-honoured custom exacted.

William L. Wilson, Boxmaster of the Free Fishermen's Society, remembers the swimming across the harbour. 'There used to be two mooring buoys across the harbour bar and we would swim out there with a wee knife in our underpants and scrape our initials on the buoys. They looked quite small from the pier but once you had swum out to them they looked as if they were right up to the ceiling. Life in the village was marvellous. There was no such thing as vandalism. Of course the harbour was the great magnet. I remember when the sprat boats came in and us boys would get to scran the boats. 'Right, laddies, into the bilges.' A jar or a hankie laid out and the fish put in them then along East Trinity Road selling them for ld.' Then there were girds, iron hoops, and guiders, carts with wooden wheels lubricated with grease 'borrowed' from the axle boxes of railway wagons.

Most of the boys were strong swimmers. Mrs Ann Harley recalled that when her father, Tom Wilson first went to sea as a boy he had to do all the cooking and he threw out a basin of water into the harbour. 'And here was all the knives and forks and cutlery and he forgot to take them out the basin and they went over. So the old man said, 'Right, boy, down and get them.' So in he dived and swam about down there until he got the lot. Of course the boys were brought up in the boats and the older ones might row down to Portobello and cast their nets for crabs and lobsters and they used to catch seagulls and ducks, and on the way back they would have a race.'

'I remember going down to the pier as a toddler,' said Sandy Noble, 'and some old fishermen were there and they said, 'I ken wha you are, your grandfaither was Auld Wowsie.' You see they all knew you and all your folk. There was no fear, you were loved by everyone. The doors were wide open, I remember, and everybody was Auntie Carnie or Auntie Wilson and so on. Everybody was just fisherfolk. It was a long time after that we started locking the doors.

'Newhaven was a great hive of activity when I was a bairn' recalls Rena Barnes. 'There was the story about me and the lassie Maggie Pie that Cornie Bunner used to tell. She lived with Nellie Noallie and her father had a boat, a wee rowing boat. She and I went into the rowing boat in the harbour right out of the harbour and round the corner to Annfield beach. By this time the boat was full of water and we were taking our turns to empty it. We left if stranded on Annfield beach. There was a lot of sand here then and we used to swim there. We knew every rock and every pool. It was wonderful at Newhaven then.

'When it was snowing I remember sliding down in a fish box in the Fishermen's Park. Or there were big trees up there and somebody would throw a rope over and you just sat there on the swings. Then we used to play at peevers. That's these squares you made on the pavement with a bit o' chalk. You had this bit o' marble or the bottom of a glass, a thick glass and you pushed it up the six squares and you would throw it up and then you hopped up to where it was and pushed it back to No. 1 with your foot.'

Mrs Cupples quotes this children's play song the girls used to sing:

Ding dong knell
The passing bell
And goodbye to you my darlng
Bury me in yon old churchyard
Beside my own dear mother
My coffin shall be black
Six angels at my back
Two to sing and two to pray
And two to carry my soul away.

This one in more cheerful vein

What will we dae wi' the herrin's heid
Oh, what will we dae wi' the herrin's heid
We'll mak it intae loaves o' breid
Herrin's heid
Loaves o' breid
And a' sorts o' things
Of all the fish that live in the sea
The herrin' is the fish for me.

Newhaven streets teemed with shops and just looking in the lighted windows of an October night was remembered with nostalgia. Oh, the village was a marvellous place to be young in.

CHAPTER 15

The Last Word

History gives a specific date when the village began. It is possible to be equally precise about when it can be said to have come to its end, four and a half centuries later.

It was in 1959 that Newhaven, reaching the nadir of its decline as a fishing community, attracted the attention of Edinburgh Corporation. They would, they decided, recreate the village in a modern restoration which would preserve its distinctive character. Two hundred and ninety families were moved out to the concrete canyons of Pilton and West Granton and the bulldozers moved in and at a cost of several million pounds the picturesque air of the place was fossilised in concrete and harling. But in knocking down the houses they somehow knocked out the memories and what they were left with was a museum. Only a quarter of those removed in what Newhaveners compare to the Highland clearances, managed to get back to the village, the rest of the houses going to others.

Newhaven became the village that was killed by kindness. 'We asked for bread and they gave us cake.'

The Newhaven folk are scattered now. At the enterprise of winning home the sea's harvest they were a passing race and, looking back, a fine one.

At the end of the day (Photograph by George Liston).

Bibliography

Anson, Peter F., Fishermen and Fishing Ways, 1932
Anson, Peter F., Fishing Boats and Fisherfolk on the East Coast of Scotland, 1930
Bertram, J.G., The Harvest of the Sea, 1865
Black, Robin M., Society of Free Fishermen of Newhaven, A Short History, 1951
Bochel, Margaret, The Fishertown of Nairn
Bochel, Margaret, Dear Gremista, 1979
Book of the Old Edinburgh Club, Vols I-XX
Boswell, James, Journal of a Tour to the Hebrides, 1785
Brown, P.H., Early Travellers in Scotland, 1891
Buchan, David, Scottish Tradition, 1984
Buchan, John, The Free Fishers, 1936
Buchanan, George, History of Scotland, 1752
Burnett, Ian, Newhaven Church, Origins and History, 1936
Cadell, Janet S., Fisherfolk, n.d.
Chalmers, P., Historical and Statistical Account of Dunfermline, 1859
Colston, The Town and Port of Leith, 1892
Cowper, Alexandrina S., The Great Michael, (Edinburgh Room, E.P.L.)
Christie, G., Harbours of the Forth, 1955
Christie, Elizabeth, The Empty Shore, 1974
Christie, Elizabeth, The Haven under the Hill - Stonehaven, 1977
Credland, Arthur G., Whales and Whaling, 1982
Cupples, Mrs George, Newhaven - Its Origin and History, 1888
Cupples, George, The Green Hand, n.d.
Dean, Peter and Carol, Passage of Time - Queensferry, 1981
Defoe, Daniel, A Tour through the Whole Island, 1727
Defoe, Daniel, The History of the Union, 1756
Dempster, H., A History of Newhaven, 1870
Dempster, H., The Deck-Welled Fishing Boat, 1868
Dibdin, J.C., The Cleekem Inn, 1896
Dick, Stewart, The Pageant of the Forth, 1910
Dickinson, W.C., Scotland from Early Times to 1603, 1961
Douglas, Hugh, Crossing the Forth, 1964
Fraser, David, The Christian Watt Papers, (ed.) 1983
Fraser, Duncan, Edinburgh in Olden Times, 1976
Fraser, Duncan, The Smugglers, 1971
Geddie, John, Romantic Edinburgh, 1929
Graham, H.G., Social Life of Scotland in the 18th Century, 1899
Graham, Rev. J., Eventide Meditations, Sermons of the Rev. Wm Graham, 1887
Grant, James, Old and New Edinburgh, n.d.
Grant, James, The Old Scots Navy, 1914
Grant, James, The Yellow Frigate, 1855
Gunn, Neil M., The Silver Darlings, 1941
HMSO, Modern Smuggling and Its Detection
Hunter, T., Woods, Forests and Estates of Perthshire, 1883
Johnson, Dr. Samuel, Journey to the Western Islands, 1775
Irons, J.C., Leith and its Antiquities, 2 vols. 1897
Irving, J., The Story of the Great Michael, 1929
Knox, J., A View of the British Empire, 1784
Lindsay, Robert, of Pitscottie, History and Chronicles of Scotland, 1437-1575

Lobley, Douglas, Ships through the Ages, 1972
Lockhart, Sir R. Bruce, Scotch, 1966
McGregor, Forbes, Salt-Sprayed Burgh - a View of Anstruther n.d.
McIver, Rev. D., An Old-Time Fishing Town - Eyemouth, 1906d
Mackie, R.L., King James IV of Scotland, 1958
Mackie, R.L., Letters of James IV, (ed.) 1953
McLaren, Moray, Edinburgh, Capital of the North, 1938
March, E.J., Inshore Craft of Britain
Marshall, Rev. J.S., Old Leith at Work, 1977
Marshall, Rev. J.S., Old Leith at Leisure, 1976
Mason, T., History of Trinity House of Leith
Munro, Henrietta, They Lived by the Sea, 1983
New Statistical Account of Scotland 1845
Nicholson, R., Scotland, the Later Middle Ages, 1974
Ordinance Gazeteer of Scotland 1882
Paxton, John, and John Wroughtson, Smuggling, 1971
Pennant, Thomas, A Tour in Scotland, 1772
Prebble, John, The Lion in the North, 1971
Reade, Charles, Christie Johnstone, 1853
Reid, Ruby H., The Story of the May Island
Reid, W. Stanford, Skipper from Leith, 1962
Ritchie, J.T., The Singing Streets, 1964
Robertson, D., The Bailies of Leith
Rule, Margaret, The Mary Rose, 1982
Russel, J., The Story of Leith, 1922
Rydon, John, Oysters with Love
Scott, Sir Walter, The Waverley Novels, (1829 ed.)
    Guy Mannering
    The Antiquary
    Rob Roy
    Heart of Midlothian
    Old Mortality
    Bride of Lammermoor
    Redgaunlet
Sgann Microforms, (Wm Johnston), Henry Dempster (1807-1875)
Sillett, S.W., Illicit Scotch, 1965
Simmons, Jean, Scottish Smugglers, 1975
Simper, Robert, Scottish Sail, 1974
Sinclair, J., The Statistical Account of Scotland, 1791
Slater, James, A Seafaring Saga
Smout, T.C., A History of the Scottish People 1560-1830, 1969
Stevenson, R.L., Edinburgh, Picturesque Notes, 1879
Sutherland, Iain, Wick Harbour and the Herring Fishing
Taylor, J., Life of James IV, 1913
Taylor, Jas., Pictorial History of Scotland, 1859
Tucker, Thomas, Report on the Settlement of Revenues, etc. 1656, 1824
Thomas, James, The Scottish Fisheries, 1849
Thompson, Paul, Living the Fishing, 1983
Turner, R., One Hundred Years New - Port Seton, 1980
Varende, Jean de la, Cherish the Sea, 1855
Victoria School Centenary Programme 1944
Watson, Sir Daniel, Memorials of Edinburgh in Olden Times
Williams, Neville, Contraband Cargoes, 1959
Wilson, G., Scottish Fishing Craft, 1965

Other Sources:

Museums:
Aberdeen Maritime Museum
The Royal Scottish Museum, Edinburgh
The Scottish Fisheries Museum, Anstruther
Wick Heritage Trust Museum

Libraries:
Edinburgh Room, Edinburgh Central Library
   Boog Watson Notes
   Press Cuttings Files
   Photographic Files
Edinburgh University Library
Leith Library
National Library of Scotland:
   Accounts of the Lord High Treasurer 1473-1566 (ed. Thomas Dickson and Sir James Balfour Paul)
   Acts of the Lords of Council in Public Affairs 1501-1544
   Calendar of State Papers
   Register of the Privy Council of Scotland
   Exchequer Rolls of Scotland 1264-1600
   Map Room
The School of Scottish Studies

Newspapers:
The Edinburgh Evening News
The Edinburgh Evening Dispatch
The Scotsman
The Leith Herald
The Leith Burgh Pilot
The Leith Observer
The North Briton
The Daily Express

Magazines:
The Scots Magazine
The SMT Magazine

Minutes of Town Council of Edinburgh
Minutes of Town Council of Leith
Scottish Records Office
Records of The Free Fishermen's Society of Newhaven
Records of Newhaven United Free Church (St Andrews)
Records of Customs and Excise
North Leith Parish Records
Various Census report 1841 onwards
1st Scottish Statistical Account 1793
2nd Scottish Statistical Account 1845

Appendix I

OFFICE BEARERS OF THE SOCIETY

COMPILED as far as possible from the records of the Society. Before 1816 there was no Preses.
With Acknowledgements to 'A Short History of the Society'.

Boxmasters:

1693	Alex Brown
1697	Alex Carney
1743	John Liston
1744	James Martin
1748	Robert Paterson
1752	Robert Paterson
1754	George Johnston
1755	John Wilson
1763	Thomas Hume
1764	Walter Lundie
1766	William Durham
1767	William Siton
1770	William Siton
1771	William Siton
1772	James Young
1773	George Durham
1774	Alex Lundie
1775	William Ramsay
1781	Robert Young
1782	John Johnston
1783	Alex Martin
1784	Alex Noble
1785	David Durham
1786	James Watson
1787	William Begg
1788	Robert Carnie
1789	William Bisset
1790	Robert Wilson
1791	Robert Wilson
1792	George Durham
1793	John Wilson
1794	John Wilson
1799	William Liston
1801	James Wilson
1802	Andrew Carnie
1803	John Liston
1804	William Seton
1805	William Liston; Secretary, Robert Wilson
1806	James Noble; Secretary, Robert Wilson
1807	John Liston; Secretary, Robert Wilson

1808   John Carnie; Secretary, Robert Wilson
1809   Henry Liddle; Secretary, Robert Wilson
1810   Thos Paterson; Secretary, Robert Wilson
1811   Thos Wilson; Secretary, Robert Wilson
1812   Alex Johnston; Secretary, Robert Wilson
1813   George Linton; Secretary, Robert Wilson
1814   James Logan; Secretary, Robert Wilson
1815   William Main; Secretary, Robert Wilson
1816   Preses William Liston; Boxmaster James Flucker; Secretary Robert Wilson
1817   Preses Jas Flucker; Boxmaster David Wilson; Secretary Robert Wilson
1818   Preses Jas Noble; Boxmaster Thos Aitken; Secretary Robert Wilson
1819   Preses Philip Flucker; Boxmaster Jas Durham; Secretary Robert Wilson
1820   Preses John Carnie; Boxmaster John Wilson; Secretary Robert Wilson
1821   Preses Jas Carnie; Boxmaster Wm Ramsay; Secretary Robert Wilson
1822   Preses Robt Young; Boxmaster James Carnie; Secretary Robert Wilson
1823   Preses Thos Wilson; Boxmaster John Flucker; Secretary Thos Wilson
1824   Preses George Linton; Boxmaster Wm Watson; Secretary Thos Wilson
1825   Preses Wm Liston; Boxmaster John Liston; Secretary Thos Wilson
1826   Preses Neil Drysdale; Boxmaster Philip Flucker; Secretary Thos Wilson
1827   Preses Wm Main; Boxmaster John Johnston; Secretary Thos Wilson
1828   Preses Thos Wilson; Boxmaster Walter Lyle; Secretary Thos Wilson
1829   Preses James Logan; Boxmaster Robert Young; Secretary Thos Wilson
1830   Preses John Young; Boxmaster James Seaton; Secretary Thos Wilson
1831   Preses Jas Flucker; Boxmaster David Main; Secretary Thos Wilson
1832   Preses Robt Carnie; Boxmaster John Linton; Secretary Thos Wilson
1833   Preses Jas Carnie; Boxmaster John Logan; Secretary Durham Liston
1834   Preses John Young; Boxmaster John Seaton; Secretary Durham Liston
1835   Preses John Liston; Boxmaster Wm Hamilton; Secretary Durham Liston
1836   Preses Jas Seaton; Boxmaster David Wilson; Secretary Durham Liston
1837   Preses Geo Flucker; Boxmaster Rennie Liddle; Secretary Durham Liston
1838   Preses Jas Flucker; Boxmaster Andrew Liston; Secretary Durham Liston
1839   Preses Walter Lyle; Boxmaster Thos Combe; Secretary Durham Liston
1840   Preses David Main; Boxmaster Wm Watson; Secretary Durham Liston
1841   Preses John Johnston; Boxmaster Geo Flucker; Secretary Durham Liston
1842   Preses Thos Wilson; Boxmaster Thos Young; Secretary Durham Liston
1843   Preses John Noble; Boxmaster Adam Rutherford; Secretary Durham Liston
1844   Preses Wm Ramsay; Boxmaster Watson Carnie; Secretary Durham Liston
1845   Preses David Wilson; Boxmaster Wm Combe; Secretary Durham Liston
1846   Preses Wm Combe; Boxmaster Robt Dryburgh; Secretary Durham Liston
1847   Preses John Linton; Boxmaster Martin Ramsay; Secretary Durham Liston
1848   Preses Robt Young; Boxmaster Thos Wilson; Secretary Durham Liston
1849   Preses Jas Carnie; Boxmaster Daniel Flucker; Secretary Chas Kerr
1850   Preses Robt Combe; Boxmaster Daniel Flucker; Secretary Chas Kerr
1851   Preses Robt Combe; Boxmaster Daniel Flucker; Secretary Chas Kerr
1852   Preses Wm Bisset; Boxmaster John Carnie; Secretary Leslie Carnie
1853   Preses Jas Johnston; Boxmaster Boreas Lyon Hall; Secretary Leslie Carnie
1854   Preses Thos Young; Boxmaster Thos Latta Main; Secretary Leslie Carnie
1855   Preses Jas Wilson; Boxmaster Wm Wilson (Wilson); Secretary Leslie Carnie

1856   Preses Wm Watson; Boxmaster Thos Combe (Bisset); Secretary Leslie Carnie

1857   Preses Andrew Liston; Boxmaster Liston Carnei (Dores); Secretary Leslie Carnie

1858   Preses John Linton (Lyle); Boxmaster David Lyle; Secretary Leslie Carnie

1859   Preses Alex Rutherford (McPhail); Boxmaster James Flucker (Johnston); Secretary Leslie Carnie

1860   Preses Wm Linton; Boxmaster Wm Bisset; Secretary Leslie Carnie

1861   Preses David Wilson; Boxmaster Adam Durham; Secretary Leslie Carnie

1862   Preses Alex Johnston; Boxmaster Henry Rutherford; Secretary Leslie Carnie

1863   Preses Jas Main (Flucker); Boxmaster Thos Wilson (Young); Secretary Leslie Carnie

1864   Preses John Noble; Boxmaster Jas Johnston (Dryburgh); Secretary Leslie Carnie

1865   Preses David Main; Boxmaster William Logan; Secretary Leslie Carnie

1866   Preses Henry Liddle; Boxmaster Jas Wilson; Secretary Leslie Carnie

1867   Preses Robt Young; Boxmaster Wm Main (Wilson); Secretary Jas Wilson

1868   Preses Robt Young; Boxmaster Alex Johnston; Secretary James Wilson

1869   Preses John Wilson (Young); Boxmaster Rutherford Durham; Secretary James Wilson

1870   Preses Robt Carnie (Liddle); Boxmaster Jas Main (Flucker); Secretary James Wilson

1871   Preses Wm Wilson (Main); Boxmaster David Dryburgh (Hume); Secretary James Wilson

1872   Preses Wm Wilson (Main); Boxmaster John Noble; Secretary James Wilson

1873   Preses Geo Seaton; Boxmaster John Linton (Lyle); Secretary James Wilson

1874   Preses Robt King; Boxmaster Alex Rutherford (McPhail); Secretary James Wilson

1875   Preses Jas Watson; Boxmaster John Wilson; Secretary James Wilson

1876   Preses John Lyle (Linton); Boxmaster Jas Flucker (Carnie); Secretary James Wilson

1877   Preses Jas Logan (Combe); Boxmaster David Wilson (Linton); Secretary James Wilson

1879   Preses John Young (Wilson); Boxmaster Geo Carnie (Thomson); Secretary James Wilson

1880   Preses John Liston; Boxmaster Wm Linton; Secretary James Wilson

1881   Preses Watson Carnie; Boxmaster Wm Noble (Liddle); Secretary James Wilson

1882   Preses Watson Carnie; Boxmaster Evan Rutherford; Secretary James Wilson

1883   Preses Wm Noble (Liddle); Boxmaster Jas Flucker; Secretary James Wilson

1884   Preses Alex R Dryburgh; Boxmaster John Young (Wilson); Secretary James Wilson

1885   Preses John Logan; Boxmaster Thos Wilson; Secretary James Wilson

1886   Preses Wm Main (Hunter); Boxmaster Wm Ramsay (Johnston); Secretary James Wilson

1887   Preses Wm Wilson (Wilson); Boxmaster Jas Wilson (Cunninghame); Secretary James Wilson

1888   Preses David Main; Boxmaster Watson Carnie; Secretary James Wilson

1889   Preses Alex Liston (Combe); Boxmaster Robt Wilson; Secretary James Wilson

1890   Preses Geo Johnston; Boxmaster John Logan (Carnie); Secretary Alex Johnston

1891   Preses Thos Wilson; Boxmaster Geo Seaton; Secretary Alex Johnston

1892   Preses Peter Murray; Boxmaster Jas Rutherford (Liston); Secretary Alex Johnston

1893   Preses John Liston; Boxmaster Wm Wilson; Secretary Alex Johnston

1894   Preses David Wilson (Young); Boxmaster Thos Paterson (Wilson); Secretary Alex Johnston

1895   Preses Thos Dryburgh (Nicol); Boxmaster Robt Carnie (Young); Secretary Alex Johnston

1896   Preses John Dryburgh (Carnie); Boxmaster John Watson (Flucker); Secretary Alex Johnston

1897   Preses David Dryburgh (Noble); Boxmaster Jas Watson (Liddle); Secretary Alex Johnston

1898   Preses Robt Lyle (Wilson); Boxmaster Wm Liston; Secretary Alex Johnston

1899   Preses John King; Boxmaster Walter Lyle (Wilson); Secretary Alex Johnston

1900   Preses Wm Logan; Boxmaster Wm Combe (Paterson); Secretary Alex Johnston

1901   Preses Thos Young; Boxmaster Thos Liston; Secretary Alex Johnston

1902   Preses Chas Wilson; Boxmaster Robt Carnie (Liston); Secretary Alex Johnston

1903   Preses Jas Main (Carnie); Boxmaster Alex Wilson (Jarvie); Secretary Alex Johnston

1904   Preses Robt Paterson (Wilson); Boxmaster Jas Ramsay (Inglis); Secretary Alex Johnston

1905   Preses Wm Main (Logan); Boxmaster Andrew Liston; Secretary Alex Johnston

1906   Preses Thos Combe (Sugden); Boxmaster Robert Lyle (Wilson); Secretary Jas Johnston (Liddle)

1907   Preses Robt Rutherford (McLaren); Boxmaster Wm Main (Hunter); Secretary Jas Johnston (Liddle)

1908   Preses Robt P Tough; Boxmaster Leslie Ramsay; Secretary Jas Johnston (Liddle)

1909   Preses James L Flucker; Boxmaster Wm Flucker (Main); Secretary Jas Johnston (Liddle)

1910   Preses Linton Logan; Boxmaster Jas Ramsay (Anderson); Secretary Jas Johnston (Liddle)

1911   Preses Jas Lyle (Liston); Boxmaster Geo Seaton (Simpson); Secretary Jas Johnston (Liddle)

1912   Preses Donald R M Carnie; Boxmaster David Noble; Secretary Thomas Comb

1913   Preses Wm Ramsay (Logan); Boxmaster Wm Logan (Gay); Secretary Thomas Comb

1914   Preses James B Lyle; Boxmaster Wm H Main; Secretary Thomas Comb

1915   Preses Robt Liston (Harper); Boxmaster Robt L Rutherford; Secretary Thomas Comb

1916   Preses Donald R M Carnie; Boxmaster Adam Rutherford (Noble): Secretary Thomas Comb

1917   Preses James Watson; Boxmaster James B Lyle; Secretary Thomas Comb

1918   Preses Peter Murray; Boxmaster Wm Liddle (Watson); Secretary Thomas Comb

1919   Preses Wm Main (Logan); Boxmaster Watson Linton (Mouat); Secretary Thomas Comb

1920   Preses Watson Linton (Rutherford); Boxmaster Robt Linton (Harper); Secretary Thomas Comb

1921   Preses Adam Rutherford (Liddle); Boxmaster Jas Carnie (Young); Secretary Robt L Rutherford

1922   Preses Jas Wilson (Knight); Boxmaster Thos Wilson (Liston); Secretary Robt L Rutherford

1923   Preses Jas Rutherford (Dunnet); Boxmaster Jas Young; Secretary Robt L Rutherford

1924   Preses Alex Rutherford; Boxmaster Alex Wilson; Secretary Robt L Rutherford

1925   Preses Thos Logan; Boxmaster Jas Main; Secretary Robt L Rutherford

1926   Preses Geo Liston; Boxmaster Daniel Hall; Secretary Robt L Rutherford

1927   Preses Peter Paterson; Boxmaster John Liston (Paterson); Secretary Robt L Rutherford

1928/1929   Preses Peter Murray; Boxmaster John Liston (Paterson); Secretary Robt L Rutherford

1930   Preses Geo Wilson; Boxmaster Robt Flucker; Secretary Robt L Rutherford

1931   Preses Geo Wilson; Boxmaster Alex Wilson; Secretary Robt L Rutherford

1932   Preses Walter L Rutherford; Boxmaster David Dryburgh; Secretary Robt L Rutherford

1933   Preses Alex Wilson; Boxmaster Jas B Lyle; Secretary Robt L Rutherford

1934   Preses Walter L Rutherford; Boxmaster Wm Wilson; Secretary Robt L Rutherford

1935/1936   Preses Walter Rutherford; Boxmaster John Lyle; Secretary Robt L Rutherford

1937/1938   Preses David Dryburgh; Boxmaster Jas Rutherford (S); Secretary Robt L Rutherford

1939/1940   Preses Walter Rutherford; Boxmaster Carnie Logan; Secretary Robt L Rutherford

1941/1942   Preses Walter Rutherford; Boxmaster Liston C Wilson; Secretary Thomas Main

1943-1961   Preses Walter Rutherford; Boxmaster Liston C Wilson; Secretary Mrs M Colley

1962-1967   Preses Walter Rutherford; Boxmaster Henry Rutherford; Secretary Mrs M Colley

1968-1974   Preses Carnie S Logan; Boxmaster Henry Rutherford; Secretary Mrs M Colley

1975   Preses Carnie S Logan; Boxmaster Walter Liston; Secretary Mrs M Colley

1976-1978   Preses Wm W B Lyle; Boxmaster Walter Liston; Secretary Mrs M Colley

1979-1981   Preses Wm W B Lyle; Boxmaster & Secretary William L Wilson

1982-1983   Preses John R Wilson; Boxmaster & Secretary Wm L Wilson

1984   Preses Andrew Hall (decd) & John K Liston; Boxmaster & Secretary Wm L Wilson

Appendix II

THE NEWHAVEN STORY IN DATES

1143   David I gives fishing off Leith to Holyrood Abbey and St Cuthberts
1313   Edward I burns boats at Leith
1329   Bruce grants Edinburgh rights to oyster beds off Newhaven
1330   Trinity House instituted
1349   Outbreak of bubonic plague ravages country

1401   Recurrence of plague
1424   Customs duties on exports at Leith £900
1425   Commercial treaty between Scotland and Netherlands
1438   Charter of James I places tax on all boats
1450   Recurrence of plague
1475   Bad plague year at Leith. Hospital on Inchkeith
1480   First mention of Yellow Carvel skippered by Andrew Wood
1483   Our Lady Kirk (South Lieth) founded
1489   Andrew Wood captures five English men of war
1490   Andrew Wood routs three English warships
1490s   Rise of powerful class of shipowners/master mariners at Leith
1429   James IV exhorts burghs to build fishing boats
1493   Charter by James IV for building of North Leith Church
1493   Abbot Ballentyne of Holyrood erects N. Leith church of St Ninian (St Nicholas chapel already in existence. Patronised by mariners and fishers)
1493   James IV requires coastal burghs to construct vessels up to 20 tons to compete with Dutch in North Sea herring fishing
1495   Andrew Wood knighted
1495   Inchgarvie fortified to protect herring fishing

1502   Scottish shipbuilding starts seriously with arrival of French shipwright John Lorans followed by others including Jaques Terrell
1504   Plague returns to Scotland
1504   Famine of wood in Scotland deplored by Parliament
1504   James IV decides to build naval dockyard at Newhaven. 163 large trees brought from Inverleith to build village, bulwarks erected and dock excavated
1504   Andrew Wood has further naval successes against English
1505   Margaret launched at Leith. Harbour found too shallow
1505   James purchases superiority of 143 acres at Newhaven from Abbey of Holyrood
1505   Ropeworks established at Newhaven
1506   James writes France for timber
1506   Andrew Barton sends James barrel stuffed with heads of Dutch freebooters
1506   Chapel of Our Lady and St James commenced (dependency of St Anthony's Leith) Sir Andrew Cowie appointed chaplain
1507   King knights Andrew Barton of Barnton
1507   New dock excavated. Start made on the Michael
1508   Chapel completed. Sir James Cowan appointed priest

240

1510   James conveys superiority of Newhaven on Edinburgh
1511   The Michael launched
1511   Andrew Barton slain by the English at sea
1512   Plague returns
1512   The Michael fitted with new masts. Later same year commissioned
1513   (May) James promises help to Hugh O'Donnell in Ulster
1513   The Scottish fleet sails for France going North-about, bombarding Carrickfergus then returning to Ayr before departing for France
1513   Flodden
1513   Remains of fleet struggles home from France (Nov)
1514   The Michael sold to Louis XII of France
1515   Sir Andrew Wood dies
1518   Sir David Wilson appointed priest at St Mary's Chapel (St James's)
1530   Plague at Leith and Newhaven. Area isolated from Edinburgh
1541   Leith staple moved from Bruges to Veere
1544   Hertford's ships land at Newhaven, sack Newhaven, Leith and Edinburgh.
Return 1547
1550   Visit of 60 galleys and ships off Newhaven for departure of Queen Regent for
France to visit her daughter
1554   Gibbet at Newhaven to hang four English pirates
1554   £500 spent by Edinburgh Corporation on repair of Newhaven Harbour
1555   Trinity House Leith built
1556   John Balfour chaplain of St James (St Mary's) Chapel (new secular
appointment)
1559   St James Chapel destroyed in Reformation (?)
1564   Great storm at sea
1567   Three Englishmen given land at Newhaven to pan salt
1568   Mary Queen of Scots spends night at Newhaven on escape from Loch
Leven
1568   Plague
1572   Society of Free Fishermen of Newhaven - first records extant
1574   Severe outbreak of plague along shores of Forth
1581   Leith made chief fishmarket in Forth for landing fish
1585-7   Severe outbreak of plague in Edinburgh and Leith
1591   Convention of witches alleged
1592   First Society records oyster fishing
1595   James Balfour named chaplain of St Mary's (St James) Chapel (now
ruinous)
1595   St Ninian's Church rebuilt, completed 1600

1606   North Leith erected into a parish (St Ninian's becomes parish church)
1606   Union Jack first hoisted in Leith
1608   Four men fined for playing golf in Leith Links during sermon
1609   James VI forbids foreigners to fish off Scottish coasts without licence
1609   27 English pirates hanged at Leith
1614   St James Chapel (St Mary's) conveyed to South Leith Parish
1614   Golden Charter - Newhaven united to Edinburgh
1620   Racing on sands at Leith begins
1622   Bridge over Water of Leith
1625   Charles I proclaimed king at Leith
1630   Lord Drummond pursues spulzie against Newhaven fishermen for tiend
fish (tax)
1631   Newhaven joined to North Leith parish

1631   Society of Free Fishermen gives first bond to Church to look after poor of 'town'

1633   Newhaven-Burntisland ferry founders with Charles I's silver

1636   Charter of Charles I grants Newhaven fishermen rights to oyster bed

1639   North Leith comes under jurisdiction of Edinburgh (previously under Holyrood)

1642   Litigation between Society and Edinburgh Corporation on oyster beds

1645   Severe plague (typhus?) in Leith - 2320 die in 8 months

1650   Cromwell takes possession of Leith

1652   Privy Council impress Newhaven men for navy

1656   General Monk erects Citadel at Leith removing St Ninian's Chapel

1660   Hackney coaches between Leith and Edinburgh

1663   Lease of Links to Jas Davidson for ropeworks

1664   Privy Council impress men for Navy

1667   Dutch men o' war in Forth - bombard Burntisland

1672   Privy Council impress men for Navy

1679   275 Covenanters shipped to Barbados from Newhaven

1681   Viscount Newhaven created by Charles II (extinct 1728)

1682   Ropewalk transferred to North Leith

1688   New ropeworks established at Newhaven

1697-9   Famine bad in Leith

1698   Darien expedition sails from Leith

1707   Ratification of Society's obligation to poor of village

1707   High duties on salt imposed after Union cause hardship in fishcuring

1710   Herring plentiful in Forth

1710   Evan McGregor who owned lands of Newhaven, entails all his lands

1715   Proclamation forbidding Newhaven fishermen to ferry Jacobite rebels over Forth

1717   Proclamation forbidding operation of ferries on Sundays

1718   George I introduces bounty system for fishing industry

1725   Herring desert the Forth

1741   Edinburgh issues proclamation limiting oyster fishing

1745   St Ninian's Church used as ammunition store because of suspected Jacobite leanings of parishioners

1746   Fishing restricted following Jacobite Rebellion

1750   Newhaven Ropery closed

1750   (circa) Newhaven important as cross-Forth ferry terminal

1752   Gregorian Calendar introduced to Scotland

1760   Fight between "Edinburgh" of Leith and French privateer

1760   Oyster production reaches peak of 30 million - thereafter declines

1761   Bathing machines first used at Leith

1764   Fisherrow oyster dregs seized by Newhaven fishermen

1765   Rev Dr Johnston inducted at North Leith

1766   Ground including old chapel and burial ground and area where Free Church eventually built in Newhaven acquired by Society

1767   Thomas Peacock establishes Peacock Inn

1767   East Coast herring fishing begins to challenge Dutch

1774   Highest tide in memory sweeps away houses in Newhaven

1775   Herring reappear briefly in Forth

1779   John Paul Jones attempts raid on Forth

1781   House of Lords decrees tiends due to minister of North Leith

1788   Newhaven men fight with Prestonpans fishers over oyster beds

1789   Encroachment of sea makes road to Leith dangerous. Five drowned.
1791   High Court of Admiralty confirms Newhaven's rights to oyster beds
1793   Herring reappear in great numbers in Forth
1793   Population of Newhaven less than 600 (1st Statistical Account)
1794   Society acquire ground at Pierhead
1795   Martello Tower built
1797   Great storm tears away bulwarks
1797   Grant of links to Newhaven for housebuilding
1779   Silver medal from Duke of Buccleuch and County gentry to Newhaven fishermen in recognition of loyalty. Also Lord Provost and Magistrates of Edinburgh present handsome stand of colours.

1801   Inchkeith light starts operation
1801   Salt duties increased
1803   Society offer of Naval service
1806   Petition to Lords against impressment
1806   East Dock, Leith constructed
1806   200 Newhaven fishermen volunteer for service on "Texel"
1807   "Texel" captures French frigate. Letter from George III. Cheque for £250 from Edinburgh Corporation. Silver cup from Navy
1808   Road through Newhaven to Cramond begins
1810   Petition against Naval impressment
1811   Great storm, houses damaged
1811   Bell Rock lighted
1812   New slip built in harbour
1812   Custom House Leith built
1812   First steamboat on Forth
1816   New North Leith Parish Church built (Madiera St)
1816   New lighthouse on May Island built by Robert Stevenson
1816   Brigs South Esk and Venus rescued by Newhaven pilots
1817   Foundation stone laid for new school
1817   New Trinity House, Leith built
1817   New rules for Free Fisherman's Society restricting membership
1820   Steamboat runs from Newhaven to Fife
1818   New school opened
1820-1828   Attempts to exact fish tythes
1821   Chain pier opened
1821-1890   100 Newhaven fishermen drowned
1821   Last public whipping of man at Leith
1822   George IV landed at Leith
1823   Execution of 2 foreign seamen for piracy, 50,000 present
1824   Great fire of Edinburgh
1826   Leith Dock Commission take over Newhaven Harbour
1827   Watch at churchyard to foil bodysnatchers
1827   Lord Provost and Magistrates hold court at Newhaven
1828   End of tiends payments
1828   Crawley water supply led to Newhaven
1830   Charles X of France lands at Newhaven on abdication
1832   Sir Walter Scott lands at Newhaven
1832   Houses in Newhaven sold as bathing quarters
1832   Plague outbreak. General fast declared
1833   Newhaven becomes part of Leith
1836   Edinburgh-Leith railway commenced
1838   First steamer to cross Atlantic sails from Leith
1838   Newhaven Church erected. Rev Jas Fairbairn inducted

1838	Granton Pier opened by Lord John Scott
1839	Oyster beds let to English Company
1840	Great catches of herring at Kirkcaldy
1840	Ferries transferred from Newhaven to Granton
1842	Old burial ground closed
1842	Queen Victoria's first visit to Newhaven
1843	Congregation seceeds. Rev Jas Fairbairn moderator
1843	Victoria School opened
1844	Skeleton together wth coins of Philip II of Spain found at Wardie
1844	Granton railway extension completed
1845	There were 300 fishermen and pilots at Newhaven
1845	Agreement with Edinburgh on oyster beds
1845	Society introduces new rules
1848	Free Fishermen's park obtained from Admiralty on 999-year lease
1849	Free Church building started
1849	Society in abeyance
1850	Rev Wm Graham inducted to Newhaven Church
1852	Free Fishermen's Society reconstituted after lapse, gets its own lease
1852	Newhaven United Free (afterwards St Andrews) Church completed
1853	Charles Reade publishes Newhaven novel "Christie Johnstone"
1854	Over 100 fishermen volunteer for Navy during Crimean War. Most served 5 years
1859	Revival Movement (Brethren)
1859	Newhaven Church becomes Quoad Sacra Parish Church
1860	Religious revival in Newhaven
1860	The "Edinburgh" steamship lost with all hands
1864	Fishermen form own breakwater
1864	Population now over 2000; 300 families
1866	Cholera rages
1866	First Royal Commission exonerates trawling
1867	Lamp first lighted on Newhaven pier
1867	Shoal of whales in Forth. 16 brought to Newhaven and sold from 10s to £4.15s. Total £33.3s
1867	Annual Fishermen's Procession revived
1867	Anderson got Duke of Buccleuch's oyster scalps
1868	New pierhead clock installed
1868	Battle of the oyster scalps. Newhaven men rout the intruders
1868	Severe storm, five boats wrecked. Very extreme tides
1868	Society erect tenement at Fairbairn Place
1868	Fishermen's clock erected by the Society
1869	13 Newhaven fishermen drowned over winter months
1869	266 boats in Newhaven
1870	First decked fishing boat at Newhaven
1871	New water pipes laid at Newhaven
1872	Queen Victoria passes thro Newhaven
1872	Paving of streets and piping of sewers
1874	Todd's flour mill destroyed by fire
1874	Last shipment of gunpowder from Newhaven following protests
1874	Main Street Newhaven laid with causeway stones
1875	English Company's sailing boats arrive Granton to trawl in deep sea but with no success and soon leave
1875	Number of fishermen in Newhaven put at 416
1876	Steam trawling begins in Forth and fish salesmen arrive at Newhaven
1876	Concrete section Newhaven Harbour begun

1878   Society's hall built on site of old school
1878   First Zulu fishing boat built Moray Firth
1878   Change of office-bearers of Free Fishermen's Society in Society's hall instead of Boxmaster's House. Soiree follows
1878   West breakwater constructed. Concrete work finished
1879   Battle with tug from Dock Commission over harbour dues
1879   Death of Dr Fairbairn. Rev David Kilpatrick appointed
1880   FFS office bearers changed January instead of November
1880   St Andrew's Free Church steeple added. Stone brought from Fife by fishing boats
1881   Dyke on Newhaven harbour finished
1881   High water in harbour at all-time low. Ships and boats could not float
1881   Great storm. 129 Forth fishers drowned, 17 from Newhaven
1882   Petition to Lords against trawling
1882   Horsedrawn tramway along Main Street to Pilrig
1882   Great Fisheries exhibition, Edinburgh
1883   Organ installed Newhaven Parish Church
1883   Steeple of St Andrews Free Church finished
1883   Fight to restrict trawler operations
1883   Second Royal Commission on trawling
1883   Steamer "Iona" of Leith stranded on Herwith Rock for 7 months
1883   Great Fisheries Exhibition Wembley. 18 Newhaven fisherwomen visited London. Entertained at Windsor. Received by the Lord Mayor
1883   Weather bell hoisted Newhaven harbour
1885   Newhaven had 33 first-class boats and 170 second class boats, 425 fishermen and boys
1885   Annfield laid with causeways
1885   Free Church bazaar raises £1510
1886   Explosion Todd's Mills - six killed
1886   Trawlers banned from Firth of Forth following Newhaven initiative
1888   Fast days abandoned
1888   Great storms: many ships wrecked
1889   Free Fishermen's Society clear of debt
1896   Newhaven fishmarket open
1898   Chain Pier blown down
1899   Newhaven boats now using seine nets. Skipper fined

1907   First motor fishing boat (paraffin)
1907   Society gives up Queensferry oyster scalps
1917   Dr Kilpatrick retires
1919   War Memorial unveiled in Parish Church
1928   Newhaven has 32 boats, 132 fishermen
1928   Last Newhaven-built boat launched
1935   War Memorial to 78 men killed in war unveiled
1959   City Council decides to rebuild Newhaven
1974   Two churches joined. St Andrews closed
1975   Rev Alex R Aitken appointed to joint charge

Appendix III

NEWHAVEN FISHING BOATS AND THEIR OWNERS

Excerpted from the Register of the Custom House, Leith 1868

Wm Watson, Planet; Wm Bisset, Probity; Henry Rutherford, Enterprise; David Main, Minnie; Wm Linton, Esk; Alex Linton, Helen: David Wilson, Olive Branch; Geo Wilson, Johnston's; Walter King, Janet Linton; Jas Flucker, Janet; James Flucker, Isabella; Alex Carnie (Liston) Four Brothers; Andrew Liston, Ann; David Ramsay, Fox; Robert Carnie, Jean; James Ramsay, Helen and Mary; Thos Carnie, jr., Hawk; Robt Lyle, Ortive; Thos Linton (Morrison) Sisters; Thos Linton, Young Thomas; Geo Wilson (Johnston), Good Intent; George Wilson, Catherine; Robert Young, Vivid; Thomas Gray (Wood) Water Witch; James Ramsay, William and Mary; James Murray, Carnie Wilson; Daniel Hall, Elizabeth; William Main, Robina and Margaret; William Main, Robina; James Carnie, William and Ann; Wm Carnie (Carnie), John; Robert Dryburgh, Sunbeam; Alexander Noble, Janet; Carnie Seaton, Jessie; William Liston, Jean; Alex Young, Margaret Carnie; Wm Linton jr., Lively Jane; John Gillon and Donald R. McGregor, Ariel (steamer); Wm Hall, Mayflower; Liston Carnie, Golden Fleece; James Main, Brilliant; Adam Durham, Comet; Wm Logan, Britannia; David Dryburgh, Isabella; George Carnie, Star of Peace; George Flucker, Integrity; Wm Carnie, Isabella; Robert Noble, Euphemia; Robert Liston, Newhaven; John Carnie, Diamond; Wm Ramsay, Favourite; John Liston, Ellen and Jane; Daniel Hall, Blue Bonnet; James Main, Dayspring; John Noble, Prompt; John Carnie, Glance; Robert Young, Reliance; James Flucker, Venus; John Noble, Lavinia; John Hume, Isabella and Mary; William Liston, Mary; Robert Young, Isabella Dores; Robert Young, Fortitude; James Johnston, Cheerful; James Wilson, Alliance; John Carnie, Christina; John Carnie, William and Ann; William Seaton, Thomas and John; William Noble, Janet; John Ramsay, Thomas and Mary; Thomas Wilson, Charlott · Robert Carnie, Catherine; Alex Johnston, Vigilant; Daniel Hall, Matchless; Robert ..oble, Euphemia; James Ramsay, Royal George; James Murray, Ann Hall; James Carnie, Seagull; James Johnston, Margaret; John Wilson, Fortitude; John Flucker, Fly; John Linton (Main), Trio; William Jarvie, Mary; Clarence Noble, Aid; B Watson, Margaret; Alex Linton, Sisters; Wm Ramsay, Helen and Jane; John Liston, (Combe) Isabella; James Hall, Marion; David Paterson, Rose; Martin Ramsay, Dayspring; Adam Durham, Jane; George Carnie, Design; David Dryburgh, Prince Consort; James Cunningham, James and David; James Methven, Paratoo; Walter Carnie, Morna; William Ramsay, Volunteer; Robert Linston, jr., Phoenix; James Methuen, Leith, Emu; Peter Murray, Robina; David Dryburgh, Twins; David Dryburgh, Brilliant; William Hamilton, Comely; John McInnes, James Duncan; Geo Anderson, Vanguard; John Wilson, Thomas and Janet; John Carnie, Perseverence; Seton Hall, Marion Noble; James Methuen, fishcurer, leith, Wolf; James Methuen, Stag; John Carnie (Leslie) Only Sister; A.G. Anderson, Edinburgh, Enterprise.

Appendix IV

MONEY AND MEASURES

£1 Scots had parity with sterling in the 14th century. Gradually reduced in value due to debasement at mint. At time of Union of the Crowns it was worth 1s 8d sterling (or put another way, the Scots shilling was worth a penny sterling). On the Union the Scots currency was recalled - all £900,000, including foreign and counterfeit currency.

1 Old Fathom = 7 1/2 feet
1 Scots mile = 9.5 English miles
1 Scots pint = 2 English quarts
1 gallon = 20 full-size herring
1 bushel = 8 gallons (dry measure)
1 anker = 8 gallons (liquid measure)
1 barrel = 32 gallons of herring
1 basket = 1/4 cran
1 cran (3 1/2 cwt or 800-1000 herring depending on size)
12 barrels = 1 last (or 4000 lbs)

Appendix V

NEWHAVEN RECIPES

Newhaven Herring

1 fillet of cooked smoked herring

1 peeled cooking apple
2 cold boiled potatoes
1 tablespoon shredded celery
3 tablespoons minced beetroot
French dressing as required
8 canapes
8 cooked button mushrooms

Chop herring. Core and chop apple. Slice and chop potatoes. Mix till blended. Stir in celery and beetroot, and French dressing to moisten. Divide equally between 8 canapes of toast or fried bread. Dredge lightly with paprika. Top each with a cold fried mushroom in centre. Serves 4.

Newhaven Cream

1lb steamed, boned smoked haddock
4oz. (1 cup) breadcrumbs
4 oz. (½ cup) butter
¾ pt. (1½ cups) milk or light cream
3 eggs
salt and pepper
For the sauce:
1 heaped tablespoon butter
2 tablespoons flour
1 pt. (2 cups) warm milk
2 tablespoons chopped parsley
salt and pepper

Flake and mash fish. Add breadcrumbs. Season to taste. Melt butter in milk and pour over, mix well. Add well-beaten eggs. Pour into large buttered basin or several small ones, put foil over top and steam over boiling water for 1 hour or half hour if small ones. Remove foil and put warm plate on top. Tip over to unmould. Serve hot with sauce. Serves 4.

To make sauce. Melt butter and stir in flour. Cook for 1 minute. Pour in warm milk gradually, Stirring all the time until smooth and thick. Season to taste and add parsley. Pour over the cream and serve at once.

Small creams may be used as first course, served cold.

(From 'A Taste of Scotland' by Theodora Fitzgibbon.)

INDEX

249